ABOUT THE AUTHOR

Dr. Ronald S. Federici is a Board Certified Developmental Neuropsychologist and regarded as the country's leading expert in the neuropsychological evaluation and treatment of severely disturbed children, particularly children from post-institutionalized settings who have experienced profound early childhood abuse, neglect and trauma. Dr. Federici lectures nationally and internationally on the damaging effects of institutionalization and deprivation which affects psychological and neuropsychological development. He has developed innovative diagnostic concepts and treatment programs for "Neuropsychologically-Based Attachment Disorders" in addition to a new subgroup of autism specific to the post-institutionalized child now referred to as "Institutional Autism: An Acquired Syndrome."

Dr. Federici serves as Clinical Director of Neuropsychological and Family Therapy Associates in Alexandria, Virginia, which is a multi-discipline mental health facility specializing in complex neurodevelopmental disorders of childhood and adolescence. Dr. Federici has appeared on numerous talk shows such as *Dateline (one of their most popular shows entitled "Saving Dane, Saving a Family"), Night Line, Turning Point, 20/20, The Oprah Winfrey Show, The Maury Povich Show, Fox Morning News, British Broadcasting Corporation*, various radio talk shows, while writing numerous articles for national and international journals, magazines and newspapers.

Dr. Federici is President and CEO of "Care For Children International," a charity comprised of a team of world experts in International Adoption Medicine. Care For Children works all over the world providing training, humanitarian aide and rehabilitation programs for children housed in the most deprived conditions. The team has de-institutionalized thousands of children worldwide and is regarded as a pioneering group of experts committed to child welfare and human rights issues.

Dr. Federici resides in Alexandria, Virginia, with his family, 3 dogs and 3 horses. The Federici's have four adopted children, Elena and Kolea from Ukraine, and Petrica and Marcel from Romania in addition to three foster children, Victoria from Belarus; Tazia and Crina from Romania, who divide their time between the Federici's home and their respective countries.

HELP for the HOPELESS CHILD
A Guide for Families

With Special Discussion for Assessing and Treating the Post-Institutionalized Child

SECOND EDITION

Dr. Ronald S. Federici

Dr. Ronald S. Federici and Associates
400 South Washington Street
Alexandria, Virginia 22314

Help for the Hopeless Child: A Guide for Families *With Special Discussion for Assessing and Treating the Post-Institutionalized Child*

Second Edition, August 2003

For publisher information address:

Dr. Ronald S. Federici and Associates
400 South Washington Street
Alexandria, Virginia 22314
Phone: (703) 548-0721
Fax: (703) 836-8995
e-mail: DRFEDERICI@aol.com
www.drfederici.com

Library of Congress Cataloging-in Publication Data

Federici, Ronald S.
Help for the Hopeless Child: A Guide for Families

Includes biographical references and index

ISBN 0-9667101-0-8

1. Psychology and Psychiatry 2. Self-help 3. Attachment 4. Child Rearing 5. Discipline of Children

Printer: Signature Book Printing, Inc.
841 Cessna Avenue, Suite 132, Gaithersburg, MD 20879

FOREWORD

"It is important for adoptive parents to remember that you can take the child out of the institution, but it may take a much greater amount of effort to take the institution of the child."

The most common complaint parents present to a mental health professional is that their child's behavior is inappropriate and in need of treatment. It is extremely common nowadays to hear parents describe their children as being completely out of control--often to the point where parents feel they are no longer able to manage the child within the home. The most common presenting problems are defiance of authority, uncontrollable temper tantrums and aggressive behaviors, manipulative and deceitful actions, substance abuse and sexual acting out, and chronic academic underachievement. Family relationships can become quite strained to where parents have considered relinquishment or totally giving up. Family dynamics often become adversarial and disengaged.

This book consists of a very comprehensive, aggressive and innovative assessment and treatment program for those families having children who have been deemed "hopeless" or "untreatable." There has been a tremendous increase in the amount of children, both biological and adopted (United States and internationally) who present with significant cognitive, emotional and behavioral disorders; including "reactive attachment disorders" based on the profound effects of severe medical, nutritional, environmental and social-emotional neglect.

HELP for the HOPELESS CHILD: A Guide for Families (with Special Discussion for Assessing and Treating the Post-Institutionalized Child) offers a somewhat controversial and provocative approach in dealing with the most difficult children and their troubled families. Let me forewarn readers that my treatment program can be very rigorous and require great patience, diligence and dedication toward the concept of recreating family cohesiveness and unity.

TABLE OF CONTENTS

ACKNOWLEDGMENTS

This book is dedicated to all the families I have treated over the years who have endured emotional pain and despair in their efforts to reorganize their family. These families never accepted that their child was beyond treatment.

This book is also dedicated to all the children in orphanages and institutions, particularly the most deprived children residing in the Neuropsychiatric Institution in Siret, Romania. These lost souls continue to be subject to destitution that we cannot even begin to fathom.

Most importantly, this book is dedicated to my family, especially our children, Elena, Kolea, Petrica and Marcel, and our adopted-foster children, Victoria, Tazia and Crina, who have endured my long hours and sometimes my over-dedication to the job of emotional healing and humanitarian aid. These seven unique children have proven beyond a doubt that there is hope and recovery from the damaging effects of institutionalization. A strong brain and strong soul prevail.

Most grateful appreciation to my friend and editor, Cari Ugent, whom I have watched develop from a brilliant kindergarten student to a brilliant editorial advisor and survivor in her own respect. Kathleen Tucker also deserves my highest praise and thanks for her loyalty, enduring support and long hours in transcribing and co-editing this work.

Additional acknowledgments go out to my close personal friends and professional colleagues, both in the United States and in Romania, who have provided me with valuable medical information and research regarding the damaging effects of institutional care.

Acknowledgments are also given to the Care for Children International volunteers from the States and abroad, especially our Romanian colleagues, who have spent countless hours in the most difficult conditions in an effort to improve the life of institutionalized children worldwide. The Parent Network for the Post-Institutionalized Child (PNPIC) and Friends of Russian and Ukrainian Adoptees (FRUA) deserves special appreciation for all of their dedication in supporting thousands of families across the globe who have struggled with special-needs children.

ACKNOWLEDGMENTS

PREFACE

A treatise on the appropriate diagnostic and treatment approaches for the post-institutionalized child has been sorely needed for some time. No one can do this more comprehensively and expertly than Dr. Ronald Federici. The reader is about to gain an in-depth understanding of the problems facing these children and families, as well as acquire rational and practical skills to overcome their problems.

During February 1997, I was personally privileged to participate in a humanitarian project in which our team, led by Dr. Federici, traveled to Romania to collaborate with the wonderful workers from the England-based Romanian Challenge Appeal to provide consultative and treatment services for the children at the Neuropsychiatric Hospital in Siret. This is the most dismal of the orphanages in the Eastern Bloc. The medical neglect and psychosocial abuse which permeate the facility reaches an abhorrent level of brutality. Progress is being made to the credit of the unsung heroes of the Romanian Challenge Appeal, whose tireless efforts defy the banalities of institutional and bureaucratic policies, regulations, and the like. It was Dr. Federici's creativity and vision which led to our rescue of two ill brothers with untreated hemophilia, transferring them from the orphanage to multidisciplinary, lifesaving, state-of-the-art care in the United States.

The experiences of evaluating and treating hundreds of children from the post-institutionalized setting, plus an inquisitive and keen mind, led Dr. Federici to formulate an appropriate diagnostic and therapeutic program for these children, as well as identify the syndrome of institutionalized autism, which is discussed in this book and is now being added to the differential diagnoses of the autistic spectrum disorders. Himself a father of four children, two children adopted from a Ukrainian orphanage and two from the Irrecuperable Institution in Siret, Romania, Dr. Federici is uniquely qualified to provide much needed insight to many readers, including adoptive parents, prospective parents, and the biopsychologists and neurodevelopmental physicians who are interested in this newly burgeoning and exciting study of the human brain, together with its vulnerabilities and endless possibilities.

Phillip L. Pearl, M.D.
Clinical Associate Professor of Neurology and Pediatrics
The George Washington University School of Medicine
Children's National Medical Center, Washington, D.C.

Introduction

Recreating Hopefulness in the Midst of Despair: There Are Always Possibilities

After continual failures and chronic despair, it suddenly becomes irrelevant as to how or why a child or young adult has reached the point of being totally impossible for families to manage. Instead, what takes precedence is that you, the parents—who have been completely dedicated to your child for years—have finally reached the devastating and crucial point of viewing your child as "hopeless" and the family unit as "helpless" in breaking the repetitive cycle of problems. For years, maybe even for the child's entire life, you have put forth incredible effort; but now you are at the point where you find it difficult to try, even just once again, to improve a situation that seems beyond improvement.

It is extremely important to remember that you are not alone in this type of dilemma. Every human being has the capacity to reach his or her "breaking point" which results in being totally overwhelmed and frustrated to where giving up is preferable and easier than putting forth any more time, finances, effort or emotional investment.

I wrote this book because I wanted to create an easy-to-read manual that instills hope and motivation back into families. This book is based on my 20 years as a developmental neuropsychologist where I have devoted my career to working with the most difficult children imaginable. In addition, I practice what I preach in my own home. We have the personal experience of raising seven post-institutionalized, internationally-adopted children who each presented with their own unique set of problems. Interestingly, while each child was very unique, they all had very similar traits regarding their perception of a new world, a new environment, relationships and a family system—things that were quite foreign to all four of them. Most importantly, I was able to observe firsthand as our newly-adopted children struggled to find a new identity after many years of being lost and completely abandoned in Eastern Bloc orphanages and institutions where they did not experience any sense of the outside world. Their perception of the future was nonexistent as they lived "for the day." There was no looking ahead to make plans for school or a career, nor was it helpful to look at the emotionally-painful past. Day-to-day survival was their way of life.

I began working with the most difficult children imaginable in graduate school during the graveyard shift in a hospital-based psychiatric treatment program in Chicago. The whole field of child psychology and neurological development had always fascinated me, especially the concept of how the brain and personality develop. This probably stemmed from having grown up in a very mixed-ethnic neighborhood where I observed many different ways families raised their children: there was the old school that believed in harsh punishment and total parental control; there was the entitled school that revered children and allowed them to do whatever they wanted; and then there were the families who struggled incredibly to make ends meet but actually enjoyed the strongest emotional bonds; and then there were families that, because of poverty, were not able to care for their children adequately--this resulted in many developmental problems along with family chaos and confusion.

As I grew older and became more experienced, I became increasingly curious as to how and why some of the children I grew up with survived and did well as adults, whereas others got lost along the way and ended up dependent on drugs, in vagabond life styles, in nonproductive relationships, in dysfunctional families, or even in psychiatric programs. Thus began my yearning to gain a better understanding of children whose families entered the mindset of "giving up." These families were totally drained and the children became lost in the family's despair and hopelessness.

During graduate school, I became frustrated with the generic brand of "psychiatric disorders" that seemed to be dished out along with various medications and nonproductive therapies. I wondered if perhaps there was something missing in the assessment and treatment of these children despite the best efforts by treatment professionals.

In my post-graduate training, internships, fellowships and Board Certifications, I waded through thousands of psychological reports and research, searching for an answer to why there were so few focused assessment and treatments for chronically unmanageable children. What I discovered, however, was that the answer only became more complicated and convoluted in the midst of psychiatric and psychological literature. The most brilliant scholars and professionals certainly have written outstanding work, but it often seemed far beyond the comprehension of the average family, let alone the family that was emotionally overwhelmed and needed a very concrete and highly directive approach. It was my gut feeling, however, that there had to be much more to the riddle of the out-of-control child, and even more so, the hopeless child. The more I delved into the complexities of assessing children, the more I realized that children just cannot be placed in any one category, diagnosis or catch-all phrase, such as the infamous "Attention Deficit Hyperactivity Disorder Syndrome (ADHD)," which has been used for many years with the hopes of explaining any and all type of misbehavior of children. Also, "Reactive Attachment Disorder (RAD)", Oppositional Defiant Disorder (ODD) and Borderline Personality Disorder (BPD) have been used so frequently to "check off and describe" behaviors instead of explaining causality and treatment. Children have very complex brains and a complex psychology. The best way I found to deal with complexity was to break it down into very simple and manageable terms--information families could better digest and use in their day-to-day life.

Despite the fact that none of the traditional psychological theories, research or treatment approaches addressed what I was beginning to realize, I held fast to the belief that unique children require unique approaches which do not fall into any one theory but require a collection of thoughts and ideas that can be implemented in a most aggressive and innovative manner. My new insights allowed me to see that children really needed someone who could literally "take charge" and help them begin their emotional life over, re-learning correct thoughts, emotions, behaviors and modes of social interaction.

I utilized the skills I had learned from working as a diagnostician and sorted out the most complicated childhood personality types based on standardized neuropsychological and psychological tests. I also spent a great deal of time with these "unique children" who were termed chronic, unmanageable and "hopeless." I began to look more carefully at how brain functions affect every aspect of human emotions, and I began lecturing on the fact that there are groups of unique and highly complicated children for whom traditional therapeutic methods are simply not enough. Specifically, certain difficulties in children (most probably neurologically and psychologically based) are so deeply ingrained that they just cannot get better or disappear with the standard "talk therapy approach."

I began to welcome the most difficult cases into my practice. Almost always, by the time families made it to my office, they had already seen anywhere from two to as many as ten treatment professionals and had spent months, if not years, along with countless dollars, only to be left feeling no significant progress had been made. The children had long since reached the stage of being looked upon as "hopeless cases." Almost everyone around them-- including teachers and therapists-- had given up, and it was clear to me that the parents felt equally helpless and hopeless. What was happening was the child was being left alone to fend for him or herself. I directly correlated this with the reason we lose so many children to state run-institutions, the criminal justicc systcm, runaways, prostitution, or to foster care or adoption programs. And, I believed, what truly would make a difference was an aggressive, intensive, confrontational and highly-structured treatment program for those lost, alone and hopeless children.

Since then, I have worked with children who suffered in ways no one, especially a child, should suffer. I have seen everything from physical, sexual and emotional abuse, to neglect, injuries and illnesses, total abandonment, and deprivation and institutionalization, where children never gained a sense of reality or the ability to respect themselves or others. I have been personally moved by the amount of emotional and physical pain children and their families have experienced and tolerated. In 1994, I became impassioned enough to put my training and experience to work on my own home front. We adopted a brother and sister who had lost everything in the way of family relationships and hope for the future in their native Ukraine. We began our quest to "undo" the emotional damage they had faced growing up abandoned and neglected in deprived conditions. Would these two children ever be able to accept another set of parents? Would they ever again be able to trust, love and respect? Would they always want to go back home and find out what happened to the parents who left them? What were the "hidden disabilities" or the genetic problems these children may face in the future? Would all of my professional training and experience in working with this exact population of children pay off in my own home?

Well, I soon learned that my professional training certainly gave me the intellectual understanding, but it was nothing in comparison to the need for practical "hands-on combat training," which I deemed an appropriate term in working our new children. We re-learned the words "consistency," "structure," "discipline," "directive," "rewards," and most importantly, we re-defined the entire meaning of love and affection. I, the accomplished doctor, had returned to being a student, learning from the child.

What quickly became evident was the hard-cold truth: love truly is not enough nor is it an adequate starting point in working with children who have been through pain and trauma. There were times love was only a word we kept to ourselves as a possibility for the future. The words "commitment," "re-developing," "dedication" and "safety" replaced the common phrase "I love you," as the former words describe much better ways of raising these special children.

Now, I can speak not only as a professional, but also as a father: over the course of time, and through much effort, an aggressive treatment approach involving trial-and-error, creativity and persistence allows children who were once thought to be "helpless and hopeless" to improve. But, there are **absolutely no short cuts**. None whatsoever. Believe me, we looked and found none.

I continue to work with struggling families throughout the country and have spent extensive time working alongside the Romanian Department of Child Protective Services/Child Welfare. I head up a team of American doctors from all different disciplines who work in the most dismal of Romanian orphanages in hope of providing proper medical and neuropsychological evaluations which give the child a "new diagnosis" as opposed to their long-standing diagnosis of "irrecuperable." Our humanitarian efforts, which have been greatly received and appreciated by the Romanian Department of Child Welfare with monumental work initiated by the former Secretary of State and Minister of the Department of Child Welfare, Dr. Cristian Tabacaru, are aimed at de-institutionalizing children who have been improperly diagnosed and severely mistreated. It often felt that our work was like chipping away at an iceberg, but after several humanitarian aid missions, we were able to properly evaluate and recategorize many children--some of whom were then allowed to enter group homes, vocational training programs, or even become eligible for adoptions. We also worked in conjunction with the Romanian-French organization "SERA" under Dr. Tabacaru's leadership, along with the British humanitarian group, the Romanian Challenge Appeal, directed by a very high spirited Irish woman named Monica McDaid. These projects aimed at de-institutionalization of Romanian orphans housed in the worst of conditions during the Ceaucesecu regime have received worldwide attention and concern due to human-rights violations.

In 1997, we took on another challenge: we rescued two Romanian orphans abandoned to the Neuropsychiatric Institution for the Irrecuperable in Siret, Romania, and decided to raise them as our own. These two brothers were destined to die from untreated hemophilia. The boys had been institutionalized for so many years that they could not even remember when they arrived there. They had no sense of time, people or the outside world.

Although I have collaborated with many experts from across the country who have extensive experience working with severely damaged children, it is worth noting that my aggressive assessment and treatment approach has been termed somewhat controversial. While I have received much praise, I also have critics who frown at the degree of aggressiveness. The only thing I can say is that children who are rapidly deteriorating and reaching a point of no return need to be aggressively treated and have a functional family recreated. Time does not wait and the more a child is allowed to "practice" unacceptable behavior, the more deeply ingrained the behavior becomes. Remember the phrase "practice makes perfect," well, this is not the kind of perfection families want. If a child is allowed to practice incorrigible behavior, they truly can become "irrecuperable."

I hope that one day, all educators and treatment professionals will become more open and less critical toward my unorthodox and somewhat provocative treatment approaches. It would be excellent if we could all come to the consensus that a multi-discipline treatment approach *does* work and that the most important aspect lies in the appropriate comprehensive assessment of the unmanageable child's brain/cognitions and emotions.

It must be acknowledged that before treatment begins, we must understand what we are treating. **Parents need to first increase their knowledge of how a child's brain and emotions work, then parent need to accept what I call the "80 Percent Solution." There may never be complete recovery. Success may be where a difficult child has moved up to functioning appropriately 80 percent of the time, leaving 20 percent of the remaining time problematic. <u>There is no such thing as perfection</u>, and anyone who seeks perfection with their child is not realistic. The goal is to strive to reach 80 percent.**

If your child has severe behavioral problems which include aggressive and violent tendencies, chronic defiance of authority, uncontrollable temper tantrums, verbally assaultive behaviors, manipulative and deceitful characteristics, chronic lying, substance abuse, sexual acting out, or academic underachievement, this book may serve as a great resource. If your child has fallen into the target group of children deemed "lost causes," "untreatable and unresponsive," "hopeless," or with severe Reactive Attachment Disorder, the program I am offering here should inspire new hope that your child's brain and emotions can be rehabilitated to where he or she may become manageable once again.

However, many families have found therapists who often opt not to label a child as "bad" or "hopeless." Rather, there is a tendency to emphasize finding some "goodness" within all children even if they exhibit grossly inappropriate behaviors that fall beyond the scope of parents' management. Most parents who have reached a level of being overwhelmed are actually ready and willing to take on any type of new or innovative treatment approach as long as there is a possibility or hope for change. Many therapists have told distraught families to be "supportive and patient,"even though the family is falling apart and in dire need of a change in treatment approaches. Many families continue in unproductive therapies with the trust and hope that the "problem child" will spontaneously recover or benefit from the current treatment program.

One of the principal goals of this book is to illustrate that many children, regardless of age, are extremely difficult to manage and exhibit a chronic pattern of asocial and amoral behaviors which require very vigorous and innovative assessment and treatment programs not typically available or accepted through standard counseling techniques.

What I have developed is a three-step program that any parent can follow—so long as he or she is extremely dedicated and, most importantly, does not give up. There will be detailed discussions on children who act out but continue to fall within the normal range of development, to children and adolescents who show behaviors which are far out of the norm.

Throughout the book, we also follow the lives of three special children: Angela, Chris, and Sergei, all of whom come from very different backgrounds, but all of whom were once considered "hopeless." We proceed step by step with these children and their families, watching both their struggles and their triumphs, many of which may parallel your own lives.

As I am sure you have experienced, mental health professionals today (i.e. social workers, counselors, pastoral services, psychologists and psychiatrists) often have very different opinions and views regarding children. Frequently, typical adjustment issues are over-exaggerated. Principal examples are the diagnoses of the 80's and 90's: Attention Deficit Hyperactivity Disorder (ADHD), Reactive Attachment Disorder (RAD), Oppositional Defiant Disorder (ODD) and Borderline Personality Disorder (BPD). Many children who are completely unmanageable are called ADHD when, in fact, their true emotional difficulties go far beyond the ADHD pattern.

Because I have seen case after case of children who are incorrectly grouped into these catch-all diagnoses, I will place extra emphasis throughout the book on clarifying children's neurodevelopmental and neuropsychiatric disorders. More importantly, this will also prevent incorrect treatment such as overuse of medication or counseling programs which may not be effective or intensive enough for the more difficult child. **Only after parents understand the principal causes of a child's uncontrollable behaviors will the proper treatment program be able to be quickly facilitated**. To reiterate, it is of utmost importance to have full knowledge of the child's brain and emotional capacities and work at their level of functioning, not our expectations as parents/adults.

There will also be a great deal of emphasis on "special populations" of children such as those who were unfortunately raised in severely abusive and neglectful environments, or those who have been institutionalized. International adoptions will be discussed at great length as these children are highly complicated, challenging and beyond the term "unique." This book will also be very important for families who have children with complicated neuropsychological and psychiatric problems, such as mental retardation or multiple learning disabilities.

Let me forewarn you, the innovative treatment approaches I offer are rigorous and demanding. Families must never give up. I am often called the "Combat Neuropsychologist" for **the methods I believe in and have seen work in thousands of cases will be like a form of boot camp for both you and your child. Treatment will require patience, diligence and dedication**. This program will not be easy, but whoever said life was easy? There are no guarantees with children, biological or adopted.

If you as family members persevere with my treatment approach, you will be supplied with new hope and momentum that can generate results.

Dr. Ronald S. Federici

Chapter 1
Understanding the Problem

Arrival at Hopelessness

"Hopeless" goes hand in hand with such descriptions as: desperate, discouraged, incurable and irreparable.

The hopeless child is one who has exhausted all family and professional interventions. It is very difficult for both parents and professionals to accept that a child is not treatable. It is a crucial part of a treatment professional's responsibility to continue to try to provide therapeutic services even if the child is non responsive, or to refer a child to a specialist who can possibly try another treatment approach. Unfortunately, there are children with such aggressive, violent, self-destructive/self-mutilative behaviors, in addition to uncontrollable rage, and bonding and attachment problems, that they can no longer be effectively managed by family members or professionals. A child who reaches this point has most likely been evaluated several times and has received several different "diagnoses" by experts.

Interestingly, many children who fall in the category of "hopeless" have had so many different psychiatric diagnoses and interventions that it is almost impossible for a new treatment provider to really understand what the problem is when the child arrives for further services. What I have found in my own practice is that children who have been deemed hopeless and non-responsive to professional interventions have often been improperly diagnosed or even overly diagnosed. For example, as I mentioned earlier, many, many children are called Attention Deficit Hyperactivity Disorder (ADHD) or Reactive Attachment Disorder (RAD) with coexisting oppositional-defiant behaviors. These children are often out of control and require constant interventions. What is being missed, though, is that many of these children have significant neurological and neuropsychological conditions well beyond a diagnosis of ADHD or RAD which have gone undetected and require more aggressive medical and psychiatric care in addition to practical psychological care. This approach is far different from the commonly used, and often ineffective, method of simply medicating the child with Ritalin and providing family therapy to try and control the child's behaviors.

Many children have also been given numerous diagnoses ranging from ADHD, RAD, learning disabled, oppositional and defiant, conduct disorder, bipolar mood disorder or just delinquent, when, in fact, these children actually have an undiagnosed developmental disorder, cognitive deficits, or bonding or attachment disorder which has prevented them not only from respecting themselves, but also from connecting with others in a healthy way. Children who have undiagnosed cognitive or bonding and attachment deficits often present with multiple, complex and continually "changing" diagnoses since their behavior can shift from person-to-person in an effort to prevent any type of solidification in their attachments. We will focus in depth on bonding and attachment disorders later.

Over the course of time and without proper assessment and treatment, these children with undiagnosed problems become even more complicated as they seem to "pick up" more problems along the way, including substance abuse, aggression and criminal behaviors, sexual promiscuity, and a general disregard for societal rules, as well as for their own personal safety. **Therefore, improper diagnosis and treatment often results in a child escalating to more severe destructive behaviors, while at the same time, deteriorating in terms of self-control, academic, social and family performance.**

Finding a way out is, by itself, almost an impossible task, as families feel totally trapped into a stagnant routine. Moving forward with another treatment attempt often produces feelings of anger, frustration, doubt and apprehension. I cannot stress enough that these are normal feelings and only further support the notion that a new, aggressive, structured and supervised treatment program may yield new hope and optimism.

Again, for families who are literally "starting over" this new approach may not produce 100 percent recovery; but the family needs to push forward with the goal of at least 50 percent improvement over their current situation—and the hope for 80 percent.

Meet Chris

I first met Chris when he was eleven years old. He came to me after he and his parents had seen almost a dozen of the top psychiatrists in Washington, D.C. Chris was the only child of Anne, a prominent attorney, and Richard, a top corporate executive of a large company. The family lived in a large, meticulously kept home in one of the wealthiest suburbs of D.C. Chris was raised in the most lavish lifestyle, but, because his parents were extremely busy people, he was often left in the care of nannies and babysitters. When his parents were with Chris, they tried to make up for the times they were not there by spoiling him, buying him whatever he wanted. His room looked like Disneyland, filled with toys, computer equipment, a television and a shelf full of videos. The parents even bought pets that Chris wanted, all of which ended up being cared for by the housekeepers and nannies. Chris was very bright and articulate and he entered a private preschool. His parents made certain he went on to attend only the most prestigious and exclusive schools thereafter. When Chris started seventh grade, he was sent to a boarding school where he lived Monday through Friday. Chris was also involved in many sports and social-recreational activities: golf, tennis, swimming, karate, music lessons, for which he was shuttled to and from by his caretakers.

Anne and Richard were pillars of respect in their community. They were members of country clubs, active in their church, and known for being charitable and conducting fund-raisers. They were occasionally featured in city magazines. The only problem was that the family's reputation began to change as Chris hit puberty. He was rapidly deteriorating and engaged in the most unusual and uncontrollable behaviors. Aggression, defiance and rage controlled the home.

How and Where to Find Help: Who is the Right "Guide"?

Chris's parents certainly took him to the top specialists, and by the time they arrived in my office they were very cynical. "We thought we were seeing the best but no one has been able to help," they lamented.

This certainly can be true. There are many excellent professionals out there in all aspects of mental health who try their best to work with families having very difficult children. Professionals will range from licensed counselors, family therapists, social workers, psychologists, psychiatrists and school guidance counselors (See Chapter 2 for descriptions of each), all of whom should be working to the best of his or her abilities. I want to emphasize, though, that finding the right person to guide the helpless and hopeless child and family is quite a task—but it *is* doable if families give it the importance it deserves. Equate the task to interviewing for a job, or buying a new home, both of which you intend to keep for the rest of your life. An important factor to keep in mind is that not all therapists are able, willing or equipped to deal with children who are categorized as hopeless. Therefore, it is going to be very important for families to be very directive with their questions and go on a search for professionals who meet the following criteria:

(1) First and most importantly, the therapist must have actual "combat experience." What I mean is the therapist needs to have been on the front-line, directly working with the most severely disturbed children who have been aggressive, violent, and who have had multiple psychiatric and psychological diagnoses. Even a "seasoned therapist" should be evaluated since families are looking for a very aggressive, energetic, highly verbal and somewhat compulsive therapist to help the hopeless child.

(2) Education and training is very important. Ask specific questions regarding the type and quality of education that the person has received, in addition to the amount and type of practical experience. Also, ask focused questions regarding the therapist's experience in psychological testing, child development, basic understanding of how the brain interacts with personality, and how "practical" their treatment strategies tend to be. Parents need to be ready to seek another avenue if they encounter therapists who just want to sit and talk about all the problems as opposed to rapidly formulating a plan of action which encompasses a willingness to try anything and everything to help the child and family. This also means the therapist must be open to reading, researching and seeking out additional supervision from experts around the country who have a reputation in working with the most difficult cases.

(3) Families need to find a therapist who is available by appointment and by phone for emergencies and additional support. Families who have reached

rock bottom need constant support, supervision, structure and encouragement as "giving up" is often easier than trying at this stage of despair.

(4) The treatment provider (much like a good job and well-built house) must be strong, sturdy, and come with excellent benefits. The therapist must have a wealth of information which can be consistently provided to the family. Books, articles, journals, conferences, videos or any type of adjunctive material should be at the family's disposal at any time. Also, the therapist needs to be knowledgeable on a wide variety of subject matter and not afraid to ask for additional help from others. Families want to beware of the treatment professionals who believe they can "fix everything" all by themselves. Even the most experienced therapist needs support and guidance at times.

(5) There has to be a degree of personal as well as professional "attraction." Family members and treatment professionals should generally like each other and be able to be open and expressive even if it means being critical and angry. There absolutely needs to be an open line of communication without reservations or boundaries (otherwise known as, "I am the doctor and you are the patient, and you must do what I tell you"). Children and families need to be active participants with mutual respect given at all times. While everyone may be working together, families must learn to trust their new treatment provider and follow guidelines even if they may not initially agree. Trust is a very personal aspect of the treatment program and must be of paramount importance.

(6) It is also very important to find a treatment provider who is not afraid to share his or her own personal experiences. Families in treatment need to realize that they are not always "psychiatric patients" and that everyone goes through adversity on occasion.

(7) It is also very important to have a treatment professional "hook up" the family with other families in the same position. Families often appreciate this group support from others dealing with the same trying issues.

Meet Sergei

Sergei was an adorable six year old whose sad puppy dog eyes tore at Peggy's heartstrings when she first saw him on a videotape of abandoned Russian children. Peggy, a government worker, and her husband, Bill, a graphic illustrator, had one nine-year-old son and desperately wanted more children, but were unable to have any. The little boy with the sad eyes and no one to love him seemed the perfect addition to Peggy and Bill's little family. The adoption agency that had taken the video said Sergei was healthy and happy—he just needed parents to love him.

The adoption was arranged and Peggy and Bill prepared for their trip to Russia to pick up their new son. What the agency did not mention, however, was that the adorable little boy had been severely abused and neglected by his biological parents, and then in the orphanage. Additionally, his biological mother, a known alcoholic and drug abuser, was clearly using damaging substances heavily during her pregnancy.

Sergei was even cuter in real life than on the video, and Peggy and Bill quickly whisked him away from the dirty and deprived Russian orphanage back to their comfortable New York home. For the first few days, Sergei was quite scared and remained quiet most of the time. Peggy and Bill showered him with love and attention and toys, trying to make him feel more comfortable, thinking it would just take time and plenty of affection. But then Sergei began to have rage attacks, lashing out at his new parents, throwing toys and hitting and biting his older brother. This behavior only became worse and more frequent. The parents called their adoptions agency who told them to "get counseling", but offered no follow-up.

What is Medical and What is Psychological?

Many families with the most difficult children have known from the time their child was born that there was something "different." There are certainly physiological and genetic origins to many children's aberrant behaviors. For these reasons, it is extremely important for families to find proper medical experts in the areas of pediatrics, neurology and psychiatry to work in close contact with psychological treatment experts.

Families should be very cautious in starting any type of new treatment plan that calls only for medication and not additional organized therapy. While medication is certainly a very important intervention and will be discussed at greater lengths in subsequent chapters, it should not be considered a starting point. This is particularly important given the fact that many families with grossly unmanageable children have gone through the gamut of medications and typically get tired of hearing about another change in medication or another dosage increase.

Before starting any treatment program, it is vital the family of a child with special needs understands the full range of medical, neurological and psychological issues involved. It is certainly possible for a child to go through a variety of medical and psychological evaluations, but often, the most difficult children are either over-diagnosed or under-diagnosed.

The starting point in any new, creative and innovative understanding of a child is for families to take a step back, agree to start over, and to gain a new opinion about their child in order to feel hopeful that other interventions, such as this one, will be helpful.

What is Normal Anyway?

One of the most difficult, yet essential, areas for families to understand is exactly which behavior problems in their children are "normal" and which signify that the child is off-track and headed for big trouble. Childhood problems run on a continuum from mild to moderate to severe. Accepting the severity of a problem is the first step to treatment and, hopefully, to recovery and rehabilitation.

Families with a heavy genetic history of emotional difficulties, such as alcoholism, drug addiction, major psychiatric disorders such as schizophrenia or manic-depressive illness, learning disabilities or even ADHD, need to be very carefully monitored as their children are highly vulnerable. It is also very common for children to show these vulnerabilities early on in their childhood development.

Meet Angela

I cannot even talk about Angela's early life without feeling a pang in the pit of my stomach. Angela was born into a world of chaos, confusion, abuse and neglect. Her biological mother was a drug addict, alcoholic and prostitute. Her biological father, whom she never knew, was also a drug addict. Child Protective Services intervened several times as Angela was often left home alone, unfed and unbathed. She was underweight and had failure-to-thrive syndrome. From the time Angela was born, her mother would leave her in one room while throwing wild parties in another. Angela witnessed open displays of sexual activity and was likely sexually abused, as well as physically beaten when she would make any type of noise in the home.

When Angela was six, she was placed in custody of social services and was then put in foster care with an aunt. Angela had trouble fitting in and would often scream and flail her arms and legs. Other times, Angela would retreat to her own world and not speak or acknowledge anyone at all. At school, she was just plain defiant. This went on for two years, until her aunt gave up.

Angela traveled the foster care circuit. Her next placement lasted only a month since she would not stop screaming. Her second, third, and fourth foster homes never lasted for more than six months. Angela knew how to keep everyone at a distance and sabotaged any attempt at stability.

Angela had been through numerous psychiatric evaluations. She had as many diagnoses as she did foster homes. It was clear no one knew what was actually wrong with her or what treatment she needed.

When I finally began to work with Angela, she was 13 years old and living with her maternal grandmother, but she continued to be a completely lost and alone child—even in the company of someone she knew. Angela's way of maintaining an impenetrable defense or "barrier" in which no one was allowed to pass through, clearly typifies that she was unable to move close to or trust anyone on a genuine level. Her entire perception of people was skewed as she had become more comfortable remaining in her "lost and alone world."

Bonding and Attachment as the Key to Stability

One of the most important areas to evaluate is the early bonding, attachment and cognitive development of infants through the toddler stage. Children absolutely require the physical comfort, support, control, and visual and verbal role models of parents in order to gain the initial perception that the world will be organized for them. The concept of bonding and attachment, and having a "healthy brain" is often not brought up enough in the therapy of young children, but it is clearly the foundation of any child's emotional stability. Much has been written on the effects of children raised in extended day care programs, foster care, or other types of institutional settings. It has been found that many children with difficulties have bonded to another caretaker aside from the parents in their early years. This was one of the first things I discovered with Chris. He had had a string of nannies and babysitters from birth. He would become attached to one just as she was replaced by someone else.

Children are totally reliant on their primary caretakers for physical nurturing and safety. **When the parents are not readily available, it is common for children to start off life by feeling insecure and afraid. This insecurity and fearfulness often causes a child to engage in intense temper tantrums as a way of gaining attention when these feelings arise.** Additionally, a typical problem of parents is to allow the infant/toddler extended time away from them while they are either working or engaged in other activities. Certainly, there are families where both parents must work, but it is very important to understand that certain sacrifices must be made in order to ensure the emotional well-being of a child, particularly during the first 2-to-3 years of life which are deemed a "critical bonding period." Otherwise, it is very common for children to quickly "forget" what their primary caretakers look like, feel like or how it is to be held by them. This is the start of "separation anxiety" which can often become quite intense and can later manifest in the form of temper tantrums, high anxiety and opposition.

As children develop language and social-interaction skills, they look to parents and significant others to learn and imitate behavior. This is a very critical stage, and the basis for establishing appropriate behaviors begins here. During this time children are extremely impressionable and will either benefit from parents' interventions or, to the contrary, become more removed when parents are not displaying the proper form of social connection or interactions. For Angela, this was a definite root to some of her major problems. Her role models were out-of-control themselves. How could Angela, a child, be expected to learn or know anything different? The conflict certainly does not have to be as severe as Angela's case. **Even just consistent arguing or verbal abuse within a family is enough to give a child the initial "imprint" of conflict, anger and aggression as a way of relating to other people.**

In viewing childhood development in general, it is very easy to overlook "stressors" which children and families experience on a day-to-day basis. There are many areas of stress during a child's early development that may affect their behaviors. It can be as simple as frequent changes in daycare or babysitting services or the addition of another sibling in the household. Other problems are parents who are involved in intense conflict, such as divorce or separation; who are experiencing trouble at work; or those parents who maintain a cold and distant attitude toward each other, such as Chris's parents who were more concerned about their appearance and their social status than their family unity. All of these confusing emotional behaviors within the family will often give the same "message" to the child that they are a secondary consideration. Parents can sometimes inadvertently give the message that they do not have time to deal with the child's emotional needs as they are preoccupied with their own adult needs and problems.

Children who start off their life feeling frustrated, anxious and insecure can often "progress" to greater stages of anger, frustration, oppositional behaviors, rage attacks and even violent outbursts. This is particularly evident in children from institutional settings, like Sergei, or in children who may have experienced impairments in brain growth and development due to high risk pre- and post-natal factors.

Bonding and attachment continues throughout all stages of childhood and adolescence, and even into young adult life. It may change in form over the years, and may also become more obscured and even misinterpreted as many families often feel that just living together constitutes bonding, when this may actually not be enough.

In looking toward older children and the emerging adolescent, it is very typical to see an upsurge of problems in behaviors. Pre-adolescence and adolescence is quite a confusing time and can often stress and strain the family bonds. The child wants independence and to "break away" from the family, yet the child is torn because he or she still needs parental love, support and nurturing. Often, a child eats up the parent's love and support, but exercises his or her independence by not giving anything in return. This causes a tremendous degree of stress on the family system as it is perceived that these children are "selfish" and not engaging in a give-and-take relationship with the parents.

Academic struggles often surface at this stage as well as the child is more concerned about social acceptance, peer relationships and the development of sexual interest than about completing specific goals and objectives with a sense of self-discipline. It is relatively safe to say that all children going through this stage of development and transition will experience some sort of anxiety and depression that may have an impact on their psychological, physical and biochemical development. With the onset of puberty, it is very common and "normal" for a child to experience mood swings, irritability and depression, as well as a stronger set of drives in the areas of sexual preoccupation and aggression. **Families often attempt to gain very tight control over pre-adolescents who seem to be breaking away. Rather, what families need to do is try to work with their child and increase bonding and attachment during these very difficult formative years. This will help the teenager approach new situations with greater confidence knowing "support" is out there**.

This is a difficult time for parents also as it is quite easy to take personally all of the child's hurtful and callous statements such as, "I hate you!" or "I wish I wasn't part of this family anymore!" The important thing to remember is, this is a normal way for a child to try to find dignity and identity rather than continuing to be totally reliant and dependent on parents.

Very often, unnecessary power struggles result from this situation. It is important for the parent to understand that the child is still relating to them in some way, and is looking for someone to serve as a "dumping ground" for all of the chaos and confusion swelling within their emotions. For these reasons, it is so very important for families to try to maintain a close relationship while still allowing the child his or her own space. Parents need to get to know the child in the midst of the child's peer groups as opposed to just trying to force a one-on-one parental-child relationship.

Extreme bonding and attachment disorders have been seen in children who have been raised in orphanages or institutional settings devoid of any nurturing. Even children who have been institutionalized for just a brief time can still exhibit deprivation and attachment problems. This is an incredibly difficult situation for families of children adopted from institutions. Parental instinct says that there is nothing that food, clothing, shelter, stimulation such as games and toys, and plenty of love and affection cannot fix. Yet, these attempts are often in vain and sadly, continue for year after unsuccessful year. What parents do not recognize is that their child has missed vital stages of development which needs to be re-taught through a slow and arduous process of bonding, attachment and behavioral control, in addition to rehabilitating cognitive impairments.

Techniques for working with children from institutional settings warrant special attention, and the entire Chapter 4 of this book delves into this unique situation.

The "Three Strike Rule"

Families having difficult children who have not responded to treatment in the past may believe that they have "struck out" and that nothing will ever change in their lives. I would like to offer the "Three Strike Rule" as a framework which may help direct families to decide to step up to the plate one last time by utilizing an aggressive treatment program that will instill new hope and motivation.

The three strike rule is very simple. When a family has seen **three** different treatment professionals and has received **three** different opinions (diagnoses), and has tried and failed for **three** years, then it's time for something more aggressive. Families really need to keep this philosophy of when to move to another treatment program as opposed to remaining "stuck"in their current unproductive therapies. Many families may have been told to "keep up the therapy" even though their current treatment program may only be providing day-to-day management as opposed to long-term improvement. Remember, life always moves forward and so must families. Families having difficult children must push forward even harder by learning from their mistakes and be willing to continually take on new approaches and ideas.

Summary

Any child, regardless of age, is going to experience a degree of acting-out behaviors that cannot be categorized as psychiatric or incorrigible without looking at many factors. Most vulnerable are children who have experienced problems with cognitive growth; bonding and attachment; children from families with a heavy genetic history of emotional difficulties; and children from families where there is considerable conflict. The family's ability to manage and allow for certain developmental difficulties is of utmost importance. Families need to pay close attention to assessing the root of the problem and the efforts made to change it.

Chapter 2

Problems and Causes

I cannot stress enough how important it is that families have a proper understanding of the problem before any treatment program can work. **To fully evaluate the problem, individual, family, social, educational and medical assessments are necessary.** All these factors are essential in a complete evaluation and, by leaving out just one, a major source of the problem can be missed.

Let us take Chris for example. When Chris was in elementary school, he was described by his teachers as "very bright, but not working up to his potential." His parents, Anne and Richard, brought him to a psychiatrist considered the best in the area. The psychiatrist focused on the educational aspect, observing that Chris had trouble staying focused and attentive, had poor motivation and work habits, was restless and fidgety and periodically would blurt out in class or talk back to teachers. Chris was diagnosed as Attention Deficit Hyperactivity Disorder (ADHD) and was started on Ritalin. Interestingly, in the family's upper-middle class community, there were many children on Ritalin therapy who were also seeing the same "best" psychiatrist. Chris would be taken to his weekly counseling appointments by his nanny or baby-sitter who would wait in the lobby chatting with the other nannies and sitters who had brought in children from Chris' neighborhood. Anne and Richard only attended the medication management appointments.

What was clearly missing was an assessment of other factors: the family dynamic, Chris' social interactions, and bonding and attachment issues. As the family would later discover, not addressing the real problem initially would only pave the way for Chris to slowly, but surely, begin to deteriorate. It often turns out that many children categorized as extremely unmanageable were later discovered to have had some type of undiagnosed medical or neurological condition (such as dementia, Fetal Alcohol Syndrome/Alcohol-Related NeuroDevelopmental Disorder, low IQ, seizures, head injuries, learning disabilities, severe hyperactivity or autism) that was actually the root of the behavioral problems. A "masking" set of behavioral problems can often mislead families and professionals into thinking the child only needs to be disciplined or better handled rather than treated for the real cause of the problems. Therefore, I always mandate a complete, multi-discipline evaluation by all medical, psychological and educational specialists before embarking on any new treatment plan with a difficult child. Remember, this book emphasizes the concept of starting over in order to move forward in a more productive treatment program.

Additionally, there are many children from institutional settings who have spent years without proper physical and nutritional care which has significantly affected their overall brain development. Without the development of a "healthy brain," emotional problems typically emerge as all of the "systems" are just not working within the child's body and mind. There must be a harmony between the brain and personality before children can develop strength and stability.

Sergei was one of these children. His parents, Peggy and Bill, had sought out numerous mental health and medical specialists after they could no longer control Sergei's spitting, biting, and throwing things. The specialists noted learning problems and developmental delays in language and academics. Sergei was given a slew of labels, from ADHD to learning disabled. He was placed on numerous medications, none of which helped. All the while, his behavior was worsening; he was purposely breaking things and trying to hurt others and animals. Sergei was also adept at manipulation. He would feign affection toward his family when he was being evaluated. He would vacillate from being completely withdrawn and isolated, to domineering over anyone who came near. He was even hospitalized on an inpatient psychiatric unit, but came out unchanged. By this time, Peggy had quit her job to try to deal with Sergei. She and Bill would cry at night, wondering what things would be like had they never adopted Sergei.

What was actually the root of Sergei's problems was twofold. There has been a great deal of research over the past few years on post-institutionalized children, such as adoptees from the former Soviet Union and Romania, who experienced profound medical and psychological neglect which impacted their brain development. Many of these children have a history of prematurity and low birth weight; small brain size (microcephaly); fetal alcohol syndrome; delays in speech, language, and motor skills; and untreated medical conditions such as ear infections, seizures or other types of viral and parasitic disease. These very subtle medical and neurological conditions are often missed in standard medical, psychological and educational evaluations and become a critical factor in understanding and treating the most difficult child's behavior.

For Sergei, the evaluation needed to involve pediatrics, pediatric neurology, audiology, occupational and physical therapy, and a complete neuropsychological evaluation. Then the second part of the puzzle had to be addressed: the family. What had happened was that Peggy and Bill actually gave too much too quickly.

What Do I Do?

One of the biggest pitfalls for families is that they often wind up getting only a single opinion and picking an approach for treating their child which they are told they need to stick with for months—or even years—even if positive results are not noticed. A prime example is when a child is diagnosed with ADHD by a physician, put on medication, and told to continue the medication even though there have only been slight improvements in behavior control.

What I preach to every family who enters my office is: **There is no such thing as a "quick fix." I often use the metaphor that children are like computers. Difficult kids are complicated machines and need complicated "repairs." If we consider the brain like a computer, then something in their "hard drive" is not working properly. Brains and emotions need to be continually tuned, upgraded and repaired just like any other piece of machinery.** Another example is when a family with a problem child only seeks out short-term family counseling when actually, the child has a more severe psychiatric or neurological disorder. I have designed the following assessment program and recommend it be followed by all families with a difficult child. For families with post-institutionalized children it is important to find professionals who specialize in this area and have seen many of these "special children."

The following list indicates types of essential evaluations your child will need:

(1) A **Comprehensive Developmental Pediatric Evaluation** to assess height, weight, growth parameters, laboratory studies, allergies and asthma, food sensitivities, and any type of general physiological abnormalities. Serological testing for hepatitis, HIV, lead testing, thyroid, and parasites, and any other chronic or contagious medical condition is recommended. It is also important to have the child monitored frequently by your pediatrician as any prescribed medication may have side-effects that also need to be addressed. A qualified Developmental Pediatrician will also be able to assess a child for possible Fetal Alcohol Syndrome and make any type of additional referrals to specialists, such as pediatric neurologists, eye-ear-nose and throat specialists (ENT), ophthalmologists, infectious disease specialists, gastroenterologists, and geneticists.

(2) A **thorough Audiological and Visual Examination** are essential as vision and hearing are necessary "clinical sensors" for learning and emotions. An audiological examination should include an ENT consult with a tympanogram. A visual examination should be completed by an ophthalmologist and developmental optometrist who specializes in potentially learning disabled or developmentally delayed children.

(3) A comprehensive **Pediatric Neurology Evaluation** to rule out any type of overt or subtle seizure disorder which can range from either grand mal or absence seizures; Tourette's or a pattern of tics and/or stereotypic movements; explosive disorder, which may be related to brain dysfunction; autism; or depression and/or manic depression, which may be related to neurological and biochemical factors (possible partial-complex seizure disorder). Often, very subtle neurological disorders can either cause or exacerbate behavioral and emotional problems. Also, a pediatric neurologist can help diagnose ADHD which is really a neurological condition affecting a child's ability to concentrate and focus on tasks. This consultation will often involve blood and lab studies, an electroencephalogram (EEG) and, if warranted, an MRI or PET scan of the brain. There is a great deal of research currently taking place on examining brain scans of difficult children in an effort to pinpoint areas of impairment which produce problems. Visiting a competent pediatric neurologist is a very important step, yet the majority of parents often overlook it.

(4) **Genetic studies** if determined necessary by the attending physician. There are multitudes of very complicated and obscure genetic conditions that can be contributing to learning and behavioral difficulties. Also assess for Fragile X chromosomal pattern which can be a condition producing mental retardation.

(5) A **Comprehensive Neuropsychological Evaluation** which assesses a child's higher-level thinking, reasoning, intellectual capabilities, memory and learning, attention, and personality factors. Many children who have average emotional and behavioral presentations often have very subtle "neuropsychological impairments" which effect their logic and reasoning skills. Additionally, attachment disorders may actually be "neuropsychological attachment disorders" where a subtle brain weakness prevents appropriate thinking and reasoning, including the ability to sort out and understand emotions, verbal interactions, and body language. Even subtle neuropsychological learning problems subject a child to developing emotional, depressive and attachment-disorder problems.

Make sure that the clinical psychologist or psychiatrist requests formal neurocognitive and psychological testing as opposed to just "diagnosing" the child after a basic screening or a rating scale. Neuropsychological disorders typically comprise the largest segment of difficult children. A neuropsychologist is a true "specialist" in differential diagnoses of brain-related versus psychiatric problems.

A list of recommended neuropsychological tests is included in the Appendix of this book.

(6) **Speech and Language and Auditory Processing Evaluation** should be completed in the child's native language via an interpreter. The importance of assessing a child's language comprehension, memory, reasoning abilities, and expressive speech is critical and should be done immediately upon arrival. Current research shows a high incidence of language disorders in post-institutionalized children. Speech and language therapy is often highly recommended in conjunction with "English as a Second Language" (ESL) services. It is a tactical mistake on the part of many school systems to keep a language-impaired child from another country in continual ESL when they need speech therapy and language remediation.

(7) **Comprehensive Educational Evaluations** to assess a child's learning potential or evidence of a learning disability syndrome in any area of language, reading, writing, math or processing. Many older adopted children have not had any educational experiences and may require a very intensive school-based remediation program since they are literally starting from the first stage of school and socialization.

(8) **Physical and Occupational Therapy** to evaluate fine and gross motor coordination, sensory perceptual skills, movement, gait, balance and sensory integration. Children with even subtle occupational and/or physical problems can often be very defensive and impulsive. There has been a very strong movement to include "sensory integration therapy" with occu-

pational therapy, which aims at stimulating vestibular and proprioceptive functioning (sensory input and regulation).

(9) Have a **Family Therapy Assessment**. Either a qualified clinical psychologist or a trained family therapist and/or clinical social worker can provide a very comprehensive assessment of the strengths and weaknesses within a family system. While a very difficult child may have individual problems, there are often family-interactional patterns which clearly contribute to a child's out-of-control behaviors. Hierarchy, structure, communication patterns and levels of motivation need to be discussed, as well as including additional evaluations of individual family members if they exhibit problems which may be negatively impacting the child. For example, a parent who is clinically depressed or other family members who have psychiatric problems, need to be assessed and treated prior to or simultaneously with treatment for the child.

If family member's problems go untreated, the likelihood of a child improving on treatment is slim to none. Also, if parents are burned out or completely worn down by the difficult child, they are apt to be inconsistent in working on a treatment plan so, there needs to be work with the parents first before starting treatment for the child. This is important as it avoids the likelihood of a parent quickly becoming pessimistic and giving up again. Additionally, if parents are preoccupied by other life issues such as work, finances, grief and loss, etc., those issues serve as a distraction to the primary focus which has to be the difficult child. It is often very painful for families to accept that their own emotional issues have contributed to or reinforced the child's difficulties. Parents need to realize that difficult children often "capitalize" on other family members' emotional distress because it takes the focus off the child's bad behavior.

Where Do I Go?

Many families with difficult children have gone through countless therapists and therapies only to walk away feeling helpless and hopeless themselves. All together, the three families we are focusing on had consulted with over a dozen professionals before they found their way to my office.

I have often found that traditional psychological and psychiatric interventions alone are <u>not</u> effective and that the very difficult child requires the most innovative, aggressive and, at times, unconventional treatment program. Find professionals who really know children, especially difficult children. If the therapist only sees one or two difficult children a year, this does not constitute adequate experience for your needs. Positive results will not be seen unless parents fully understand the different types of therapies and practitioners. What follows is a list of standard types of practitioners and the services they offer:

Pediatrician or Family Practice Physician: A pediatrician or family practice physician is a medical doctor who specializes in childhood and adolescent developmental disorders, and typically treats routine conditions. This doctor is often referred to as the "primary care physician" who will be responsible for ordering additional laboratory studies, diagnostic procedures and coordinate referrals to other specialists.

Clinical Psychologist: A clinical psychologist is a doctor with a Ph.D. or Psy.D. in psychology. The clinical psychologist has usually completed courses in general development, psychological testing and measurement, as well as psychotherapy counseling and techniques. Many clinical psychologists develop a subspecialty in child and adolescent development, psychological testing and family therapy. Not all psychologists do in-depth testing. Also, it is important that a treating psychologist have post-doctoral training in childhood disorders.

Clinical Neuropsychologist: A Clinical Neuropsychologist has undergraduate and graduate level training in biological and medical theories pertaining to human behavior. Neuropsychologists complete graduate (Doctoral) studies in Clinical Neuropsychology with post-graduate specialty training (Fellowships and Board Certifications) in the assessment and treatment of adult and child neurodevelopmental disorders, neurological and medical conditions, traumatic brain injury, learning and memory disorders, with the most important role being an expert in the differential diagnosis of organic (brain-related) conditions versus psychiatric/ psychological disorders. Often, the neuropsychologist assesses true "neuropsychiatric conditions" in which both the brain and emotions produce a complex array of symptoms. The Clinical Neuropsychologist often coordinates care with other allied medical, neurological and mental health professionals in order to coordinate the most appropriate cognitive (brain) rehabilitation program, psychiatric care (medication issues) and psychological therapies.

Psychiatrist: A psychiatrist is a medical doctor who specializes in the evaluation of major psychiatric and emotional disorders that may require medication. Psychiatrists complete medical school and post-graduate training in psychiatric disorders, along with subspecialties in child and adolescent psychiatry. The primary focus of psychiatry is in medication consultation and management, with only a few psychiatrists actually having formal training in psychotherapy, counseling or other interventions to address childhood behavioral and emotional disorders. Many psychiatrists work with or refer patients to specialists in child and family evaluation and therapy.

Clinical Social Worker: Clinical social workers complete a Master's Degree in Social Work which emphasizes the structure of the family and the child's interactional strengths and weaknesses. Social workers typically focus on social, educational and family adjustment issues, but do not have formal training in psychological testing. Many social workers complete additional training and licensure to be able to offer counseling to individuals and families.

Marriage and Family Therapist: Marriage and family therapists have a Master's Degree in counseling techniques that mainly focus on relationships, families and couple problems. Family therapists focus on communication building, and structure and boundaries within the family.

Occupational and Physical Therapist: These allied medical specialists evaluate motor, sensory-perceptual, and sensory-integration skills, as well as gait and balance. Most of these therapists are available at major hospitals.

Audiologist and Speech and Language Pathologist: These are licensed specialists who evaluate and treat receptive and expressive language disorders, articulation disorders or children who may be formally "hearing impaired".

Ophthalmologist and/or Developmental Optometrist: These specialists will assess primary visual acuity deficits and secondary visual-perceptual problems which often contribute to learning disabilities.

Autism Specialist: This group of therapists is highly trained in dealing with children having all variations of autism and focuses on speech, language, social-interactional skills with an emphasis in Applied Behavioral Analysis (ABA). Autistic specialists are often utilized both at home and at school and help arrange intensive treatment programs to better manage the child with an autistic diagnosis.

Educational Advocate: This is a very new specialty in which the educational specialist reviews all evaluations and treatment recommendations and incorporates the material into the appropriate "Individualized Educational Program." The advocate accompanies the parents to all school meetings and helps negotiate the most appropriate replacement and school-based interventions for the special-needs child.

Signs and Symptoms of the Most Important Problem: Bonding and Attachment Disorders

So far, we touched on bonding and attachment as one source of a child's out-of-control behavior. I really want to drill in this concept though, because I find, more often than not, it is at the root of a child's problem. This bonding and attachment concept should always be kept in the back of parents' minds. Think of Chris, Sergei and Angela. All of them, in different ways, had bonding and attachment disorders. For Chris, his parents were unavailable and the bonds he did form would often be severed when nannies would change shifts or leave. For Angela, the only people in her life to bond to were chaotic. And for Sergei, there was no one to bond to at all. Assessment of bonding and attachment should be done over the course of time *and* with the input of multiple specialists to determine cognitive and emotional abilities.

It is very important in the early stages of assessing a child's difficulties to determine if the child is "attached" or "detached." The concept of attachment needs to be viewed on both the individual and the family level, as parents can be detached from their children, and children from their parents.

Often, parents are emotionally and physically unavailable to meet a child's needs. A parent who travels as part of his or her job, a parent who is a substance abuser, or a parent who is preoccupied with his or her own emotional difficulties may be emotionally "detached" from the child and the family system. While the majority of families make a very strong effort to bond and attach, many unforeseen circumstances occur in which parents themselves "inadvertently prioritize" who is in the family system and who will be the recipient of the majority of available physical and emotional care.

This, in no way, makes parents inadequate or neglectful; but what happens is that the child may perceive that he or she is being abandoned by the family member. The key here is that children need to perceive that they are physically and emotionally bonded to their parents. If this happens correctly, there will be less tendency towards acting out and fewer feelings of abandonment, depression and insecurity.

Bonding and attachment occurs on several levels:

1) caring for physical needs
2) loving and nurturing
3) consistent discipline
4) teaching moral values, standards and "right from wrong"
5) educating and training in sensitivity, empathy, caring and generosity

Children and families require a great deal of glue to bond and attach to each other. Imagine trying to build a house by only putting walls on top of the ground without a foundation. Without that firm foundation, the entire structure will soon fall apart. Likewise, if children start off with an unstable foundation, it is very difficult for them to develop any sense of trust or feelings that relationships are the basis of safety and security.

The early stage of bonding and attachment disorder always starts off with a child being frustrated since his or her basic needs are not being met. Children who do not have parental love, attention, affection and soothing often progress into stages of depression as they feel life is emotionally unrewarding and typically a "chore" to live.

The following are some symptoms of the unattached child:

1) Engaging or charming in a superficial way; an overall sense of phoniness and sneakiness
2) A general lack of eye contact
3) Indiscriminate affection with strangers
4) A lack of ability to give and receive affection (a non-cuddly child)
5) Destructive to self and others and cruel to animals
6) Chronic crazy lying even in the face of reality
7) No control over impulses
8) Easily distracted

9) Lack of cause-and-effect thinking
10) Lack of a conscience
11) Abnormal eating patterns; often stealing, hoarding and gorging food
12) Poor peer relationships
13) Preoccupation with fire, blood and gore
14) Asks persistent nonsensical questions, chatters incessantly and has abnormal speech patterns
15) Inappropriately demanding and clinging

It is also important for parents to understand the individual temperament of a child. The simple fact remains that some children are just born more sensitive and anxious and require a tremendous amount of attention. This type of child can often slip into very deep states of depression early on in life and may later show separation anxiety, fear of strangers, lethargy or unmanageable rage attacks.

If a child perceives that he or she is somehow deprived or neglected, an inner sense of anger and rage toward the parents begins to develop. This type of rage can begin very early in infancy. When children feel frustrated, depressed and unhappy, they will often throw a temper tantrum even when the parents are not in close proximity. This may be the child's way of trying to express feelings of abandonment and rejection. Primitive emotional outbursts and sometimes aggressive and destructive behaviors are often the only way a child can relate his or her feelings. In the institution where Sergei lived, the children who had been neglected from birth often regressed to banging their heads against the walls or rocking back and forth; futile attempts at self-stimulation.

Over time, depression may seem to fade and the child becomes more angry, externalizing the rage in the form of under achievement, school refusal, running away, physical and sexual acting out, violence and often delinquency. Relationships begin to be looked upon as another potential source of hurtfulness, to the point where the child may either stay away from others completely (called Attachment Disorder, Inhibited-type), or be extremely demanding, controlling, gregarious and aggressive towards others (Disinhibited-type).

Unfortunately, by the time the child reaches a delinquent level, he or she is only viewed by others as being hopeless. It is a common, yet unfortunate, pattern: the child's despair and depression have seemed to disappear but what remains is anger and rage, which becomes the critical focus of the family and professionals. What is actually happening is that the root of the problem, the depression, has not disappeared but has only "progressed" into rage. Too often, treatment providers become overwhelmed and unable to get past the child's rage. Once again, the real problem goes unaddressed while the symptoms masking the problem are targeted, medicated or ignored.

Assessing Bonding Integrity

Attachment disorders may seem to be very complicated psychiatric conditions, but are actually quite common in children who have been described as being incorrigible and unmanageable. If a family has the ability to allow a treatment professional to evaluate the complete family system, it will likely be surprising how patterns of behavior, family relationships and general dynamics that may have led to an attachment and bonding disorder are easily identifiable. This evaluation is a very important starting point since understanding the problem means the family is already halfway toward resolving the problem.

The first step is to understand who the child's role models have been. Are there one or two parents? What other authority figures have been involved in raising and disciplining the child? It is very important to understand the quality and consistency of the parent's or caretaker's response to the child's physiological, emotional and social needs.

Often in this evaluation stage, families tend to minimize the amount of tension and conflict that has occurred in the home, along with how these experiences could negatively impact a child. A child who has watched or heard their parents in conflicts or catastrophic situations, such as poverty, substance abuse, physical or sexually inappropriate behaviors, or indiscriminate socialization where a multitude of people are in and out of the home, may be traumatized to the point where he or she feels angry and confused. Or, parents who are very young or involved in their own emotional problems and unresolved childhood issues can often project their own anger, frustrations and depressions onto the child, leading the child to feel extremely insecure and afraid.

The Lost and Alone Child

What we have been discussing thus far are the traits and characteristics of children with attachment and bonding disorders. I want to take a step backward now and look at what has been happening emotionally within the child since early development. We already know that most of out-of-control children have experienced a tremendous sense of rejection and abandonment by their primary caretakers, and these feelings may eventually spread out and be directed toward their relatives or other authority figures. It is very common for children who have experienced deep depression, despondency and a feeling of detachment to see relationships not as sources for comfort and soothing, but more like objects which need to be controlled. Therefore, many deeply depressed and despondent children relate to others on a superficial level, or even a very manipulative level. It is hard for them to trust anyone. Who really wants to be hurt or neglected again? Aloneness is preferable to these children.

A common statement I hear children say is, "No one really loves me anyway." I look at this closely for it is the principle reason why a child is acting out at home.

What the child is trying to communicate is that he or she feels detached and empty. Herein lies the understanding of the most difficult child.

In Search of Jiminy Cricket

Children who exhibit a chronic pattern of asocial and amoral behaviors tend to lack the formation of a conscience. These children have not gone through the stages of cognitive and psychological development where they would have learned to trust others and to internalize the role model which had hopefully taught them guilt and remorse for wrong doings. This situation requires, again, an assessment of the family system. The concept of developing a strong moral sense filled with appropriate guilt, remorse and a solid conscience or, as per Freud, a "superego," may have been absent in the child's life. Basically, a child may not have developed the ability to differentiate right from wrong, and may not have learned how to respect the needs and wishes of others. They may have developed a rather self-serving thought pattern and behavioral presentation as they are trying to "survive" in a world that has been extremely painful and difficult for them to understand. This was most evident with Angela and Sergei, both of whom had no appropriate role models and both of whom saw nothing wrong with lying, stealing and hurting others.

Often, families feel that children should be able to care for themselves at very early years. There are a great deal of children who attempt, and succeed, at surviving in deprived and damaging environments, but their survivorship often results in their becoming cold, indifferent and very angry. Survivorship always has a price attached.

Crazy Lying

Children who are detached and have not yet developed a solid sense of self or integrity often engage in "crazy lying." This means they lie in order to get their way and will hold their ground even when faced with indisputable reality or evidence. Peggy once told me she was in the same room with Sergei when he purposely stomped on a glass, breaking it. Just seconds afterward, with the broken glass scattered on the floor, he denied having broken it. This pattern of crazy lying and asocial behaviors sabotages any effort at close interpersonal relationships and promotes an additional state of anger and rejection between child and parent. To take it a step further, this develops into a vicious cycle where the child who is engaged in crazy lying and deceitful behaviors recreates continual rejection and abandonment by parents. Chaos and confusion turns into a way of life for these children, while interpersonal relationships become equally chaotic. Crazy lying is truly habitual-- and remember, "practice makes perfect."

Tug of War

At this point, you may be asking why a child who desperately needs attachment and bonding from parents continually pushes them away by inappropriately acting-out. Clearly, this reaction seems a paradox and irrational, and in truth is one of the most complex and difficult questions I encounter from parents. I find that often the only answer I can give is that the child is confused and that his or her perception and ability to feel safe and secure in relationships is altered. For these reasons, the child may vacillate from being appropriate and cooperative to being very manipulative, angry and unpredictable. I also stress that parents need to redirect their thinking in trying to understand how, at an early stage, their child may have felt completely insecure and afraid. This is often difficult for the parents to do since, likely, they were never aware of the depth of the problem. Parents can sometimes become very defensive if they feel "blamed" or in some way responsible for the problem. I try to emphasize that problems develop over the course of time and that "everyone is involved and everyone interacts." This happened with Peggy and Bill. Of course, they knew that the conditions Sergei was raised under were dark, dirty, and often lacked proper food, but they never really understood that there was a strong likelihood their son was hardly ever touched or given affection by a caretaker. I will never forget the look of horror on their faces as I described what life may have been like for Sergei. They did not want to hear what I had to tell them, but they could deny it no longer.

For Chris and his family, seeing the whole picture was even more difficult because there was a lot of guilt. Anne and Richard had to reflect upon the way they had raised Chris, the priorities they had set, and the dynamic of the entire family. Sometimes, families give up trying or are just too "burned out" to continue. Without the family, the child is totally lost and will regress further.

Childhood Depression

Many people, including mental health professionals, are still very confused regarding the entire concept of childhood depression. People often think that children who are depressed should cry all the time, be sullen and somber, and are always thinking about killing themselves. While this is certainly an extreme form of childhood depression, the typical form of depression in youths is one which is "masked" or hidden. Even mentally retarded and autistic children get depressed--a concept which eludes many professionals and parents.

Children who are going through a very difficult stage in their development often slip into states where they are generally unhappy, negative and pessimistic. Also, they are just not able to keep up with environmental and interpersonal demands and pressures. Add to this insecure feelings about being shorter, thinner, fatter, or taller than the norm, which may subject a child to social rejections and feelings of inadequacy about their overall appearance. Then, top it all off with the fact that children are innately immature in their problem-solving strategies and just do not know how to deal and cope with demands and pressures placed upon them, and you have an intense mixture of frustration and anger just waiting to explode.

Many children who have depression are also impulsive, hyperactive, have poor attention span and concentration, and are distracted easily. This is why many children who actually have depression are given other labels, particularly ADHD or just a "behavior problem." Depression runs deep in the heart and soul of the troubled child.

Acting Out: A Symptom of a Bigger Problem

We have all been in the check-out line at the grocery store when a child is lured by the strategically-placed candy and throws a temper tantrum when told, "No, put it back, you cannot have that." Of course, it is normal to encounter some resistance. But a parent needs to take notice when the child does not forget the situation relatively soon after and dwells in constant complaining, whining and crying when his or her needs are not immediately met. **This extreme sadness and negativity is the first warning sign.**

The next stage of frustration and unhappiness is the temper tantrum in the younger child and the more intense emotional outbursts with the older child. While occasional temper tantrums or outbursts are normal and to be expected, more frequent ones or long-lasting ones may the direct byproduct of unresolved frustrations and sad feelings within the child and with the family system. If severe or frequent temper tantrums and angry outbursts are allowed to continue without proper intervention, children rapidly move toward increased aggression, and provocative and unmanageable behaviors. This can take the form of destructive and violent outbursts against property or other people.

Destructive behaviors are very typical in children who have a long history of depression and frustration. Again, we know children are looking for any type of "outlet" to expel their feelings. Since they cannot organize and vent these feelings in a more appropriate manner, they act out.

This can turn into violence if children are allowed to continually to display problems over the course of years. These children wind up in a highly aggressive, destructive and even "predatory" phase in which they stalk out other children and try to violently control them; an example is the chronic delinquent who steals, hits, assaults, and is in constant police trouble. These children view intense aggression and violence as ways of establishing dominance and control over a situation when, in fact, these children are completely out of control themselves. This is the child people are afraid to be around.

A child who exhibits aggressive and violent tendencies often is sent to juvenile detention or criminal court where he or she receives punitive instead of professional interventions. It is very difficult for authority figures to view a violent and rageful child as a child who had depression and despondency. Often the authorities' only goal is to prevent any additional violent behaviors by controlling the child. This is certainly an appropriate starting point, but many of these children who are in the "violent cycle" are often lost in the criminal justice system. It is the same issue for long-term psychiatric hospitalization: do they really improve?

I also try to view the violent and aggressive child from a more medical and neurological standpoint. Many of these children have some type of underlying brain difficulties, possibly a chemical imbalance, which causes them to become extremely agitated and volatile in their moods and emotions, thus resulting in violent and aggressive behaviors. Some children are driven by intense mood swings, agitation and depression, which cause them to be very hyperactive, impulsive and out of control. Others have undiagnosed psychiatric conditions such as Bipolar Disorder (manic-depressive illness), Schizophrenia or other major emotional disturbances which are causing them to completely "break down." The resulting aggression and violence is merely a manifestation of a feeling of total loss of internal control and a great fear that they are "losing their mind" or losing control of themselves.

Chris' acting-out behavior was allowed to progress. Soon, his occasionally disrupting behavior in class turned aggressive and he would steal, push and shove classmates and generally treat everyone as second-class citizens. He would blatantly refuse to do homework, telling his teachers "I already know it." Chris' psychiatrist increased his dose of Ritalin for ADHD and told Anne and Richard that should do the trick. Anne and Richard felt the boarding school was overreacting to Chris's behavior and that, after four years, the school was obviously just not understanding him and unwilling to work with him. So, Chris was transferred to another top school and, after one semester, was dismissed for belligerent behavior. Anne and Richard found yet another private school that had a more structured setting and was even more expensive. The expense was looked upon as "finding the better school" and Chris was then enrolled.

Anne and Richard constantly received phone calls from the new school about Chris' behavior. They changed psychiatrists, and Chris was put on different medication. No difference. They changed psychiatrists again. New medication, still no difference. Another psychiatrist and along with that, a new diagnosis: bipolar mood disorder. Suddenly, with a more serious diagnosis, Anne and Richard looked upon their son as "sick." He was given more leeway and was allowed to throw tantrums. They gave him every toy, privilege and freedom he demanded. He would play with a toy for a while, then destroy it and ask for more. Anne and Richard felt sorry for Chris and viewed him as a "very misunderstood child."

But then, Chris began to deteriorate rapidly. He started setting fires and abusing animals, and he began to smoke. He stole alcohol from his parents' bar and he stole petty things from grocery stores and from his classmates. He also began to wet the bed. Behaviors went from bad to incorrigible.

Probably the most odd of Chris's behaviors was that he actually found pleasure in the smell from his soiled pants. He began to wet his pants at school and found it amusing when his classmates made fun of him. In a demented way, he was in control.

Control began to rule Chris' life. He went after his mother one day with a baseball bat yelling, "No one is going to tell me what to do." Anne and Richard ran to the psychiatrist asking for stronger medications. The psychiatrist recommended family therapy also, but everyone backed away because they were intimidated when Chris intensely screamed over and over, "There is nothing wrong with me! Everybody needs to leave me alone!" Even the family therapist felt overwhelmed.

Again, Anne and Richard went doctor shopping. They were looking for a miracle cure, some medication they could give their son that would make him normal again. What they had not realized was that this was not a problem that could be solved by medication alone. Chris had reached the point of becoming a "hopeless child" and one caught up in the eternal roller coaster of unproductive assessment and treatment.

Summary

It is essential to understand that acting-out behavior in children can often signify a deeper issue, such as a bonding and attachment disorder, or a form of depression, both of which may be a "starting point" in children who engage in disruptive, aggressive and potentially vigorous and violent behaviors. The m may lack the cognitive integrity to actually "get it". Understanding the problem is the first step toward solving the problem. Choosing the right guide is essential for this process to begin. Different mental health providers have different degrees of expertise and areas of focus, it's vital to find the one that best fits your needs. The next chapter will focus on more of the specific psychiatric signs and symptoms which may indicate that a child's deviant behavior is the direct cause of an emotional disturbance requiring aggressive care.

Chapter 3

What is A Psychiatric Disorder?

The last two decades have brought tremendous knowledge in the area of psychiatric diagnoses. Research institutions across the country have studied every psychiatric disorder known to mankind ranging from ADHD, depression, anxiety, manic depression, schizophrenia, alcoholism, drug addiction and obsessive-compulsive behaviors. With all of this research occurring regarding mental illness, children nowadays are often quickly slapped with one of the aforementioned "diagnoses" when they may have nothing more than a simple behavioral problem. If we line up all of the symptoms for psychiatric disorders, a child may exhibit one, if not all, symptoms depending on the day of the week or their attitude at any moment in time. As an example, literally thousands of children are diagnosed with ADHD and it is to the point now that this "illness" or "condition" may actually be a catch-all for any type of depression, anxiety, PTSD, mood or major psychiatric disorder, or for any child who has grown accustomed to being disruptive, aggressive, or generally frustrated with school (often due to undiagnosed learning disabilities).

A true psychiatric disorder is still defined as one in which there is a strong tendency towards some type of medical/neurological/biochemical problem. For example, a true diagnosis of ADHD is believed to involve problems in chemical activity in the brain adversely affecting the ability to pay attention, concentrate and control hyperactivity and impulsivity.

A true psychiatric disorder will also cause a ripple-effect in many other areas of a child's life. For example, children who have clinical depression often have difficulty sleeping, eating, paying attention and concentrating, and are either hyperactive or under-active. They also tend to be pessimistic, moody, irritable and intolerant. Depressed children can appear exactly like a child with ADHD, with behavior problems, or just a bad attitude. Many depressed children also have great difficulty with bonding and attachment and may appear withdrawn, isolated and shy, or overly disinhibited and hyperactive-impulsive.

Understanding Medical Conditions

Documented medical conditions in children can clearly impact psychiatric and emotional functioning. For example, children who have chronic illnesses, physical abnormalities, neurological problems, or another condition with a clear physiological basis, will often struggle with a great deal of sadness, frustration and depression which can impact behavior and social skills.

Children with medical conditions, such as seizures resulting from brain injuries, previous head injuries or post-neurosurgery, or children who have recovered from such illnesses as meningitis and encephalitis can typically have a great deal of anger, irritability, low tolerance, attention and concentration problems, hyperactivity, and personality changes. Additionally, medical and neurological conditions such as Tourette's Syndrome, retardation and autism can produce coexisting hyperactivity and attention disorders, multiple tics, high anxiety and obsessive-compulsive traits, as well as clinical depression. All of these offshoots are the direct result of the child feeling "different" in comparison to his or her peers.

Other medical conditions such as chronic asthma and allergies, diabetes, chronic fatigue syndrome or percocious puberty, which require regular medication, can often result in a child feeling generally tired and irritable. Particularly, asthma medications and treatment may result in hyperactivity, depression and irritability. There are also endocrine problems, genetic disorders or some types of neurological condition that can send a child into a downward spiral. High risk pre- and post-natal factors, such as fetal alcohol/drug use, smoking, viruses or trauma can cause major problems that can surface later in a child's development.

Children can play very roughly with each other which increases the likelihood of head injuries that may go undetected. Head injuries can be a principal factor in children who have erratic and aggressive behaviors. A very careful developmental history involving the degree and frequency of a child's "accidents" needs to be included in the overall assessment. Poor pre- and post-natal care can also result in a child being born with brain damage, which leads to major cognitive and behavioral issues.

Feeling overwhelmed? Of course, which is why multiple specialists are needed to really get to the root of what is going on with your child. For Sergei, what we discovered was that he had some fetal alcohol problems, he also had blocked out his years of being abandoned and neglected in Russia and was left with tremendous rage and depression which he took out on everyone around him. What was also a very important revelation was that Sergei's thinking was extremely concrete and he had difficulty benefitting from previous experiences. This was the principle reason why therapy and all of Peggy and Bill's attempts had failed in the past.

Understanding Genetics

Family history also plays a role in the development of psychiatric disorders. Alcoholism, drug addiction, depression, anxiety, schizophrenia or manic depression in family members often results in children who are highly vulnerable to developing some type of emotional problem. There is a great deal of research on trying to "trap" family genetic backgrounds. For example, learning disabilities and attention disorders tend to run through several generations. Many children who may show early signs of aggressive or violent tendencies, depression or anxiety traits, or even bizarre behaviors often have family members who have had a similar pattern.

A family history of alcoholism, or more specifically, a mother who drank or used drugs during pregnancy, puts a child at high risk for developing fetal alcohol syndrome or fetal alcohol effects (now referred to as Alcohol Related Neurodevelopmental Disorder). These are true psychiatric-neurological conditions in which a child's brain may not have developed properly. Sadly, this was the case with both Sergei and Angela.

Understanding the Family

It is important that the entire family be psychologically evaluated for the child's problem may actually be a "family disorder." The focus of a family evaluation should be on understanding how the family has grown up together, how they communicate, how discipline and correction works, as well as who has assumed the role of the dominant force and/or the parent. It is also important to understand who else is involved in the child's life, such as additional caretakers or other relatives and how often or how long the child spends away from these important figures. Remember, the family is the only thing a difficult child has for support and to give him or her a new beginning.

Family members must also assess their own personal psychological difficulties. Many times, a child's set of difficulties mirrors a family member's set. For instance, a child who is quick-tempered often has a parent who is quick-tempered. Depression and anger disorders often run in families and it is not uncommon for me to see a family in which all members are very depressed or are acting out in some way.

All family members need to lower their barriers and be open to discussing their own personal issues-medical, neurological, or psychiatric-for the sake of the child. As I will stress continually, a child will <u>not</u> improve if there are untreated conditions within the family. Family members <u>must</u> deal with their own issues in order to help their child. Remember, this is a "Family Intervention" to help their unmanageable child. Without parental stability and strength, the child will remain unstable.

Understanding Cultural Aspects

Another area that is important to look at is a child's cultural background. Each ethnic and religious background has a direct impact on a child's behavior. Often, problems arise when parents hold very traditional beliefs that conflict with the child's ability to "fit in" with society or peers. Internationally-adopted children have a great deal of acculturation as they are typically stepping out from deprivation and poverty and stepping into the "over-stimulation of America."

Enter Peggy and Bill. They wanted to make up for Sergei's deprived childhood (all of the food, experiences and relationships he missed). They decorated his room with cartoon characters and they bought him toys and games and stuffed animals. They took him to McDonald's and movies and even Disneyland. But what happened was that Sergei literally could not handle it all. He had never seen such things before and the wealth and newness, the colors, the attention, and the stimulation scared him. He had never even done simple things, like ride in a car, play with any games or be outside for more than a few minutes. Imagine how he must have felt in the middle of Disneyland! In spite of Peggy and Bill's best effort, Sergei was only more confused and expressed this confusion through acting out. Sergei's brain "computer" had become overloaded with confusing stimuli and shut down. Did you ever have your home computer freeze up on you? Frustrating, isn't i? When you see this happen, what is your first inclination? Get angry, what else! Now you are really understanding the computer "hard drive" of the difficult child. React when frustrated.

Understanding Social Aspects

Peer relationships are extremely important throughout all stages of childhood and adolescent development. Often, these can be jeopardized by things as simple as not fitting in with the norm, such as a child's perception that he or she is too fat, too thin, too tall or too short. A child who is detached and isolated is certainly at great risk for emotional and behavioral problems. In contrast, a child who is overly involved in his or her peer group is also at risk when socializing away from home takes precedence over honoring and working out family commitments.

All children need to socialize. Troubled children need to <u>learn</u> to socialize under strict parental training and supervision.

Understanding Educational Aspects

A child's ability to "fit in" to a specific educational program needs to be assessed, as a misplacement in classes that are either too easy or too hard may cause huge stress. If a child is reluctant to attend school, all aspects, such as learning problems or depression, must be taken into consideration as there most likely is a very good reason the child is resistant, unmotivated, or just plain hates school.

Nowadays, schools can be very difficult in providing proper assessments and interventions. Parents must be strong advocates for their child, and be willing to challenge the system or take on the expense of private services. It is a "pay now or pay later" concept.

Understanding Neuropsychiatric Conditions and Developmental Disorders

What Children Need

All children need a normal growth and development cycle. The principal goals a healthy child accomplishes are:

1) Achieving attachment and intimacy
2) Achieving autonomy and a sense of independence
3) Developing self-esteem
4) Developing a conscience
5) Maintaining a sense of safety and security

Infancy (birth to 18 months) is clearly looked upon as the "soil of personality development" and is the most critical bonding period. In infancy, a child is totally reliant on the primary caretaker for all needs. Also during this period, a child develops motor and sensory-perceptual skills in order to continually "inspect the world." This inspection process is actually done through the senses of the primary caretaker.

As the child moves to the toddler stage and beyond (approximately 18 months to 7 years), physical growth and development increase and the child learns to walk, talk and display much more independence and autonomy. Language is rapidly developing, along with the ability to question all aspects of the environment. This ability to question is often accompanied by episodes of rebellion. Toward the end of this stage, children should be venturing away from their parents and developing outside social relationships through school and interactional play.

When Something Goes Wrong

Children who have been separated or who have drifted apart from primary caretakers will often appear very colicky, cold and indifferent, or be very difficult to control. Temper tantrums, regressive behaviors or social and educational delays will be evident and should be viewed as "warning flags" that the child is off- track in his or her development.

Additionally, caretakers who give the child "mixed messages" (Dad says one thing, Mom says another; or household rules are inconsistent) during the critical infancy and toddler phase will often confuse the child, rendering him or her unable to solve problems rationally. This inconsistency on the part of the primary attachment figure can cause the child to look at the world in a very "black or white manner." What is actually happening here is that the child with cold, indifferent or emotionally over-reactive parents has learned to model that behavior and will begin to think and act in the same way. We can see how this affected Chris's life and perceptions as his view of his parents were ones of them being cold and unavailable; in Sergei, his new world completely contradicted his old, but "known," world; and with Angela, she modeled her behavior after people who had no moral values and could not provide any type of proper role modeling and stability.

Families who are unpredictable in their own moods and emotions, and constantly "change their mind" will typically raise an unattached child who does not know how to make decisions, or who makes decisions which are extremely irrational. One of the most difficult thing for parents to do is to accept that their child's inappropriate behaviors and poor problem solving/decision making may be the byproduct of their own problem-solving difficulties. While I do not say this to produce guilt, I do say it to jump-start change with the parents and in the entire family system.

MENTAL RETARDATION

Many families do not fully understand the importance of intellectual abilities and limitations in relationship to behavioral problems. In fact, many very disturbed children who appear to be bright, social, and even manipulative actually have levels of mental retardation. These conditions may severely restrict a child's ability to benefit from previous experiences, solve problems, fully appreciate emotions or concepts such as guilt and empathy, or benefit from parental training and discipline. Many difficult children have been placed (and maintained) in regular educational programs when, in fact, they have significant cognitive limitations, or even mental retardation.

Psychiatry continues to categorize children with mental retardation as psychiatrically impaired (Diagnostic and Statistical Manual of Mental Disorders - DSM IV). While mental retardation alone does not suggest a psychiatric condition, many children with mental retardation can develop coexisting psychiatric conditions. Retarded children can, for instance, have great difficulty understanding instructions and directions, thinking and reasoning, problem solving and organizing, and can have motor and sensory-perceptual deficits. Mental retardation can have an origin in genetics, illness, injury, Fetal Alcohol Syndrome or a multitude of medical conditions causing brain damage.

Mental retardation can be divided into the following levels of severity:

Mild Mental Retardation. IQ of 50-55 to approximately 70. Children with mild mental retardation constitute approximately 85 percent of the mental retardation spectrum. Children at this level of are considered "educable." They typically are able to develop social and communications skills during the preschool years, and are able to live successfully in the community (whether it be independently or in some type of structured, supervised community setting). Other times, however, such children may not progress in basic skills beyond the early elementary school years.

Moderate Mental Retardation. IQ of 35 to 50-55. Children in the moderate mental retardation range are also considered educable or trainable. This group constitutes approximately 10 percent of the entire population of individuals with mental retardation. Children in this range may not develop beyond the first or second-grade level in their academic subjects; however, they often enter workshop training programs and can live within the community, although they do require consistent supervision.

Severe Mental Retardation. IQ of 20 to 35. Children in the severe mental retardation range, approximately three to four percent of all individuals with mental retardation, develop little, if any communicative speech. They are able to reach only the pre-academic level of functioning, such as familiarity with the alphabet or simple counting. They may be able to develop a degree of language, mostly "survival words," but typically require constant care.

Profound Mental Retardation. IQ below 20. Children with profound mental retardation, approximately one to two percent of individuals with mental retardation, do not have the brain capacity to independently follow rules and instructions. They require constant assistance for self-care, management for intensive behavior problems, and training in doing simple tasks.

ORGANIC BRAIN SYNDROMES (DEMENTIA)

Many, many children who have been termed hopeless, unmanageable or generally non-responsive may have brain damage as the result of many complicated factors. FAS and in-utero drug exposure, poor pre- and post-natal care, malnutrition, heavy metal exposure, head trauma, metabolic and neurological disorders, medication side effects and genetic disorders may lead to brain dysfunction. In particular, certain parts of the brains "master computer" (i.e. frontal lobes and executive functioning) may have received the most injury. These highly complex areas of the brain are directly involved in attention, learning, mood and behavioral control. Now do you see why we need a multi-discipline evaluation?

Pervasive Developmental Disorders/Autistic Spectrum Disorders

A pervasive developmental disorder is actually a "group of symptoms" which involve impairments in several areas of development. These neurocognitive and psychological impairments often include difficulties in initiating and/or maintaining social relationships; problems in the appropriate development of receptive and expressive communication skills as well as deficiencies in maintaining socially acceptable behaviors, interests, and activities. Children with pervasive developmental disorders most often have underlying neurological and/or genetic disorders. Pervasive developmental disorders range from mild to moderate to severe. Principle examples of Pervasive Developmental Disorders are Classical or Kanner's Autism; Asperger's Syndrome and Higher Functioning Autism (HFA); Rett's Disorder; Childhood Disintegrative Disorder; and Atypical Autism (commonly referred to as Pervasive Developmental Disorder, Not Otherwise Specified).

Autism. Children who have been found to be extremely bizarre and inappropriate in their behaviors, may have been erroneously diagnosed as having schizophrenia, manic depressive/bipolar disorder, ADHD, or a learning disability, but may actually be autistic. Children with autistic disorders often have behavioral symptoms such as:

1) Severe hyperactivity
2) Severely short attention span
3) Severe impulsiveness
4) High levels of aggression
5) Tendency toward self-injury
6) Drawn-out temper tantrums
7) Constant repetitive actions and preoccupations
8) Attachment-disorder symptoms
9) Over-sensitivity to sights, sounds and being touched
10) Constant laughing, crying or rapid mood changes (often, these lead to an incorrect diagnosis of a mood disorder or ADHD)

Classical Autism or Kanner's Autistic Disorder is a very complicated disorder that involves underdevelopment or immaturity of the entire central nervous system. Autism particularly affects brain functions needed for general intelligence, acquisition of receptive and expressive language, and appropriate social-emotional development. The autistic child also has a markedly restricted repertoire of activities and interests. In fact, parents first clue may be that the child, from birth, acted somewhat odd or unusual, particularly in social interactions. Children with classical autism typically have coexisting mental retardation. Approximately seventy-five percent of children with classical autism function at a retarded level, commonly in the moderate range.

These signs and symptoms typically emerge prior to age three:

1) Marked delay in development of language, eye-to-eye gaze, and appropriate facial expressions.
2) Abnormal and unusual body posture and gestures, such as hand and finger flicking, repetitive movements, torso twisting, contortions or preoccupation with lights and/or inanimate objects.
3) Lack of spontaneously seeking out enjoyment and contact with others for play.

As the child grows, further abnormalities occur, such as:

1) Unusual or total absence of language; for example, speech patterns with unusual pitch, intonation, rate, and rhythm.
2) Repetition of words or phrases regardless of meaning; for example, constant repetition of jingles or commercials or language that can only be understood by those familiar with the child's unique communication style. Often, the child appears to be talking to him or herself.
3) Failure to respond appropriately to questions and directions or failure to understand basic humor and jokes.
4) Choosing only certain food groups or just one or two toys and completely ruling out all others.

5) Showing very little, if any, interest in establishing friendships. Being highly attached to an inanimate object as opposed to a person.
6) Having a markedly limited range of affection and emotions; vacillating from extremely sullen, withdrawn, and shy to self-absorbed, preoccupied, silly, and giddy.
7) Displaying stereotypical body movements, such as clapping of the hands and flicking of the fingers, whole body rocking, dipping and swaying, or walking on tip-toes.

Asperger's Autistic Syndrome and Higher Functioning Autism (HFA) is a subgroup of Classical autism. The critical difference is that there is no significant delay in language or cognitive development, and/or no signs of mental retardation. Another difference is that, while many of the symptoms of Classical autism may be evident, they may be more subtle and less incapacitating. These distinctions explain why many children with odd and unusual social behaviors may, in fact, have Asperger's autistic disorder rather than ADHD or general behavioral problems.

Because Asperger children may be able to communicate their feelings, they often are just dismissed as being very difficult and unmanageable. The hallmark of Asperger's syndrome is social-interactional difficulties, odd and repetitive behaviors, obsessions and compulsions, high anxiety and a "drifting" into solitude and aloneness. A large majority of Asperger's children and adults are extremely bright with often special and unique abilities in specific areas such as art, music, mathematics and memory. Remember Dustin Hoffman in "Rainman"? Many Asperger children are also referred to as "higher functioning autism" as they may have good (innate) cognitive skills, but difficulty in utilizing the parts of the brain needed for proper socialization and emotional control.

Rett's Disorder. This is a disorder in *females only*. In the rare Rett's disorder, a girl will exhibit multiple deficits which seem to surface at about four or five years old. She will have started off developing normally, but then will "lose" the majority of her cognitive and social-interactional skills. She will slow down and regress and deteriorate in both physical and cognitive functioning so that she will ultimately become as impaired as a child with Classical autism. This disorder is a true medical, neurological and, most probably, a genetic disorder.

Childhood Disintegrative Disorder. The essential feature of childhood disintegrative disorder is a significant regression in all areas of functioning following at least two years of apparently normal development. Childhood disintegrative disorder is often associated with mental retardation, although children who have experienced some type of neurological trauma, such as illness or injury, can often lose both expressive and receptive language abilities, social skills, and adaptive behaviors, as well as play activities and motor skills.

This diagnosis may certainly be appropriate in children who, like Sergei, have been living in institutional settings which are often devoid of any type of emotional or positive interaction. In this type of deprived environment, babies cries go unanswered, young children are never hugged, praised, or properly disciplined.

These factors adversely affect a child's social and cognitive development and subsequent brain functions. Therefore, it is a possibility that children who "disintegrate" in both cognitive and interpersonal skills may have brains that have been adversely affected by environmental factors producing a profound state of loss of previously acquired abilities. This concept will lead us to a later discussion regarding a newer form of autism which I have "reserved" for the institutionalized child, referred to as "Institutional Autism: An Acquired Syndrome."

CHILDHOOD LEARNING DISABILITIES

The most difficult children often have learning disabilities that have not been adequately assessed or treated. A child with learning disabilities has "mechanical problems" in processing and memorizing material, organizing activities, problem-solving, paying attention and mastering academic skills. Simply, the child is deficient in skills that would enable him or her to work towards appropriate solutions. Some signs of learning disabilities include:

1) Continued academic struggles
2) Poor attention span and concentration
3) Resistance toward school work to the point of cheating and losing homework
4) Poor time management and careless, haphazard work habits
5) Disruptive behaviors in the classroom and at home, particularly during homework
6) Signs of depression, anxiety or changes in behavior

Children with learning disabilities often have coexisting ADHD (almost 60-80% of the time). In this case, dealing with the cause of learning disabilities must take priority over dealing with the attentional disorder. More often than not, a child with learning disabilities is diagnosed as ADHD and parents are told: "Try medication first and then we will see if the child requires learning disability services." This is a very wrong recommendation because learning disabilities almost always produce coexisting attentional problems. Even when a child is on medication, he or she may also need intensive special-education services by speech and language specialists, learning disability tutors, and occupational and physical therapists. This is why, if there is a learning disability, it needs to be assessed and treated first. Children spend a great deal of time involved in school work; we need to focus on improving deficient academic skills in order to build success and self-esteem while "exercising" the child's brain.

There are <u>many</u> types of learning disabilities. For the purpose of clarity and simplicity in this book, learning disabilities are divided into two broad categories: Language Disabilities and Visual-Perceptual Disabilities.

LANGUAGE DISABILITIES

Verbal Comprehension Problems. Children with verbal comprehension problems have difficulties understanding language on a primary level. They tend to be partially deaf or at least lacking in their ability to understand what people are actually saying. An analogy would be to liken oral comprehension problems to one going to another country and trying to "figure out" the new language. You may be able to make out bits and pieces but would not understand the entire sentence or instruction presented. Children with such deficits need to have a full hearing examination to determine the extent of, if any, hearing loss.

Auditory Memory Deficits. Children with difficulties in what is called "central auditory processing" typically have problems with short-term memory. For example, learning sequences of instructions and directions is difficult and the material presented is quickly forgotten. Children may cover up this forgetfulness by stating that they do not care about or did not hear the instructions. They also can appear "lost" and become easily and highly distracted from tasks both at home and in school.

Verbal-Reasoning Deficits. Difficulties with higher-level thinking, logic, abstract concepts, and ideas are signals of verbal reasoning deficits. Examples would include problems in distinguishing similarities and differences of concepts and ideas, such as: larger and smaller, more and less, and various categories, etc. Verbal-reasoning deficits go hand-in-hand with difficulties in auditory memory. Children who exhibit this pattern make the same mistakes over and over. The parents report that the child "just doesn't get it" and seems very immature and concrete in overall thinking and reasoning when faced with a problem. This is very important when trying to understand the "language of human emotions".

Verbal-Expressive Learning Disabilities. Children with deficits in verbal expression have significant problems expressing their thoughts and ideas and relating them in a logical and cohesive manner. Within this pattern, speech disorders, such as difficulty in articulation, word retrieval, stuttering and stammering are clearly evident. Typically, children with verbal-expressive deficits also have problems in receptive language/auditory comprehension. This means the child struggles to learn and retain verbally-presented material; or, that the child may not understand single concepts and instructions. These language development deficits cause the child to be confused, frustrated and angry which can result in disruptive behaviors.

VISUAL-PERCEPTUAL DISABILITIES

Visual-Reception Learning Disabilities. Many children who have reading and writing problems miss visual details. For example, they misinterpret or confuse signs, shapes, letters and numbers. Weaknesses in visual reception often correlate with either (a) the need for corrective lenses (glasses or contacts) or, (b) secondary visual-perceptual processing deficits or the brains inability to visually "sort out" stimuli. Children with visual-reception problems will often be frustrated, as they are unable to learn new material that is presented on chalkboards, overheads, or in books and papers. Again, this could be because they are physically having trouble seeing the material, or because they are having trouble processing it.

Visual-Memory Defects. Children with visual-memory defects typically see but quickly forget signs, symbols and shapes, resulting in very poor reading comprehension. It is also difficult for them to remember facts and events necessary to complete homework assignments and examinations. The child significantly struggles just to make his or her way through school. Causes of this deficit are often genetic or medical. Treatments can be medical, surgical or intensive visual and occupational therapy to "exercise" the visual processing centers of the brain. Computer programs can be valuable training devices.

Visual-Associative Reasoning Disorders. Children with this pattern find it very difficult to create "mental pictures" which are necessary for completing math computations, creating a story, summarizing a book, or being able to grasp concepts such as how people feel or relate to one another. Without these abilities, children typically are very limited in "sizing up" or assessing a social situation and responding appropriately. A child must have adequate visual attention and visual-associative reasoning abilities to be able to"tie in" facial expressions, body language and interactional behaviors. A child's emotional development can suffer without these needed visual processing skills. Social relatedness and all attachment rely heavily on proper recognition of visual cues.

Written Expression Disorders. When children find it very difficult to copy and write, they completely give up trying to complete their homework assignments or classwork. Fine-motor coordination deficits are typically evident in children who have problems with written expression. Some neurological signs of fine-motor deficits include difficulties in left-right orientation and individual finger movement. Children who have difficulties in expressing their thoughts and ideas in a logical and cohesive written format typically have problems in both language and performance areas. If one thinks about the entire concept of writing, it involves understanding language in addition to being able to express words, phrases and sentences in a logical, cohesive and sequential manner.

DEVELOPMENTAL DYSLEXIA

Children with both language-based and visual-perceptual deficits can often have developmental dyslexia that goes unrecognized. Dyslexia actually means "a deficiency in general language, reading and writing based on processing deficiencies." There are two principle categories of dyslexia: Dysphonetic and Dyseidetic which can also occur in a combined form. These are neuropsychological terms that basically describe problems in phonics development and visual-perceptual abilities. It is essential for caregivers to obtain an accurate diagnosis to determine if dyslexia is present.

Dysphonetic Dyslexia focuses on poor phonics knowledge. Children with this disorder have significant difficulties with auditory processing and general language comprehension, sound-word discrimination, and with integrating symbols (letters or words) with their sounds. This means the child finds it difficult to break down words into their natural auditory units and sound out and blend the component letters and syllables of a word. These weaknesses in sound-word discrimination produce difficulties in phonics knowledge which can adversely affect phonetic decoding strategies needed for reading, spelling, and the formation of words.

Dyseidetic Dyslexia is poor visual-perceptual skills. For children with this pattern, the primary problem is visual recognition/visual reception, visual memory, and written expression. Rapid recognition skills are very difficult to maintain and without them, children have haphazard reading style (losing their place), slow reading rate, lack of comprehension due to "forgetting" newly read material, and grossly disorganized written expression.

Dysphonetic-Dyseidetic Dyslexic Disorder. This is a combined developmental dyslexia with more severe processing deficits in both auditory and visual areas. Children with this disorder perform at levels several years below their actual age and grade level. Many children rarely get beyond the third or fourth grade level in overall academic functioning, but can improve significantly to higher levels if intensive remediation and learning disability services are provided for a long period of time. There are excellent rehabilitation programs for dyslexic children involving approaches such as the Lindamood-Bell model and Wilson Reading Method. Families having dyslexic children can access tremendous resources via the Internet or by contacting the Orton Dyslexic Society.

ATTENTION DEFICIT HYPERACTIVITY DISORDER (ADHD)

As mentioned earlier, ADHD has received a tremendous amount of publicity. But the diagnosis of ADHD needs to be reserved for a true neurologically-based learning disability. Typically, ADHD involves co-morbid difficulties with auditory and/or visual memory, and general problems in speed and efficiency of task completion. Other signs are lack of sustained attention and concentration, hyperactivity, impulsiveness, low frustration tolerance, and impulsiveness. Moods can be labile and behaviors uncontrollable which merit the focus of treatment.

Before arriving at an ADHD diagnosis, all other psychiatric, psychological, developmental and family disorders need to be ruled out. Many children with clinical depression, anxiety, or attachment disorders exhibit behavior associated with ADHD. Virtually all autistic/pervasive developmental disorder children, for example, exhibit ADHD. Well more than half of all children with learning disabilities, particularly memory processing and language deficits, exhibit a degree of ADHD. Developmental dyslexics typically have a high incidence of ADHD patterns. ADHD goes hand-in-hand with so many childhood disorders because when a child is struggling in school, great "stressors" in the brains attention mechanism are activated, causing the child to be extremely frustrated and agitated, and to appear hyperactive and impulsive.

Although excellent research is going on there is not yet a definitive test that can pinpoint the medical cause of ADHD. The proper evaluation of ADHD involves medical, educational, family, psychosocial and neuropsychological interventions *over the course of time*, as opposed to a "quick assessment" by either a parent's or teacher's rating scale. The "quicker" the assessment, the more probability of an incorrect diagnosis.

I cannot stress how important it is to "differentiate" a child with ADHD from a child with another type of emotional or learning disorder. A general guideline is that ADHD tends to follow a more classic pattern of inattention, distractibility, hyperactivity and impulsiveness, without the emotional roller coaster of mood swings and negativity.

Based on my experience and supported by many other colleagues, it is becoming known that approximately 60 to 80 percent of children who are "diagnosed" ADHD actually have an incorrect diagnosis. Too often, families are looking for a quick fix and Ritalin is too frequently thought to be the answer. It is amazing that Ritalin distribution in the United States has increased over 400 percent in the past ten years. No wonder, since almost any child who is underachieving in school or showing some behavioral disturbance is initially referred for an ADHD evaluation (which does not actually exist, as the proper evaluation involves many disciplines).

True ADHD should have some coexisting problems as well; such as an underlying biological or neurological problem, a coexisting learning disability, a proven (consistent) attention and concentration problem, or distractibility and hyperactivity which are *not* related to another psychiatric disorder. The brain is too complex for ADHD to just exist by itself. It can occur, but we must be thorough in our evaluation and treatment before assigning this catch all label.

It is certainly common for children with ADHD to develop depression and mood problems over time as a result of their struggles at home and in school. Likewise, many children who start off with a diagnosis of ADHD are often at risk for other psychiatric disorders such as mood disorders (Bipolar disorder or Cyclothymia), depressive and/or anxiety disorders, oppositional disorders and potentially serious conduct problems. Severe ADHD can be the "precursor" for a Bipolar disorder, psychotic disorder or autistic spectrum disorder. Remember, brain chemicals are involved and affect many "systems" over the course of time. Therefore, it is extremely important to get an accurate diagnosis as the treatment for depression is much different than the treatment for ADHD, and if either go untreated or are treated incorrectly, further problems could result.

It is extremely important that Attention Deficit Hyperactivity Disorder become a "diagnosis of exclusion," that is, the last diagnosis on the list to be considered. Learning and emotional disorders must be ruled out before a diagnosis of ADHD is made. ADHD can and will co-exist with many other disorders, focusing only on this "set of symptoms" may result in parents, teachers and professionals ignoring the principle emotional and learning problems of the child. Ritalin and other ADHD medications are treatments, not solutions.

DISRUPTIVE BEHAVIOR DISORDERS

A disruptive behavior disorder is a broad category describing a series of repetitive and persistent violations of rules, rights of others and age-appropriate societal norms. This severe behavior must occur consistently for at least six months before it is thought to be a disorder.

Oppositional-Defiant and Conduct Disorder

The child with an oppositional/defiant and conduct disorder tends to be highly negative in both attitude and behavior. The child usually expresses defiance by extreme stubbornness, resistance to directions, and a general unwillingness to compromise or give in at any level. The chronic pattern of defiance toward parents and other authorities often strains caregivers to the point of giving up. Children with oppositional/defiant and conduct disorders make up the largest percentage of difficult children and those described as "hopeless."

Some of the persistent and identifying behavior patterns of these children include:

Stage 1) Loss of control.
Stage 2) Chronic academic difficulties.
Stage 3) Sabotaging school relationships in hopes of being dismissed.
Stage 4) Verbal and, at times, physical aggressiveness towards others as a means of control and vindictiveness.
Stage 5) Delinquent (or criminal) acts such as destruction of property, theft, deceitfulness, cruelty, and serious violations of rules.

Obviously, these children are not able to cooperate within school guidelines, nor are they motivated to work up to potential. Children with oppositional/defiant conduct disorders typically find school to be boring, even though it really is too much of a challenge.

The oppositional and defiant child starts off by engaging in temper tantrums and acting angry and frustrated toward anyone in authority. Blaming others for their mistakes is very common, in addition to going out of their way to deliberately annoy people. Over time, the child's behavior pattern toward authority figures turns into conduct problems, including verbally and physically aggressive acts, and violations of societal rules, moral standards and values. The adult manifestation of the oppositional/defiant conduct disorder is an antisocial or true "criminal personality."

To fully understand an oppositional/defiant or conduct-disordered child, it is very important to review the sections on attachment disorders or children from post-institutionalized settings. Many of these children have a "triad" of problems involving: 1) attachment disorder traits; 2) post-traumatic stress disorder; and 3) clinical depression.

Usually a "progression of aggression" in the defiant child occurs if problems are left untreated. The following outlines the typical stages of the progression of aggression:

1) Early frustration due to the inconsistency of parental bonding, attachment and discipline.
2) Frustration progresses to sadness and depression due to feeling lost and alone.
3) Depression gradually transforms to overt anger and defiance as a way of expressing unfulfilled needs.
4) Anger progresses to a more uncontrollable rage where the child seems "out of control" (i.e. yelling, screaming, kicking and destruction of property).
5) The rage progresses into deceitfulness or theft and violence toward

people and animals.

6) The child then turns to predatory violence against a world which is viewed as cold, rejecting, hurtful and in need of "punishment."

BED WETTING AND ELIMINATION DISORDERS

The difficult child can often display a pattern of encopresis, which is a repeated passage of feces into inappropriate places such as clothing or on floors; or enuresis, which is voiding urine into the bed or clothes. While it is very important to assess any type of medical condition, the difficult child can often have a repetitive chronic pattern of poor control, both behaviorally and physiologically.

Night-time bed wetting or enuresis is not uncommon and can often have a genetic or medical basis. In encopresis, the child has most likely engaged in a very difficult "toilet training pattern" and is attempting to maintain control over others by playing with feces and refusing (or forgetting) to use the bathroom. Many oppositional/defiant and conduct-disordered children have very little interest in changing or improving their elimination patterns which results in deliberate self-soiling as a way of being in control and provoking others. At the same time, this disorder is a symbolic representation of a child's extreme anger, rage and poor self-control.

ANXIETY DISORDERS

Anxiety disorders in children are often complicated or masked by another disorder such as tantrums, learning and attention difficulties, sleep problems, and self-soiling. Although there has been a great deal written about anxiety disorders in children, there is still a very poor understanding among treatment professionals and parents as to the role of anxiety within in the difficult child. The broad categories of anxiety disorders include: (a) generalized anxiety, (b) post-traumatic stress disorder, (c) separation anxiety, (d) obsessive-compulsive disorder, (e) panic or acute distress disorder.

Generalized Anxiety Disorder

Generalized anxiety disorder (also known as overanxious disorder) tends to be somewhat of a catch-all category describing excessive anxiety and worry regarding any type of event or activity. Symptoms may include restlessness (feeling "keyed up" and on edge), fatigue, irritability, and chronic muscular tension. Difficulties in concentrating and remembering, to the point where a child's memory "goes blank," are common. Also, over-anxious children tend to have trouble falling asleep and staying asleep. Anxious children can also have persistent enuresis and encopresis.

Generalized anxiety typically does not involve intense panic attacks or obsessive-compulsive thoughts or behavior (see descriptions below). Nevertheless, the intensity and duration of the anxiety is *far* out of proportion to the specific event or situation causing the anxiety. In other words, it is often rather routine or mundane events that can cause incredible anxiety in an over-anxious child. These children are often very insecure. They tend to refuse to go to school, complain chronically, and be highly sensitive to any type of criticism. They are also constantly afraid of what is going to happen (anticipatory or performance anxiety). They tend to be preoccupied by the outcome of tasks they do, such as the quality of their schoolwork or their performance in sports.

Post-Traumatic Stress Disorder (PTSD)

Life circumstances may have led up to a child becoming out of control. Many difficult children have been raised in violent and dysfunctional households in which bonding and attachment disorders are clearly evident. Also, children from post-institutionalized settings typically have struggled through many traumatic events. In some situations, a child from either a dysfunctional or violent home and/or institutional or even foster care setting may have been physically, sexually and emotionally abused. The outcome is often PTSD—children experience a constant state of fear, insecurity and feelings of abandonment.

Any child, even one from a healthy background, may have PTSD in the wake of an extremely traumatic event that involved direct personal experience and threatened the child's safety or physical integrity. You may have heard of PTSD in association with military combat veterans or concentration camp survivors, but it is also quite common in anyone who has experienced some type of violent personal assault, such as a robbery.

A child with PTSD will often meet the criteria for anxiety and depression, but can also be out-of-control, aggressive, or violent. The child's behavior may be sexualized or take on a repetitive pattern of chaotic actions. Self-destructive and impulsive behaviors, chronic complaints of physical illness or discomfort, as well as persistent feelings of inadequacy, insecurity, helplessness, and hopelessness may all be signs of the post-traumatized child.

One explanation for such behavior is that the child may feel guilt if he or she "survived" a situation that others did not. The child may even develop a complete avoidance of situations similar to those which caused the initial pain. For example, a child with PTSD might sabotage all interpersonal relationships if the initial trauma came from someone close to the him or her. Since the child no longer has the ability to control his or her emotions, social situations or education might be avoided as well.

Additionally, a child with PTSD can slip into states of bizarre and unusual behaviors. Children who have been traumatized have developed a mechanism called "dissociation" in which they automatically block out the very painful reality and create a new "made-up reality" that is more pleasurable and may include giddy and silly behaviors, imaginary friends, or hallucinatory experiences. The institutionalized child often finds ways to block out pervasive loneliness and despair: PTSD at its finest. Many of these "dissociated" children may appear bizarre, psychotic, autistic, mentally deficient of "unattached". Prolonged trauma can alter a child's reality and stability.

The child surviving an entire traumatic history, as opposed to a single event, has the burden of many years of painful depression. Here, we are likely to see a "progression of aggression" where depression fades away and is replaced by anger, rage, hostility and ultimately predatory violence. This is a "cycle of repetition" where a child begins to identify with the aggressor who caused the suffering. Children who have been victimized or exposed to chronic violence may experience this "imprint" of violent tendencies that becomes a part of their own personality structure, causing them to behave just as aggressively as their "role model." Despite a child's efforts, or even definite statements that they are "going to be different," it is very difficult for the PTSD child to actually think and behave differently.

Reactive Attachment Disorder of Infancy or Early Childhood (RAD)

The essential feature of Reactive Attachment Disorder is markedly disturbed and developmentally inappropriate social-relatedness as the direct result of grossly disturbed early-childhood care. Abuse, neglect, deprivation and institutionalization have all been found to have a direct impact on a child's ability to develop appropriate interpersonal relating.

RAD has become a major diagnosis in abused and neglected children and is often overdiagnosed or underdiagnosed. This is a very complex disorder that almost never exists by itself as traumatized children who struggle with attachments typically have coexisting PTSD, depression, anxiety, conduct problems, autistic characteristics, and even disordered thinking that may appear psychotic. Many children are either significantly isolative and withdrawn or overly indiscriminate. The most important consideration in diagnosing RAD is to fully assess any and all cognitive and psychiatric factors which may imitate or exacerbate the true attachment disorder pattern. For example, many children with mental retardation or autism, or even major psychiatric disorders will be mistaken for having RAD. There have been many treatments recommended for RAD, but there is no one solution or "quick fix." RAD is more of a long-term developmental disorder which requires multiple interventions ranging from cognitive, academic, family therapy and psychiatric care. Many of these children are quite resistant to traditional psychological treatment and may superficially comply with just one intervention, such as Holding Time, play therapy, or family therapy. RAD never exists by itself--there are always co-morbid disorders. With a RAD diagnosis, always ask "is my child's brain working?" Brain dysfunction takes priority in all treatment programs.

Separation Anxiety

Children with early bonding and attachment deficits can often exhibit a long-standing (if not life-long) pattern of separation anxiety. The essential features of separation anxiety are consistent states of tension; emotional distress; and at times, a complete loss of control, especially when the child is separated from the home or from the person to whom he or she is attached (or to the person to whom the child wishes to be attached).

Such children have great difficulties attending school, going to bed or working independently because they need to "cling" to their caregiver. Children with separation anxiety can often act hysterical, aggressive and destructive when they are forced to be on their own. They may also exhibit a wide variety of somatic complaints as they allow their emotional problems to impact their bodily functions. Examples are sleeping and eating disturbances, stomach problems, dizziness, aches and pains, headaches and panic attacks.

Obsessive-Compulsive Disorder (OCD)

Children with obsessive-compulsive disorders (OCD) can often be extremely intense, rigid and inflexible in their thinking, reasoning, and behavior. Such children find it very difficult to change tasks or "transition" to anything new. They are unable to allow for any type of deviation from their "plan of action."

While it is normal for children to have obsessive thoughts, an OCD child's thoughts will be consuming and will clearly interfere with the ability to complete other tasks, such as home routines and schoolwork. Many difficult children categorized under oppositional/defiant, ADHD, or attachment disorder can actually have OCD. Their behavioral manifestations are a "smoke screen," or cover, for this psychiatric disorder. OCD can truly be painful to a child and will often lead to his or her becoming nonfunctional.

Sometimes a child can be either obsessive *or* compulsive, but not necessarily both. Obsessions are persistent ideas, thoughts, impulses or images that are intrusive and inappropriate and cause marked anxiety and distress. For example, the obsessive child will have constant thoughts regarding contaminations, and will be preoccupied with fears and phobias and aggressive and horrific themes. Thoughts may often be paranoid in nature and the child may think that people are "out to get them," or that they are being scrutinized or put down by authority figures.

The compulsive child, on the other hand, repeats pattern of behaviors, such as hand washing, ordering and checking items, counting objects or repeating words silently over and over. Compulsive children find it very difficult to shift to a task which is not part of his or her compulsive ritual. They can become "paralyzed" when asked to do something new.

Panic Disorders

Children with panic (or "acute distress") disorder typically have recurrent, unexpected panic attacks which can result in episodes of excessive worries, obsessions, and compulsions along with physical symptoms. Very typically, the child with panic disorder will become completely out of control and will yell, scream, throw tantrums, engage in hyperactive behavior, and at times, make bizarre and inappropriate statements.

Panic disorder can sometimes exist with agoraphobia, which is an unrealistic fear of new surroundings. This affects the child when he or she is in places or situations from which escape may seem to be very difficult. Typically this occurs outside the home, when a child is in a crowd, standing in a line, in an open place or in an enclosed place (as in claustrophobia, a subset of agoraphobia). The child fears, that he or she is completely on their own and that something catastrophic may occur.

Dissassociative Disorder (formerly called Multiple Personality Disorder)

There have been many reports of children who have experienced severe developmental trauma ranging from physical, emotional and sexual abuse to profound environmental and psychosocial deprivation who may experience dissassociative episodes. The essential feature is the presence of fragmented and sometimes "distinct identities" or personality states that recurrently take control of a person's behaviors. During these episodes of dissassociation or personality fragmentation, children may not remember specific events, engaged behaviors, emotional outbursts, or awareness of known family members. Fragmented or alter-identities typically serve to mask and avoid dealing with the specific trauma.

MAJOR MOOD DISORDERS

Clinical or Major Depression

Among the various childhood disorders discussed in this book, quite a few coexist along with the psychiatric diagnosis of clinical depression. You may find it hard to understand or sympathize with the fact that your child is "unhappy" when he or she is acting out in a grossly inappropriate way. Parents' frustration often leaves little room for empathy for the child's emotional struggles. But keep in mind that the majority of childhood depression is "masked." Unlike adults, most children do not have the emotional or verbal sophistication to express clearly their feelings of sadness, frustration, or anger. Instead, what typically surfaces are very intense emotions and behaviors. Depression is one of the most commonly missed diagnoses in child psychology since so many of the symptoms can easily be mistaken for some other disorder.

For example, the severely depressed child will often present the exact same acting-out behaviors as a child with severe ADHD (very poor attention and concentration, impulsiveness and hyperactivity, poor planning and organizational skills, signs of learning disabilities, and general academic struggles). Other signs of the severely depressed child include:

1) A cold, withdrawn or indifferent demeanor.
2) Highly aggressive and volatile behaviors.
3) Suicidal or homicidal statements and actions and self-destructive or risky behaviors.
4) Marked changes in both appetite and sleep.
5) Complaints of bodily problems, such as aches and pains, headaches, diarrhea, dizziness, etc.
6) Increasingly resistant to others with confused logic and reasoning
7) Rigid and inflexible thinking patterns, negative and pessimistic attitudes.
8) Academic difficulties.
9) Attention and concentration disorders which resemble ADHD.
10) Gravitation towards self-destructive behaviors and a negative peer group.

11) Potential for hallucinatory and delusional experiences
12) Potential for catatonic behavior (total shut down)

It should always be re-emphasized that a child who is aggressively out-of-control has already started off along the "progression of aggression." A good statement to remember is: "When the depression fades, it turns into rage." This is particularly important in understanding the child from a post-institutionalized setting or a child who has been raised in a very violent and dysfunctional environment. All the child's built up depression and frustration have to eventually go somewhere; too often, that somewhere is in the form of aggressive acts toward anyone in the child's path.

Bipolar Mood Disorders

There has been much written about bipolar mood disorders in adults, but only now are researchers starting to understand that bipolar disorders manifest very differently in children. A common thread in children with all types of bipolar mood disorders is that they exhibit very rigid and oppositional behavior patterns that persist despite any type of interventions. Their high level of energy tends to "wear down" others around them. Bipolar mood disorders are categorized as Type I and Type II, with Cyclothymia being the "middle of the road" mood disorder pattern.

Bipolar Type I Mood Disorder or Manic Depressive Illness

The words "mania" or "manic" typically describe someone who is pressured, loud and rapid in his or her speech. A manic can have unbounded energy and thoughts that race faster than can be articulated. Manics can often be extremely distracted, self-absorbed and preoccupied, as well as grandiose and expansive to the point where judgement is very impaired. Adults with mania have an increase in goal-directed activities (they become workaholics) and can also engage in excessive spending or sexual behaviors. In children, mania presents in a different manner. Manic children can also be highly talkative and easily distracted and have a decreased need for sleep. But unlike adults, they tend to "regress" during angry episodes, throwing tantrums and becoming so disorganized in their reasoning that they cannot be engaged in conversation. They become intolerant in any type of conversation and will quickly engage another person in a verbal or even physical fight. Manic children also are extremely guarded and paranoid in their thinking, yet they are openly aggressive in their impulses. Manic children can often exhibit a "flight of ideas," grandiosity and omnipotence in their logic, reasoning and belief systems to where they may believe they have supernatural powers or have become some type of superhero or imagined figure from their fantasies. I have seen manic children believe they are everything from God to the Devil reincarnated. This is a prime example as to how mania can change reality perceptions and grossly interfere with a child's functioning in the world.

These children will often be called the most difficult children around as they are chemically driven, having supercharged energy, and impulsiveness which allows them to sustain very intense oppositional and conduct-disordered tendencies far beyond those of other children. Unfortunately, as their self-control, judgment and reality perceptions become increasingly impaired, the cycle of these children becomes extremely difficult to stop. It is very painful for families to watch their manic child in a downward spiral; hospitalization with intensive medication becomes the only hope during this crisis time.

Manic children are sometimes misdiagnosed as suffering from ADHD since both disorders are characterized by impulsiveness, inattention, hyperactivity, learning disabilities, and great physical energy. There has been a tremendous amount of new research going on regarding Bipolar disorders in children, indicating clear genetic and neurochemical links. It is very important for families to have a very skilled mental health professional help in the differential diagnosis.

Bipolar Type II Mood Disorder and Cyclothymia

Compared to manic children, these children are more in control of their moods and behaviors. Nonetheless, these children suffer a more chronic state of irritability, low tolerance, mood agitation, and volatile behaviors. Children with this type of "low-grade mania" (hypomania) are often called "temperamental" since their emotions and actions cycle between extremes that are hard to predict or counter. Chronic depression needs to be evident in order to fully diagnose a Bipolar disorder. Such children often go without proper assessment and treatment, as so much effort is spent just managing their extreme behaviors.

Cyclothymia is a very common co-existing emotional disorder in children who have also been diagnosed with ADHD or significant behavior problems. Cyclothymia actually reflects an agitated mood-disorder pattern which can produce states of irritability, low-frustration tolerance, depression, and volatility. There is a very similar "chemical make-up" between ADHD and Cyclothymic mood-disorder patterns, as both conditions often present with inattention, distractibility, prominent impulsivity and behavioral dyscontrol. It is very important to "rank order" these diagnoses as the medication and therapy treatments can often be very different.

SCHIZOPHRENIA

Some of the most difficult children who exhibit the most unusual behaviors may, in fact, have a more severe psychiatric disorder called Schizophrenia. Schizophrenia is poorly understood in children, and often parents have very little information regarding this condition. Schizophrenia typically runs in families which supports a genetic and biological link. Children whose parents, aunts or uncles have schizophrenia are ten times more likely to develop the problem compared to the general population. Genetics are the key and are being researched extensively.

However, a diagnosis of schizophrenia must be made with great caution. Equally bizarre behaviors can result from any number of other disorders, including autism or other neurodevelopmental disorders, psychotic depression, chemical dysfunction in the brain, head injury and post-traumatic stress disorder. On the other hand, schizophrenia can often be overlooked in favor of the above disorders. Likewise, a schizophrenic child may also simply be mistaken for a "loner," or someone who just has an active imagination and prefers to play by himself. The schizophrenic child exhibits a number of bizarre symptoms, both "positive," (that is, more readily identifiable) and "negative" (more passive or not as noticeable).

Among the "positive" symptoms are:

1) Gross distortions and exaggerations of thinking including delusional beliefs.
2) Auditory and visual hallucinations.
3) Disorganized language and communication patterns where speech is sometimes incomprehensible.
4) Vacillation between gross disorganization and lack of control to catatonic and totally self-absorbed states.
5) Sexual preoccupations and public displays of inappropriate behavior, such as masturbation.
6) Extreme immaturity, unpredictable mood agitation and difficulty with basic, daily schedules such as bathing, toilet use, organizing meals and getting dressed.

The more passive or "negative" symptoms of the schizophrenic child are often missed. These include:

1) An extremely flat and blunt emotional presentation, such as lethargy, apathy or no emotional expressions. Anhedonia or a total lack of pleasure from life may be present.
2) Poor motivation and lack of interest in anything in life
3) Impoverished speech that tends to be very concrete despite the child's known intellectual abilities.
4) Paranoia and maintaining an overly guarded and suspicious posture.
5) Rapid regression in social and educational functioning during which the child pulls away from all relationships and becomes increasingly shy and withdrawn, or exhibits attachment disorders.

Again, great caution should be made in diagnosing a child as schizophrenic. There are many factors which can cause a child to appear psychotic. Just read through the symptoms of autism, organic brain syndromes (dementia), major depression, bipolar disorders and obsessive-compulsive disorders to fully understand how much one disorder can mirror another.

PERSONALITY DISORDERS

Psychiatric research states that a true personality disorder cannot be assigned to a child until he or she is at least 18 years of age. It is my experience that many very difficult and disturbed children do, in fact, have disorders in which personality traits have become so inflexible and maladaptive that they interfere with social and/or school functioning and cause marked personal distress. It is very important for parents to recognize if their troubled child has reached a state of existence in which their entire personality structure is in need of reorganization. Remember, the underlying, deeply ingrained personality traits of the child support and maintain the difficult behaviors which parents may see every day. These "symptoms" have become a habitual part of the child's life since they have done a good job of practicing this behavior to perfection.

To further clarify, children with personality disorders typically have coexisting behavior and conduct problems, in addition to extremely inflexible and rigid thinking patterns. The reality the child may live in is often in sharp contrast to the realities of life and family. Even in personality disorders, depression and emotional turmoil can be evident although "masked" deep within the personality structure, rigid defenses and behavioral manifestations which push other people away. The three principle personality disorders that seem to be the most common in difficult children are: borderline, antisocial and narcissistic.

Borderline Personality Disorder. Children with this disorder experience chronic mood swings that destabilize their relationships. They go from feeling helpless, hopeless, and empty, to raging and impulsive. They have little tolerance for frustration, frequently threaten suicide, and show a skewed perception of reality. Acting out and chronically provocative behaviors are common.

These children typically come from chaotic family systems in which there may have been abuse, alcoholism, drug addiction, neglect, bitter divorce, or other circumstances in which the child has received little in the way of consistent love, affection, or nurturing and has constantly been "pulled" in a number of different directions.

Antisocial Personality Disorder. Children with antisocial personality formations tend to be very bright and articulate without any documented signs of learning disabilities. Early stages of oppositional and conduct disorders are often evident and will proceed into a chronic pattern of rule-breaking; irresponsibility and unreliability. Chronic lying, deceit, and manipulation are typical of antisocial children, who also show a need for immediate gratification and a general lack of insight into or remorse for their wrong-doings. Antisocial children constantly seek dominance and control over others and are continually "paying back" those perceived as having done them wrong or those who need to be "conquered." It is typical for the antisocial child to be very attuned to retaliation and control.

Remember the "progression of aggression"? That certainly applies here as antisocial children have often been depressed or frustrated, and, if left untreated, they progress to states of anger and rage with predatory behavior against others. In fact, there is a strong possibility these children will progress into a criminal personality type.

Behind the antisocial child, there is typically the antisocial family system. How children become antisocial is very complicated, but the pattern usually starts at early childhood development. Families that are inconsistent and over-indulge the child will produce a child who demands immediate gratification. Children who start off with temper tantrums and oppositional behaviors and who are allowed to "progress" to states of very poor conduct are candidates for antisocial personality type. Antisocial children "practice" bad conduct and wear down their families to where it's the child who runs the show.

Narcissistic Disorder. Children suffering from this disorder tend to feel grandiose and omnipotent and have very little empathy for others. The narcissistic child tends to exploit social relationships and constantly seeks compliments and praise despite grossly inappropriate behavior and conduct. This child is often high-strung, self-reliant, highly independent and the "know it all" of the group. It is very easy to recognize narcissistic children in a school setting: they tend to boast, brag and always seem to think they are able to do things better than others.

Additionally, narcissistic children typically command (and demand) that people around them cater to their every whim and, when their wishes are not immediately met, they will inflict a great deal of guilt and pressure on other people to respond immediately. When confronted or challenged, such children can become extremely angry and resist anyone's attempt to correct them.

Deep within the narcissistic personality structure is a child who has not formed a solid sense of self-esteem or an understanding of human emotions. The narcissistic child often comes from a narcissistic family. The family system is one that has supplied the child, throughout the course of development, with "material possessions" in place of deep love and affection. Families of the narcissistic child typically avoid deep commitments to one another and try to smooth over situations with gifts. Additionally, parents of narcissistic children tend to be very consumed with their own problems or interests and have difficulties setting consistent limits, rules and regulations, thereby forcing the children to raise themselves.

Avoidant Personality Disorder. Children suffering from this disorder have a personality based on avoiding social-interactional situations. There is a pattern of isolation, social fears and emotional inhibitions. It should be emphasized that the child with avoidant personality disorder is very comfortable in his or her social detachment. The only anxiety which surfaces is when people attempt to force the child to be more interactive. This personality profile can also be seen in higher-functioning autistic individuals, such as those with Asperger's Syndrome.

Dependent Personality Disorder is where the individual is extremely insecure and constantly needs others in order to survive. Their co-dependency is typically profound separation anxiety, or a fear of being alone. This personality style can be draining to others as these children tend to create constant crises and chaos in an effort to prevent being alone.

Histrionic Personality Disorder is the "dramatic" type who is always in crisis, sick, complaining or needing to be the center of attention. People with this pattern go out of their way to "grandstand" in order to feel important. The histrionic personality type has a total flair for the dramatics which can manifest in dress, spending habits and "name dropping." Histrionics call people all the time and give them their opinion regarding subjects that they may know very little about. The histrionic is much like the dependent personality as they hate being alone. Histrionics also love going "doctor shopping" as they enjoy the attention when people find things wrong with them.

Obsessive-Compulsive Personality Disorder. The most essential features are preoccupation with orderliness, perfectionism and mental and interpersonal control at the expense of being flexible, open and efficient. Children who have obsessive-compulsive personalities are often viewed as being overly rigid, oppositional and defiant, and unwilling to cooperate with rules and regulations that they deem irrelevant.

Schizotypal Personality Disorder is the "odd" or eccentric individual who presents with strange and unusual thoughts, ideas and ways of relating. There can be schizophrenic-like behaviors, magical thinking or excessive fantasy life to the point where the individual believes his or her own stories.

Summary

Personality disorders often exist with many other psychiatric and, primarily, social problems. Adults and children with personality disorder traits are very difficult to deal with and have been this way for much of their lives. They may adjust, but will never really change their true personality make-up. They fight real change as their unique personality often sees the world and relationships in sharp contrast to reality. This discrepancy between perception causes continual problems in adjustment to others and to the world in general. Unfortunately, the concept "practice makes perfect" may apply again to a child who has developed a chronic pattern of "personality traits".

Chapter 4

Understanding the Complexities of U.S. and International Adoptions

Adopting an American Child

Adoptions are a very important part of American and, more recently, other countries' cultures. We here in the U.S. have a wide range of adoption possibilities, from infants to young teens. Adoptions are big business and we use social service agencies, religious groups, agencies and attorneys who handle "private adoptions" (which have come to great media attention when things go wrong).

Even though it may seem more familiar, or even "safer" to adopt a U.S. child, parents need to realize that a good deal of these children have been abused or neglected, or the biological parents have had their rights terminated under court rulings. This means that these children may have sustained some type of physical or psychological damage or trauma that could affect them for many years. Therefore, families adopting American children should still go forth with much caution and training before and after the adoption.

The good news is that we have so many medical and psychological professionals to help us with our decisions and with problems regarding health issues, legal issues or even how to face a child's inevitable questions regarding his or her biological roots. Usually, families have the opportunity for hands-on contact with either the social service agency or adoption agency. While there still may be some problems, much information regarding the child is typically disclosed as social service agencies spend a great deal of time gathering the child's developmental information and medical and psychological documentation. Also, family home studies are required and training for the prospective family is highly recommended, although not always completed.

Medical Profile of the Adopted American Child

American children who become candidates for adoption may have a variety of medical problems. We also tend to see this in international adoptions, although here in the U.S. early assessment and treatment of problems is by far more aggressive. These problems can range from damage caused in-utero, such as poor health of the birth mother, nutritional deficiencies, illnesses such as hepatitis and HIV, or toxins such as alcohol or drug exposure (both of which are major causes of mental retardation and serious developmental and behavioral problems). What comprises the largest segments of the U.S. adoption industry are: teen pregnancies, unwanted pregnancies, victims of rape or incest, or people who just cannot afford to care for their child.

Abuse, trauma, neglect, and the "wear and tear" of being brought up in a dysfunctional family are among the main causes of emotional and psychological problems observed in American children who become candidates for adoption. Many parents in the U.S. have had their parental rights terminated because they couldn't adequately care for their children or were found guilty of chronic abuse and neglect. We have a huge population of children in U.S. foster care programs eligible for adoption, although families desiring these children should be emotionally strong and well equipped as many of these children (particularly older children) have a great deal of "emotional baggage" which will require long-term professional care.

Institutional Care

Although it exists elsewhere in the world, the classic orphanage is almost an institution of the past in the United States. When children are orphaned, abused or neglected, or when their parents are not able to manage their special needs, they fall under the mandate of the State Department of Child Protective Services and Family Services, which has the power to intervene immediately when warranted. State child-protective agencies usually are aggressive and will take total custody of children, placing them in a safe and secure environment ranging from foster homes, group homes, therapeutic group homes (where children receive intensive psychological and educational care) or even residential psychiatric facilities, if needed.

Foster Care

While the U.S. may have a rather sophisticated foster care system, we have a large problem in that many children are moved repetitively from foster program to foster program (and in some cases, from parent to parent). Sometimes children are moved because of disruptive behavior which is basically their "acting out" anger and frustration due to losing their family. The majority of foster parents are usually not equipped to deal with all of the child's psychological or behavioral issues, despite even the best training. There are certainly "therapeutic foster homes" but not nearly enough to adequately service all of the children damaged by abuse and neglect. It is very common for children who shuffle through the foster care system to increase their level of anger and rage which can seriously stress the caregivers trying very hard to provide a sense of home life and stability.

Angela spent seven years being shuffled from relatives and foster homes, one after another. First, her aunt, who was unable to handle Angela, sent her into the foster care system. Angela's first placement, with a couple in their forties, lasted just one month. Her second, third and fourth foster placements ranged from two to six months, but in the end, all of them failed and Angela was sent to her grandmother who then brought her to my office.

Foster parents are compensated financially for their services but many of them feel they are not paid enough to handle the extremely difficult child. When a child becomes disruptive, it is very common for him or her to be moved as many as eight to ten times or until legally declared an adult. Our foster care system has flaws; it is a temporary solution to a long-term problem. No child should remain in long-term foster care. Children need a home and family.

While life in foster care may protect a child from neglect, abuse or other damaging effects of a dysfunctional family, the child faces another difficult problem: the uncertainty caused by the transitional nature of such care. Because more children are remaining in foster care programs for longer periods of time, those feelings of insecurity can escalate into feelings of helplessness, hopelessness and the despair over the loss of family.

Despite the temporary nature of this care, foster children at least have some semblance of normalcy in their lives with people talking to them and encouraging them to be part of some type of family, even if it is not a great family or if it is only a temporary family. The operating principle is that any relationship at a critical stage of a child's life is better than no relationship at all. Although there may be incidents of children abused or neglected in foster care environments, the hope—and certainly the goal—is that these children are at least better monitored than they would be in their original family setting. In addition, foster children are further helped by others, such as teachers, social workers, and medical and mental health professionals. Unlike conditions abroad, the foster child in this country has a wide support system that can help. We have a very sophisticated psychiatric and psychological approach which includes hospitals, residential treatment centers, medications, state-run programs, church support systems, and community agencies--all readily available. Even with all of these "supports and safeguards", foster children in the U.S. have been without a family during critical formative years, which may leave lasting scars.

Transition From Foster Care to Adoption

In U.S. foster care and social-service systems, children are eligible for adoption regardless of the type of trauma they have experienced. Hopefully, social services or the state tries very hard to provide the child with comprehensive medical and psychological assessments and some degree of treatment prior to adoption. This is very important information to be passed on to the new adoptive family. All information should be presented.

A critical problem with adoptions in the United States is the possibility that the biological parents will try to reclaim their children after abandoning them or after their parental rights have been terminated. Incidents have occurred in which, despite the fact that the child has been legally adopted, the birth parents emerged and, using media attention, reclaimed their child. Often, this happens after the birth parents have found jobs and are suddenly able to afford the child. Other times we see parents give up a sickly or badly misbehaved child only to want him or her back after they learn the child is "better." This is why many children in the foster care system go back and forth from the parental home to foster care, often perpetuating the family dysfunction and preventing the child from becoming available for adoption.

Unlike many other countries, here in the United States it takes a great deal of effort to have the parents' rights terminated through a forced procedure by the courts. Because of the parents' constitutional rights, it is quite difficult to prove that they are permanently unfit or unable to raise their child. There has been a strong movement to terminate parental rights, but right now, as the system is set up, the parent or parents have to be deemed totally incompetent to raise a child, with no redeemable qualities or ability to improve, despite psychiatric and psychological care. Many parents who are just unable to care for their children unnecessarily litigate in order to maintain custody and, at times, continue to receive financial support from the State which they use for themselves instead of for the child. Under our current system, which is still in the process of evolving and hopefully changing this pattern of financial manipulation, families need to think about what is best for their child as opposed to being self-serving. Unfortunately, the current system still allows many unfit parents to regain custody, which frequently results in the repeated patterns of abuse and family dysfunction.

The biggest problem facing children eligible for adoption in the U.S. today is that many of them have been sadistically and ritualistically physically, sexually and/or emotionally abused. Sex abuse at very early ages down to infancy is, unfortunately, becoming common in our society. Social service statistics show there has also been a definite increase in the amount of abuse and neglect petitions filed. While the goal is to "treat" disturbed and abusive families, therapy often fails which results in children being placed in state-run programs. Sadly, the children are the ones who lose and become the statistics.

Additionally, a majority of these children have been raised in dysfunctional families where alcoholism, drug addiction and long-term generational patterns of abuse have occurred. Ongoing family dysfunction and repeated abuse becomes even more prevalent in home situations where there are cramped living conditions (i.e. multiple family members and friends residing in small housing situations) where the social environment is chaotic or where there are significant socio-economic problems. Many families with limited resources try very hard to maintain a solid family system; trying to "shield" their children from outside/environmental influences. Families in these situations are to be commended for their efforts as they are often faced with great pressures and continued worries regarding basic safety and security. **If adopting a foster child, we must respect and remember their developmental experiences.**

Adopting a Foreign Child

My personal observation regarding my visits to orphanages and state-run institutions in Eastern Bloc countries has left a lasting impression on me both personally and professionally. It is incomprehensible how children can possibly survive this system in an emotionally and psychologically healthy way. It is alarming and depressing how many "throw-away" children are sentenced to life in institutions simply because they have been abandoned by their parents or because of a medical condition.

The big picture, however, is that international adoptions have been booming since the late 1980's. In 1989, nearly 8,000 children were adopted from overseas. Nearly a decade later, the figure has almost doubled to around 14,000 adoptions, according to Immigration and Naturalization Service (INS) data. Indeed, international adoptions have become "big business." Although there are agencies that attempt to carry out adoptions honestly and effectively, there unfortunately are, some agencies that have a goal of placing as many children as possible, all the while disregarding health conditions. Often, agencies are greedy and downplay the true picture in order to complete the adoption. This is a definite disservice, and the revenues generated by agencies can sometimes color the true picture, which needs to be provided to the perspective adoptive family. Families need to have the most detailed information available which lists out all of the pros and cons and potential problems. This information needs to be provided at the beginning of the adoption process before families invest a great deal of emotional energy and financial resources.

Eastern Europe (especially Russia, Kazakhstan and Romania), China, Korea, and South America (in rank order per INS statistics) have dominated the foreign adoption scenario. For example, in 2002, Russian adoptions were approximately 7,500; China 5,000; Korea 1,800; Romania only 200 (due to restrictions); and South America around 3,000. Guatemala is a country on the rise for adoptions. Chinese adoptions have expanded to a waiting list as young infant girls are readily available. Eastern European Bloc countries continue to expand international adoption programs. India and Southeast Asia also continue to have international adoptions, with countries such as Thailand and Vietnam on the increase although there have been problems in these countries adoption procedures.

Working With International Adoption Agencies

Some parents hope that adopting a child from another country will be quicker, easier, and less expensive than dealing with the adoption process in the United States. Others look abroad because the termination of the biological parents' rights is clear and irrevocable in other countries—very different from the American system's strong protection of parental rights which often causes numerous problems later on. Also, older couples and single people can adopt foreign children when American children are barred to them. And, children from Eastern Europe satisfy the demand for Caucasian children, many of whom are not readily available in the U.S.

However, many children in other countries who have been placed for adoption come from very impoverished backgrounds and often have spent time in an institution. Numerous pre and post-natal problems often go unrecognized or are minimized in importance. Many of these children exhibit a wide variety of neuropsychological impairments which may not be quickly identified but which most certainly surface throughout early childhood development.

Unfortunately, thorough medical, neurological and psychological assessments are not typically done on a child prior to international adoption. Only sparse information about the child's medical and developmental history is provided by the adoption agency. Therefore, it is very important for the family to seek out thorough evaluations of the adopted child immediately before and after arrival in the United States. Current standards have been put in place by International Adoption medical specialists regarding pre-adoption reviews of videos and records. Throughout the United States, there are well over 25 centers, which now specialize in International Adoption Medicine, where a team of pediatric experts will carefully review medical and psychological records, the child's level of development, and potential risk factors. There are still no guarantees as to the actual medical and psychological health of the child until they are brought back to their new family, but pre-adoption counseling can certainly be beneficial and answer many questions for the prospective adoptive families.

It has been reported by many adoptive families that some adoption agencies have suppressed negative information from their child's medical record. This was apparently done in hopes that the family would not be deterred from adopting if presented with potentially negative and possibly erroneous information. Many times the translation of medical records and general information provided to the agencies regarding the child often reflects only "institutionalized problems" such as social and environmental neglect, poor nutrition or a general "lack of stimulation." Many families have reported that adoption agencies will tell them that the diagnosis on the medical record is incorrect and was only written as institutions "have to put something down on the record in order for the child to be adopted out." For example, common "diagnoses" of perinatal encephalopathy; anoxia; macrocephaly (large head size) or microcephaly (small head size); or delayed psychic and/or speech development are all instructed by adoption agencies to be ignored or downplayed. Agencies will sometimes provide videos or photographs supposedly showing a contented child when, in fact, the child may have been sedated or medicated so that he or she appears calm and pleasant for the video audience. A photograph or twenty-second video is only a "snapshot" designed for promotional use and provides very little helpful information regarding the true health of a child.

There are some agencies that do inform prospective families of "risks" but most do not follow through in offering any type of pre-adoption training or post-adoption counseling for the family. The definition of a "good agency" is one which informs parents of all the possibilities (range of cognitive and emotional problems) while also providing ongoing training and support after the child arrives with their new family. Agencies have been recently flooded with new research and data regarding cognitive and emotional issues of the post-institutionalized child.

All too often, in their strong desire to have a child, couples may be susceptible to various types of manipulation or deception during the adoption process. They also may be mislead into thinking that the child will be "fixable" if given the right environment and lots of love. In actuality, the child may have already experienced alterations in the development of brain function. Often, it is only after child has been welcomed into the new family that parents realize the severity of the child's medical and psychological problems presents a far more serious challenge than anticipated. The "give them love, food, shelter and time to adjust" is just not an accurate statement as children from deprived backgrounds who have spent sometimes many years in institutional settings need assessment and help from the first day. "Waiting and watching" may only delay the inevitable and make life even harder on the families that have a child who clearly needs early interventions.

There has been a rapid increase in families adopting children from Eastern Bloc countries following a "summer camp program" where potential adoptees are brought over to the U.S. for several weeks; hosted by perspective adoptive families who are then "pushed" to make a decision regarding adopting the child. Those of us in the field of International Adoption Medicine express great concern regarding these programs as seeing these children for "fun and recreation" in no way gives a clear picture of the child's true institutional profile. Any child will "have fun" for a few weeks, leading families to see them as "just fine". Agencies then push families to adopt based on this "snapshot". Many do, only to see the honeymoon period sadly end (rapidly) after the adoption when reality of the child's troubled past sets in and stresses the family.

Recent "surveys" completed by adoption agencies boasts very low incidences of problems with internationally adopted children. Professional analysis of these "contentment surveys" are misleading to the general public as many families, even those with problem children are "content" to have a family. Also, families often grossly under-report true problems out of guilt, anxiety and denial. This often results in inflated statistics by adoption agencies and some researchers, claiming there are relatively "few problems" with the post-institutionalized child, when in actuality, there are clearly issues that have not been disclosed.

Peggy and Bill fell victim to this system. They were not warned nor trained by the adoption agency. After they returned home with Sergei, they didn't hear from the agency again. There was no follow-up, no help, no guidance. They were on their own with a child they had no idea how to handle. Sergei was a complicated child requiring complicated treatment.

How can it happen, parents later wonder, that their seemingly healthy child with "temporary" emotional or developmental problems has turned out to be severely impaired? Although it is nearly impossible to find out the "how," we can understand the "why" by taking a close look at where the child came from.

Some Preliminary Data to Ponder

New research suggests that the longer a child is institutionalized, the more likely he or she will experience longer-term psychological and cognitive difficulties. In a recent study of mine, involving a sample of 67 internationally-adopted children who were declared by the adoption agencies as "completely healthy and normal" actually had a wide range of disabilities which surfaced as the children began to enter school. Language disorders were seen in over 60 percent of the children; learning disabilities were seen in over 53 percent of the children; attentional disorders in over 37 percent; post-traumatic stress and depression in over 66 percent of the children; attachment disorders in over 16 percent of the children; and Fetal Alcohol Syndrome in approximately 6 percent.

The take-home points that prospective adoptive families need to be aware of are the high risks of language and learning disabilities, which are typically long-term. There are certainly many children who do well, despite all odds, but one must respect the "risk factors" and the combined effects institutionalization has on brain growth and development, as well as personality.

It is important for adoptive parents to remember that you can take the child out of the institution, but it may take a much greater amount of effort to take the institution of the child. Many older post-institutionalized children find it much more stressful after being adopted, since they have many more complicated and confusing issues to deal with, such as school, family, friends, work and responsibilities, and the expectation of being productive. In the institutional environment, the expectations are to follow a rigid and inflexible schedule, which is dictated by the caretakers who merely supervise the children rather than nurture, educate and shape them

Living Conditions and Biological Roots of Overseas Orphans

Children from many of the impoverished Eastern Bloc countries such as Romania and the former Soviet Union experience a wide variety of conditions which clearly impact brain development. **Fetal Alcohol Syndrome (FAS)**, which is the result of a mother drinking during pregnancy, is very prominent in these deprived environments where society is under a great deal of stress. We know from our own United States history that, during the Great Depression, alcoholism was highest during these most depressive years. Fetal Alcohol Syndrome is truly a medical/ neurological syndrome which produces classic facial dysmorphic features which are quickly recognized by competent medical specialists. There are research centers around the country studying the medical and cognitive affects in the children whose mothers consumed alcohol during pregnancy. Medical researchers have been trying to develop a uniform method of assessing the child with Fetal Alcohol Syndrome.

Children may also have endured much more subtle **Fetal Alcohol Effects (FAE)** (now more commonly referred to as Alcohol Related Neurodevelopmental Disorder or ARND). In ARND, the physical malformations associated with FAS such as an abnormally small head size, low nasal bridge, abnormally small or separated eyes, with epicanthal folds, flat mid-face, short nose, thin upper lip and indistinct philtrum are not typically present. What surfaces are multiple impairments in cognitive-intellectual and psychological/psychiatric syndromes. Specifically, a child with FAE can look very normal and have a relatively average IQ, but may have very unusual behavioral patterns; subtle and multiple learning disabilities;

deficits in attention, memory, judgement, verbal reasoning and auditory processing, and behavioral control. Children with FAS or FAE/ARND often have very fragmented and disorganized language and are unable to communicate in a logical and cohesive manner. Problems such as mood disorders, uncontrollable rage attacks and depression are also common in the FAE/ARND child. Neuropsychologists have a great interest in this pattern of alcohol related neurodevelopmental disorders as the cognitive and behavioral disabilities are "hidden" and require very intricate, comprehensive assessment and multi-discipline treatments.

Other high-risk factors evident in impoverished environments are poor prenatal care which can result in vitamin/nutritional deficiency syndromes and low birth weight. Low birth weight and medical complications during the time of pregnancy and delivery have been found to have a relatively high correlation with later-onset learning disabilities, motor problems and ADHD. The medical manifestations of children have who experienced fetal distress can be cord compression, maternal hemorrhage and chronic hypoxia which can cause secondary problems involving cell and possible brain damage. Heavy metal toxicity (often <u>not</u> screened) is less common, but another risk which can directly impact cognitive and psychological growth and lead to a very complex pattern of difficulties.

There are many children who have been adopted from institutional settings who do no show major medical, cognitive or psychiatric problems. This depends greatly on the age of the child and the amount of time spent in the institutional setting. For example, if a child has been adopted out of an institutional setting before the ages of 12-to-18 months, they stand a much better chance of recovery from the damaging effects of deprivation and institutional care than the child who has been institutionalized for over 2 years. Therefore, it is highly critical that a child be adopted at the earliest possible age (preferably under 2 years) as he or she stands a better chance of recovery and the adoptive families may be faced with a lesser degree of problems.

When people adopt older children from institutionalized settings (ages 2-10), the children are often diagnosed, by default, as having an attachment disorder or ADHD based on their initial behavioral presentation and appearance of cognitive limitations. However, it is likely that neither of these diagnoses is completely correct. The older child residing in an institution for more than 2 years is certainly going to have attachment problems as there was no one there to adequately attach to in terms of primary caretaker. Also spending lengthy times in an institution clearly can slow down, if not damage, brain development and produce very significant learning and emotional problems. The longer the time spent in an institution, the more likely it is the child will suffer from depression, despondency and, at times, loss of acquired skills. The post-institutionalized child presents with a very complex group of developmental and psychological disorders which require immediate, comprehensive and intensive treatment.

To fully understand how the brain and emotions become affected, we must go back to basic neurobiology which dictates that the cells of a developing brain are very impressionable and can be easily influenced by internal problems (i.e. illnesses and injuries) or by environmental and external factors. The human brain clearly has an important component termed the "emotional brain". This center of emotional functioning orchestrates a child's personality and control over basic human feelings, such as anger, love, affection and, at times, rage and aggression. When the brain structure experiences some type of problem, personality changes are very typical. While there is no specific test to confirm or negate a diagnosis of brain impairment that affects emotions, there is a tremendous amount of research in trying to "track down" specific areas of the brain which seem to be most sensitive to and changeable from injury and insult. For families interested in further study, the famous Russian neuropsychologist A.R. Luria has done in-depth studies of the emotional brain and the levels of brain organization, which include: 1) mental alertness and arousal for general brain activity; 2) receiving, analyzing and storing newly processed information; 3) regulating, inhibiting and organizing new data while responding appropriately to environmental and interpersonal stimuli.

Many families, and even their pediatricians or other specialists, erroneously believe that the child only needs time to acclimate to the new language and culture and will "outgrow" the institutional delays. Instead, what should take place is a careful diagnostic neuropsychological assessment of the child. The "neuropsychology of attachment disorders" is one of the most important areas to evaluate. This new term which describes the complexities of the internationally adopted child is one I must place great emphasis on and will continue to reference throughout the book as it is a core point in understanding and treating the problem.

What Life Was Like for Your Adopted Child

Among the thousands of adopted foreign children now living in the United States, about half once lived in extreme economical, medical and psychological deprivation, often for many years. Many of these children were born into the extreme poverty of developing countries in Latin America, Asia and Eastern Europe. Many others come from industrialized nations that have experienced tremendous dislocations in their economies, affecting every aspect of society. With the fall of Communism and the break-up of the Soviet Union, many countries have suffered such enormous crises that they have an over-abundance of orphaned or abandoned children.

Southeast Asia

China has dominated Asian adoptions for the last 5 years, although there are still many children being adopted from Vietnam, Thailand, Korea and the Philippines. It is very common for a child born out of wedlock to be placed immediately in an institution as this is a cultural taboo. In China, young males tend to be more needed and desired so there are an abundance of baby girls which are not necessarily wanted by the families. There are two principal reasons why girls are put up for adoption: 1) the one-child family policy of the Communist China government, and 2) males traditionally inherit the family wealth and are responsible for caring for elderly parents.

This has prompted many adoption agencies to arrange for the placement of thousands of baby girls per year at costs which can be fairly high, from around $12,000 to as much as $20,000 to $30,000 per infant. As the demand increases for young and healthier infants, the costs rise.

In the Southeast Asian countries I have visited, hygiene and medical care in orphanages and institutions is relatively poor, although mandates still require women caretakers to feed, clothe and bathe the children. Also, abuse did not seem to be as prevalent, although it does exist but in the form of deprivation as opposed to physical or sexual abuse. Malnutrition and diseases not frequently seen in the United States, such as malaria (very rare incidences), hepatitis, rickets and various infectious diseases are widespread. Medical conditions common in China (as documented and researched in 1998) involve asthma, anemia, rickets, lead toxicity, Hepatitis B carriage, exposure to tuberculosis, malnutrition and failure to thrive. These types of medical problems are treated very aggressively in America, but produce grave crises in Asian countries. Poor medical care and health standards also mean poor maternal health, ultimately damaging an infant's physical and possible cognitive development. In Asian countries, it is common practice for the mother to work up to the last moment before childbirth and have the child at home. Due to this pattern, we really do not have the actual statistics regarding prematurity and low birth weight although we can assume that there may be "high risk factors," both pre- and post-natal. Many of these problems may not be immediately treated because many parents stay at home and attempt to deal with the situation themselves since they cannot reach or afford better medical facilities and care. The basic health care that most Americans take for granted, such as inoculations and regular treatment of common childhood ailments, is often out of reach for the average Asian child. Something as simple as an ear infection can, if left untreated, result in hearing problems and language delays.

Latin America

Most Hispanic children adopted in the 1990's have come from Mexico, Guatemala, El Salvador, Columbia, Chile, Brazil, Bolivia or Paraguay. Although Latin American countries typically have somewhat better medical care than Asia and Eastern Europe, premature birth and other risk factors due to fetal exposure to alcohol, cigarette smoke, and other neurotoxins are common. While there are no formal statistics, South American adoptees seem to have a relatively higher incidence of genetic problems because of more relationships between first cousins and increased incidents of incest/rape, but this is often screened via genetic testing.

I have not observed actual conditions in Latin American countries, although I have evaluated numerous adopted children from Central and South America. News reported by parents, orphanages, and foster care programs tends to be somewhat more positive. Abuse is not as prevalent and, if children are able to get out of a hospital setting and live in a foster program run by the state, they have a chance of being given human contact and appropriate nutrition. South American foster care systems can be quite good. Adoption in these countries are more costly as it is felt the children are better cared for and are healthier.

Eastern Europe and Former Soviet Countries

Life in Eastern European and Soviet countries was difficult even before the collapse of the USSR in 1989. After decades of oppression and neglect, a number of environmental toxins seeped into children's lives: air pollution, herbicides and pesticides, lead poisoning from water pipes, paint (children chew on either lead-based paint on cribs or ingest it through drinking the water), leaded gasoline (which is actually the number one airborne pollutant) and radiation fallout from the Belarus and Chernobyl nuclear plants. Children representing "second generation" radiation can be found to have congenital malformations such as joint deformities, skin discolorations, missing or deformed teeth, difficulty maintaining normal weight, and cognitive and learning impairments. We are now even seeing "third generation" cases of radiation poisoning. Additionally, we are now seeing the long-term effects of environmental hazards and abandonment on the thousands of lost orphans in Eastern Europe.

Misguided governmental policies also adversely affected children. Nicolae Ceaucesecu, the infamous dictator of Romania until 1989, was hopeful that women would have many children in order to expand the work force. The ensuing increase in the birth rate brought many unwanted children into the world. Many of these "decree babies" were abandoned and ended up in orphanages. Often, as a result of medical and environmental neglect, many children were born with a handicap, medical condition, or deformity. During these difficult years, many Romanian children were erroneously evaluated as "irrecuperable" and were placed for life in neuropsychiatric institutions for the hopeless. The majority of these children remain lost and a victim to a failed system of child care which is now changing very gradually.

Although the fall of Communism and the break-up of the Soviet Union was a victory for democracy and capitalism, these events triggered mammoth dislocations in national economies, spawned regional warfare, toppled legal and financial systems and threatened the very fabric of society. Suddenly, families literally lost everything they had known under their communist system. Under the new free market system, workers were now required to pay for all the housing, food and medical care they used to get from the government for free. Government agencies and enterprises were abolished or drastically cut back and, virtually overnight, many workers lost their jobs. Others found their salaries drastically reduced under the new system. One of my close Russian friends is a top-notch pediatric neurosurgeon who makes only $350 a month. Another friend is an aeronautical engineer with a Ph.D. and is making only $100 per month. The average "flat" which is merely a two bedroom apartment with a kitchen can run as high as $25 or $30 a month, leaving only a small amount of "change" for the family to actually survive on.

As a result, many workers are no longer able to provide for their children and the families disintegrate. People become homeless. Many resort to criminal behavior, prostitution or a vagabond way of life. Food scarcities cause malnutrition and illness. Pregnant women often cannot afford adequate pre- or post-natal care. Needless to say it is a vicious cycle.

Other specialists across the country and I have been gathering statistics regarding the internationally adopted child and have come up with provisional "percentages" outlining areas of problems. It is very important to emphasize that these statistics which outline cognitive and emotional-behavioral problems are typically reserved for the older adopted child (ages beyond 3 years old) who has reached a level where a formal assessment regarding brain and emotional development can be made. Neurodevelopmental and emotional delays are less prominent with infants and toddlers under the age of 2 due to lesser time in stages of deprivation and institutional care.

My current statistics reserved for the older child (beyond 3 years of age) which involves a sample of approximately 1500 children, suggests that about 20-25 percent of adopted children from countries in Eastern Europe have severe or multiple developmental delays which will require life-long services; 40-50 percent have moderate multiple delays requiring continued educational and psychological support; while only 20-25 percent are relatively free of developmental problems. These healthier children tend to have routine adjustment difficulties and expected delays yet, over time and with adequate educational and parental interventions, they typically advance on towards independence and healthy adjustment. In summary, there is approximately a 75 percent chance a child from Eastern European institutional settings will show a pattern of developmental delay which will require long-term treatments.

I have visited multiple institutions in Eastern Bloc countries and have seen first-hand that they are dismal failures. The level of dirt, infection and contagion is overwhelming. Urine and feces typically line the institution floors. Viruses such as Hepatitis B and C, HIV, meningitis, and some instances of encephalitis and cytomegalovirus (a principle cause of cognitive problems and mental retardation) run rampant. Simple colds, flus, pneumonia and chronic ear infections are rarely treated and often result in significant medical complications for the children. Food and nutrition is horrible, often just a kettle of broth with a few chunks of bread floating in it being the typical breakfast, lunch and dinner. There is limited medical care, limited medications, few sterile, or even clean, bandages. The so-called "medical director" assigned to the facility may be difficult to find, leaving the children to fight to survive. Children often receive medical care only when they are in an acute or life-threatening situation, and the little care they do receive is often inadequate and sometimes causes even more problems than the actual illness. Staff paid to care for the children often lighten their workload by delegating responsibilities to older children to. Abuse is common, with emotional deprivation being at the top of the list.

Bathrooms are so bad that I could barely walk in because of the stench.

Children are bathed only once a week in mass groups with unsanitized water. There is virtually no heating or ventilation and most of the children are crowded together, with five to a bed. Babies are often left in cribs for days or weeks at a time, wrapped very tightly in blankets so they do not crawl or get out and injure themselves. It is also not uncommon to see children who are around eight to twelve years old to be "cribbed" or tied down if they are behaving badly. The only term I can think of to adequately describe what I saw is "warehousing." Many of these children are so bored and isolated that they engage in repetitive, self-stimulation or self-mutilation, such as head-banging.

There are many orphanages which attempt to do a better job in terms of cleanliness, hygiene and general child care. Colleagues and families who have personally visited orphanages in parts of Russia, Ukraine, Bulgaria, Hungary, Latvia, Poland, Republic of Georgia, and Lithuania reported better conditions for the children that are eligible for adoptions. In Romania and Moldova, the majority of the institutions are extremely deprived and unsanitary although there are Lageanuls (or Lagens for the toddlers) which are somewhat better in terms of living conditions.

Of greatest notation is that children in these Eastern Bloc institutions are rarely, if ever, physically held, nurtured or cared for emotionally. It is very clear that the majority of the staff tolerate their job as the pay is very low and the children are high maintenance in terms of requiring care. It is not uncommon that the underpaid caretaker will steal food and clothing from the children or the institution in order to provide for his or her own family. Also, physical and sexual abuse is, unfortunately, prevalent.

Children are frequently moved from institution to institution. The first move typically comes at about age two, when a child is able to walk and get around on his or her own. By this time, the child's speech and language abilities should have developed, although due to the many moves and continuous deprivation, the child may not learn to speak the native tongue, but rather an "institutional language," a combination of gibberish and babbling.

In Eastern Bloc countries, handicapped children are viewed as both irrecuperable and irredeemable, to the point where it is believed that people should not spend ample time, energy or money working with them. To make matters worse, the orphan's health problems or developmental problems are often misdiagnosed. For example, developmental delays (perhaps a simple lag in language) can be misconstrued as mental deficiency or retardation. As a result, children may be labeled "morons" or "imbeciles" or the old word, "Oligophrenic" (which means mentally deficient) and placed in neuropsychiatric facilities where conditions are abysmal. Once placed, children often remain there for life.

Children with crossed eyes, malnutrition/anemia and physical deformities or orthopedic problems that are easily treated in the United States are placed in hospital-like institutions, as are children with complicated medical conditions such as hemophilia or congenital malformations and deformities. Instead of receiving proper care, these children get placed in an institution where they frequently encounter infections, many of which result in death. ***There is no such thing as a good institution, however some are better than others.*** Many institutions try very hard, despite meager resources. They are to be commended for their efforts and caring for the lost children of communism.

The Downward Spiral of Institutionalized Children: Hopelessness Sets In

The anger and frustration that such a child in these circumstances feels gradually turns to deep depression and despondency, helplessness and hopelessness. At the same time, these children's psychological problems may be transferred to the form of aggressive and out-of-control behaviors. When a child experiences extreme loneliness and despair, he or she will often resort to bizarre behavior as a way of compensating for the lack of human contact and stimulation everyone needs. The child may find some degree of pleasure in such behavior as incessant rocking, or flapping and waving of the arms.

I have seen children whose physical and mental development had slowed to the point that it was impossible for me to accurately determine their age. Many children appeared to be six or seven years old when, in fact they were actually in their early or middle teenage years. This is an example of classic "Psychosocial Dwarfism," which means the physical and medical neglect has grossly altered growth and development. Eventually, many children disintegrate, losing a vast majority of motor, sensory, language and general intellectual-cognitive skills. Once this regression begins, it tends to become progressive and insidious. While there is no precise measurement to assess how long this takes, a rough rule of thumb is that for every year of life in an institution, a child will experience a rapid rate of regression—as much as six month's worth—in psychological and cognitive functions. The rule of thumb for children under 2 years is: for every three months in and institution, there is one month of loss in development. Therefore, children who have been institutionalized for one year may be delayed three months; children institutionalized for two years may be delayed a minimum of six months, and so on.

THE ULTIMATE TRAGEDY:

INSTITUTIONAL AUTISM--AN ACQUIRED SYNDROME

When a child's memories of the few positive experiences of life gradually fade away, he or she may regress to the most infantile stage of development. In my visits to many Romanian institutions, I have observed children who have retreated into a fantasy world and have become extremely regressive in both their cognitive and psychological development. This regression can ultimately lead to a very infantile and autistic state in which the child exhibits an emotionally detached or preoccupied attitude. Being "cribbed" or totally secluded is the ultimate deprivation and isolative experience. Alone and scared. Scared and alone.

Children who "learn" to become autistic as a direct result of being institutionalized often have little, if any, language. They may be able to express five or ten words, but typically tend to grunt, moan, yell and shriek. Many tend to rock, sway and pick at themselves. These self-stimulating behaviors are the way they communicate and fill in the gaps of loneliness, boredom, and deep despair in their lives. Because these children have spent the majority of their formative years with other children who were similarly abandoned, it is understandable that they imitate the behavior around them. Eventually, these children regress to such low levels that they appear truly mentally deficient. For children who started out in life relatively normal, this is, indeed a tragedy.

This type of autism however, does not fall into any of the classic definitions of autism, Rett's Disorder, or even Childhood Disintegrative Disorder (although there is certainly "disintegration and regression").

A unique and institutionally specific pattern of behaviors which constitute Institutional Autism often meet the following criteria:

(1) Actual loss of physical height, weight and growth. Many of these children are not even represented on the growth charts or curves by which we estimate average growth. This is again referred to as Psychosocial Growth Failure. The profound negative effects of malnutrition, untreated medical problems and social deprivation take their toll on the body and mind/cognitive development. Early onset puberty is also common as the brains "time clock" has been altered. Many of these children started off their institutionalization in somewhat stable medical condition or having only minimal difficulties. These problems intensify the longer the child's in the institution.

(2) Does not look to be anywhere near actual age. In assessing many institutionalized children, I was unable to discern the actual age of the child; teenagers looked like 6 or 8 year-olds. This is why, often, children are assigned an age upon adoption, but are actually much older. Many of the girls have short hair and are dressed in boys clothing, even making gender difficult to determine.

(3) Loss of previously acquired language, or the use of language which is extremely regressive to the point that it resembles "infant babbling." This is commonly referred to as "institutional language." Along these lines, intellectual capabilities diminish to the point where the child can appear mentally retarded or autistic.

(4) Rapid deterioration of behavior to the point where the child exhibits primitive acting-out. This may include aggression and assaultive tendencies, hoarding food, urinating and defecating on themselves, and/or playing with urine and feces.

(5) Various illness, injury and malnutrition can profoundly affect the body and brain development, resulting in a condition similar to the confusion of Alzheimer's dementia. As the brain experiences more trauma, the child continually loses more and more intellectual and cognitive capabilities.

(6) Major regression to self-simulating behaviors, such as rocking, head banging, hair pulling, picking at their own body, thrusting themselves into walls and windows, or enuresis and encopresis, playing with urine and feces. These severe behaviors imply that the child is trying to find a way to maintain internal physical and psychological "movements" which serve as a level of stimulation and as a way of passing the time. Rage, emotional outbursts, obsessive behaviors and self-stimulation may just be more ways to "keep busy" while also reminding themselves that they have no real identity or purpose in life.

(7) The ultimate Institutional Autistic syndrome is a complete regression to these self-stimulating behaviors and loss of acquired skills. Autistic characteristics serve as a way of filling in the gaps of loneliness, deprivation and despair. Over the course of time, if left to continually "practice" these behaviors, a child develops a repetitive pattern of newly learned movements, mannerisms and speech and social interactions. The regression to the most self-absorbed and isolative way of life may be the "ultimate defense" in blocking out pain and suffering. Post-Traumatic Stress Disorder and Disassociation at its finest?

A better understanding of this unique and highly complex syndrome may help families approach the entire concept of international adoptions with more awareness. Many families are so anxious to adopt that they do not take the time or responsibility for learning about the complicated medical and psychological health issues before they adopt. So very often, many families finally reach qualified specialists after two or three years and multiple evaluations which have cost them thousands of dollars. By the time the proper diagnosis is made, families are often very angry and depressed. They tend to blame adoption agencies for misleading them and telling them their child did not have any significant cognitive and psychiatric/psychological problems and that "love would be enough." Love is an important intervention but it typically is not the recommended starting point for children coming from institutional backgrounds that do not understand the abstract concepts of human emotions. The word love needs to be "reframed" and used in a more helpful context which may be better termed "providing structure, safety and security."

The earlier the assessment and interventions, the better the outcome for the internationally adopted child. We know very well that children adopted out of the institution under the age of two years old stand a much better chance of rehabilitation or recovery. Remember our previous statistics for the older internationally adopted child which indicated that approximately 75 percent may be deemed "high risk" for long-term developmental problems, with only approximately 25 percent appearing to be relatively unscathed or at least able to recover from institutionalization. This leaves a very large percentage of the "walking wounded" who are survivors but with a great deal of brain and emotional baggage. A strong brain and strong soul appear to be the critical factors in surviving an institutional life.

These statistics are, indeed, very concerning as the damaging effects of institutionalization are clearly seen impacting the medical and emotional growth of the child. Today, the new subspecialty of "adoption medicine" continues to provide valuable research, education and interventions for families pursuing international adoptions.

Unfortunately, severe diagnoses of autism, mental retardation, fetal alcohol syndrome/fetal alcohol effects or multiple learning disabilities will often persist until adulthood. It will take a very strong and dedicated family to help the child cope, work through these difficulties and find the proper adjustment and vocation. Therefore, before engaging in international adoptions, families must be well informed of all the risks and long-term effects of institutionalization. Children from institutional settings clearly need to be considered a "high-risk population." No child who has been institutionalized will emerge unscathed. The younger the child (preferably under the age of 18-20 months) who can be removed from the institution via adoption will have a better opportunity of improving developmental delays at a more rapid pace, although the long-term effects of even short-term institutionalization will not clearly be evident until the child reaches school age years when learning aptitudes and abilities are assessed. Research being conducted in Romanian institutions by the MacArthur Foundation is showing us that cognitive and psychological regressions are evident in children as young as 9-to-12 months old. It should be emphasized that, the lesser amount of deprivation will increase (but <u>not</u> guarantee) the chances of recovery or smooth sailing. There are no guarantees. Remember, life offers no guarantees—only challenges.

What Adoption Agencies and Adoptive Families Can and Should Do

(1) Adoption agencies should have a better awareness of Institutional Autistic Syndrome and the concepts pertaining to Post-Traumatic Stress Disorder. On my wish list, I would set up a "task force" of trained professionals to work in the institution where children are being adopted out would be beneficial, as this may help better "prepare" and "desensitize" the child prior to adoption. These professionals should be trained in syndromes of severe abuse and neglect and should work with the prospective adoptive child for a minimum of three months before the child is allowed to be placed with his or her new family.

(2) Families with an adopted child from an institutional setting should be required to attend intensive pre and post-adoptive training programs to learn how to deal effectively with the problems that will arise. The Parent Network for the Post-Institutionalized Child (see Appendix) has done an outstanding job of setting up various training programs around the country, along with information and training videos.

(3) Families need to address specific treatment issues which are highly specialized and germane only to the post-institutionalized child who may possibly suffer from Institutional Autism. A unique and innovative family therapy approach should be arranged immediately upon the child's arrival to the United States.

Before Adopting a Foreign Child: How Parents Need to Prepare

As noted earlier, adoption agencies sometimes give only very brief information or "filter" the actual medical records. It is often very difficult for families to get completely accurate translations as this can be very costly and time consuming, particularly if the families request the entire foreign medical record of "dossier" on the child. But families have the right to ask for any and all medical records and get their own independent medical opinions prior to adopting the child. Agencies will often tell the families that this is not possible but this can certainly be secured if families are aggressive and demand that the agency find a way to contact the overseas coordination or institution director. Extended videos can also be arranged if families are willing to pay the extra price. Remember, many things abroad can be arranged for an additional cost— overseas coordinators and assistants need the extra money and just need to be instructed what needs to be done, such as retrieving additional documents or making longer videos. It is very important to find a way to obtain the child's foreign medical record and periodic video tapes through stages of development, even if it is month by month or at the very least at 3 month intervals while the family is waiting to adopt. Trust me, it is worth the extra money in the long run. Also, many families are now securing their own medical experts in other countries to perform independent medical and psychological evaluations of the child. I think the best is to bring over your own United States physician who may have experience in internationally adopted children. I realize the cost is certainly a burden, but this initial evaluation will provide invaluable information and help the family make a better decision regarding adoption as the majority of families would prefer not to have a seriously delayed child.

Families should take a very careful look in person at the institutional setting of the child they wish to adopt. This will give them a better idea of how the child has been living for months or years as opposed to just seeing the child in the "Director's Office" which is often a very nice showcase. While viewing the institution and spending <u>ample</u> time with the child, I would like to provide a word of caution to prospective parents and their medical consultants who are assessing the child: pay attention to the very subtle neuropsychological syndromes that are loosely described in the child's medical record. Do not downplay the significance, for research clearly indicates that these syndromes are linked to difficulties which often do not emerge until later; well after the child has been adopted and families are beginning to struggle.

Adopting parents should discuss with their medical experts how to set up early intervention strategies after the adoption has been finalized. It goes without saying that it is very important for families to find an international adoption agency that can give them a wide variety of opinions, training and education, in addition to follow-up and supportive services after the adoption process has been completed. Too often, adoption agencies tend to mysteriously disappear, offering no help or support to the new parents.

Parents need to prepare themselves for the difficulties which lie ahead so that they will be fully ready to handle a wide range of issues that are unique to the institutionalized child. Parents should enroll in pre-adoption counseling as well as familiarizing themselves with training for early detection of multiple medical, cognitive and emotional problems in the child. Understanding concepts related to learning disabilities, mental retardation, autism and attachment disorders should be a mandatory requirement before adoption. To help the entire family, a unique and innovative family therapy approach should be arranged immediately upon the child's arrival in the United States.

The Parent Network for the Post-Institutionalized Child (known as PNPIC and directed by two adoptive mothers: Thais Tepper in Pennsylvania and Lois Hannon, also in Pennsylvania) has done an outstanding job of setting up various training programs around the country, in addition to having regular newsletters, mailings and research readily available to families in need.

Another outstanding organization, Friends of Russian and Ukrainian Adoptions (FRUA), provides national and international support and training for families who have adopted children from Eastern Bloc countries.

The PNPIC and FRUA are nationally recognized support groups that provide the most comprehensive information to families having internationally-adopted children. It all started with a few families getting together during the critical Romanian and Russian adoption years in the early 90's. When disabilities in the children began to surface, the parents began to talk. Over the past ten years, the PNPIC and FRUA have evolved to approximately ten-thousand members. Experts from around the country are involved in consulting with the groups, and hold workshops and intensive training programs several times a year, both in the U.S. and abroad.

The amount of information which has been brought up regarding the plight of Romanian and Russian orphans, or any child raised in an institutional setting, has been tremendous. Families that have difficult children are finally receiving proper help and guidance. Additionally, the PNPIC and FRUA have been keenly involved in providing professional guidance and support to multiple agencies and medical facilities, and have also been involved in providing critical information to overseas countries regarding the follow-up problems of the post-institutionalized child.

Adoption Agencies Must Do a Better Job Preparing Parents

Adoption agencies need to have a better awareness of the Institutional Autistic Syndrome and Post-Traumatic Stress Disorder. They should set up a task force of trained professionals to help prepare, not only the parents, but the child as well. It is my feeling that experts trained in severe abuse and neglect syndromes should work with prospective adoptive children for a minimum of three to six months before they are allowed to be placed with their new families. Agencies need to advise families of all the risk possibilities and not just selected information or the catch-phrase, "love and a good home will fix the delays." Also, proper post-placement surveys should focus on cognitive and emotional strengths and weakness as opposed to "family contentment" which has little to do with assessing, treating and supporting the child and families. Agencies need to stay in touch as many families report that, after adoption, they never hear from anyone again. Parents who are struggling with a newly adopted child often feel overwhelmed, afraid and alone. They feel embarrassed and tend to hide their problems as they sometimes feel they have "failed" as a new parent. New parents, particularly parents having a developmentally delayed child, need a great deal of support, encouragement and professional guidance which should be an integral part of the "adoption packet."

Bringing Your Child Home

It is very important to ensure the help of doctors who have some experience with the post-institutionalized child. Otherwise, you run the risk of receiving misdiagnoses. I can recall one specific case where a post-institutionalized child had Fetal Alcohol Syndrome, but instead of viewing the big picture, the American psychiatrist diagnosed every "symptom." For example, the child was medicated for: ADHD, obsessive anxiety, a sleep disorder, and depression. The correct diagnosis of Fetal Alcohol Syndrome was eventually made after taking the child off all medication and placing the child on the proper (single) medication. There are hundreds of cases similar to this with the most common "mistakes" in diagnosis being ADHD and bonding and attachment disorder.

Upon returning to the U.S., the child should have the following exams:

(1) Medical and Neurological examinations
(2) Infectious Disease consultation
(3) Endocrinological consultation
(4) Developmental Neuropsychological and Psychological evaluations
(5) Educational and Learning Disability testing
(6) Developmental Speech and Language evaluation
(7) Physical and Occupational therapy evaluation
(8) Sensory Integration Evaluation and treatment
(9) Audiological and Developmental Optometry evaluation
(10) Family Therapy evaluation to assess bonding, coping and adjustment strategies

Post-Traumatic Stress Disorder (PTSD) in the Post-Institutionalized Child

It is very common for older children who have resided in institutional settings for at least 2-3 years to have PTSD following their adoption. In fact, the majority of institutionalized children over the age of three, will likely have a level of PTSD.

As a child develops and attempts to adjust to their new family, the child with PTSD often appears very angry, frustrated, moody, irritable, self-destructive and completely lost and alone in this new world filled with new people, rules, values and emotions. The child is overwhelmed and over-stimulated. All of these major depressive indicators, in addition to a child who tends to constantly worry and "obsess" regarding problems, are very typical characteristics.

These children often push others away out of fear of additional abandonment, rejection and neglect. Again, the erroneous diagnosis of attachment disorder is often made as the child is trying to stay away from people who may hurt them once again. It is also very common for children who have been abused and damaged during their early years to "repeat" the cycle of abuse and neglect which was done to them. This may take the form of aggressive and violent behaviors towards new siblings and new adoptive parents. It is important to remember that many children who have been raised in very destructive institutional settings have only witnessed depravation, anger and abuse, and may be repeating the cycle that was the initial "imprint" or role model presented to them during their early formative years.

Bonding and Attachment Disorders in the Post-Institutionalized Child

Bonding and attachment disorders are very prevalent in children who have spent time in institutional settings or who have been shuffled from primary caretaker to primary caretaker. This disorder is based on very poor early childhood care. These children have been basically disregarded and were neglected of basic physical and emotional care, such as comfort, nurturing, affection and proper stimulation in order to develop cognitively and emotionally.

It is often hard for parents to comprehend that some children just cannot understand or express feeling and emotions. To make it easier to visualize, pretend you are trying to work a computer that does not have all the software installed. You are trying to use this computer, yet there is a lack of a solid data base. The only way to get the computer to function is to consistently upgrade and add the appropriate software. Likewise, with these children with attachment disorders, the "software" is just not there and these children may need a complete cognitive rehabilitation and re-education in order to learn the meanings of happiness, sadness, sensitivity and genuine expression. Because bonding and attachment disorders can manifest themselves in very severe and confusing ways such as destruction to self and others, it is imperative that parents have a complete knowledge and understanding of the disorder. Please pay close attention to the complicated and multiple symptoms of this syndrome and re-read previous sections of this book addressing attachment disorders.

Depression in the Post-Institutionalized Child

Another problem not to be taken lightly is the fact that many of these children may be severely depressed on both a biological and psychological level. Chronic stress, elevated cortisol levels, malnutrition and deprivation can clearly lead to changes in brain neurochemistry leading to a Major Depressive Disorder. Once again, the added stress of the child leaving the institution further contributes to the depressive cycle. These factors need to be addressed immediately since unchecked depression can often turn into rage. A child from an institutional setting should be assumed to have a degree of depression and despondency. After all, he or she had been living in deprivation and aloneness. Please refer to the sections on childhood depression in the earlier portions of this book.

Post-institutionalized children often have very intense depressions, mood swings, irritability, low frustration tolerance and, at times, total lethargy and despondency. Many children look totally psychotic and out of control. Many are over or under-diagnosed, and placed on aggressive medications too quickly. For these special children, we must use caution, conservative treatment approaches, patience and continual assessments at regular intervals. It took years for this level of damage to occur. It will take years for the child to recover but, in many cases, partial recovery is the most that can be expected.

Innovative Treatment for the Post-Institutionalized Child:

Detoxification from Institutionalization

I want to expand on a very important topic which I tend to call "Regressive Therapies for the Post-Institutionalized Child." In particular, children from institutions need to be gradually and consistently "detoxified," slowly retrained and rehabilitated-medically and psychologically-from their past damaging life which has altered their cognitive and emotional structure and development. These children have literally missed years of their life and it is our job to put the pieces of the puzzle back together if possible. This takes tremendous time, patience, persistence, empathy and, most importantly, assertiveness and structure. Structure and rehabilitation supersedes love and affection for the damaged post-institutionalized child.

Once a child has come from an institutionalized setting, many parents, like Peggy and Bill, try to provide love, stimulation and the appearance of a normal household with the hope this will rectify all of the problems the child has experienced. Again, although this sounds heartless to say, love is just not enough. It is in the best interest of the child to detoxify and retrain first. Then, hopefully, the child will be able to comprehend basic concepts of love and affection. The younger child who has been adopted under the age of two stands a much better chance, whereas the child beyond three has experienced longer lasting trauma based on deprivation.

Many children are delayed in receiving the proper assessment and treatment programs as families are often told by adoption agency officials and medical specialists to "wait and see," and allow the child a period of time to "adjust and develop." Many people have been told that it is "just too early" to determine the level of the problem during the child's first couple years. With the child under the age of two years old, families certainly have to wait until the child enters school to see if there are any cognitive problems; but for the child three years and above, an assessment should be made immediately.

I disagree totally with the "wait and see advice" and take the stance that, based on statistics of the older post-institutionalized child, there are <u>most</u> <u>definitely</u> going to be problems and the best thing for both the child and the parents is to address these potential problems immediately. As a result, I have created a very innovative and unorthodox treatment program especially for the post-institutionalized child. Many families find it very difficult to follow as they feel they want to rapidly integrate the child into their home instead of instituting a program. Additionally, many families may find it difficult to practice the rather strict techniques on a child who has just come from such a horrendous background. I can only offer sympathy in this area, for it is tough. As a parent, you want to welcome your child with love, but as a parent of a post-institutionalized child you need to be able to shift gears.

For the child who has been institutionalized for at least 2-3 years, I recommend the following detoxification treatment approach:

(1) Prior to retrieving their adoptive child, the family should prepare for the difficulties ahead. I mandate that pre-adoption and pre-placement counseling be undertaken in the field of adoption medicine. Parents should be well aware of the high risk factors in children from institutional settings and be trained in early detection of children who have multiple medical, cognitive and emotional problems. Understanding concepts pertaining to learning disabilities, mental retardation, autism and attachment disorders should be mandatory as well.

(2) Parents should be prepared in meeting and greeting the child for the first time. Many parents hope that the child will immediately bond to them or that they will completely fall in love with their child. This often is not true and leads to a great deal of disappointment for parents.

Many children from institutional settings do not care to be around their adoptive families initially. They are still very attached to the caretakers speaking their native language. They may show some initial signs of "liking" their adoptive parents but this is mostly to gain some type of favor, toy, game or food which is often brought for them.

(3) Parents should not try to fix everything while they are abroad as this "fixing" will actually be life-long recovery for the child. Parents should just try to keep matters calm and cooperative while in the other country and allow the native-speaking caretaker to deal with the child. Make sure, however, that the caretaker gradually and concisely explains to the child he or she is going to be with a new family that does not speak their native language, and lives in a different place. The initial focus should be on preparation for the long trip ahead. It is very wise for parents to consult their local pediatrician and bring along proper medications as children can often be sick with a cold, flu, constipation, diarrhea, scabies and lice, to various types of cuts and bruises.

It is also very important for parents to be prepared that the child may need some type of sedation on the long flight home. Many parents absolutely refuse to do this and many doctors also refuse to give medication, but it is very necessary to have a child calm if he or she has never been on, or even seen, a plane before. Imagine being a child, not speaking the same language and then being strapped into a seat and taking off. Wouldn't you be terrified? It is also very common for children to be completely out of control on the airplane due to over-stimulation and/or the close, confined quarters. While this may sound very cold and heartless, sedation is better than a fight requiring physical restraints.

Again, families should be instructed in proper and safe holding techniques with the unmanageable child in their pre-adoptive training program (see Holding Techniques in the next chapter). Many families are totally ill-equipped to deal with this and allow the child to run loose throughout the plane and disrupt everyone. The more informed and equipped the parents are prior to retrieving their child, the more smoothly the plane ride home and initial transition will be.

Your newly adopted child needs a full neuropsychological and psychological evaluation immediately, in their native language which serves as a "baseline". This evaluation will help determine strengths and weaknesses while further developing a "road map" to treatment and recovery from institutionalization.

(4) Upon arrival home, it is very important for families to absolutely and unequivocally **not** over-stimulate the child at any level. Therefore, the child's room should be kept **extremely** basic (if not stripped) and somewhat consistent with his or her room in the institutional setting. Your child's room should be relatively stripped of stimulation, colors, sights, sound, toys and, primarily, food. Remember, even though this seems cruel to you and me, it is all the child knows and it is what feels familiar. We all feel most comfortable when things are what we are used to. You are actually doing your child a favor by initially supplying only the bare minimum. Remember, children who have resided in an institutional setting are used to having nothing. Changing things right away will only confuse the child and begin the process of the child becoming "attached" to new and over-stimulating inanimate objects instead of the new parents. Making it Christmas year round for the new child is an issue that benefits the parents as opposed to helping the child. It is human nature to want to give everything to a deprived child with the hopes of making up for all the years of deprivation. But remember, we are trying to rehabilitate and detoxify the child, so we must keep in our minds what the *child* needs, not what the *parents* need. As time passes, you can gradually expose your child to new things, This will be discussed in detail in the next chapter.

(5) Immediately, the child, regardless of age, should be placed on a very well-structured routine. Many families allow the child to constantly play and be the "center of attention." This is also not very helpful as it gives the child too much stimulation and exposure to adults and relationships which he or she just cannot handle all at once. When my wife and I first brought our two children home, all of our friends and family arrived with colorfully wrapped gifts for the kids. We allowed the kids to keep about a fourth of the toys, mostly videos and books. As for the rest, we took our kids to the local hospital and passed the toys out to children there. We made it very clear that, in our home, people came first and toys were not a requirement (remember, they did not have any consistent playful stimulation in the past). We also have made a point to involve our kids in

packing up toys to send to the institution they came from.

(6) Families should stay at home with the child for as long as possible and have only very few people around, primarily close relatives. Children need to have primary exposure to both parents for the initial 2-3 months with an extra recommendation for onc parent to be at home with the child for a minimum of 6-12 months before returning to work.

The thought of extended day care immediately upon arrival is an absolute accident waiting to happen. Many families adopt a child and then go back to work a few weeks later, dropping the child off at day care which only promotes further emotional detachment, abandonment and anger within the child.

(7) Over the course of the first 2-3 months, if at all possible, parents should try to find a way to communicate with their child in his or her native language. Many families try to force the child to speak English right away when it is much better for the child to gradually learn English over time, with the help of tutors and plenty of patience. Even poor Russian or Romanian on the part of the parents is better than no Russian or Romanian at all. Children typically respond very well to short and concise instructions and directions which can be learned by parents via tapes or even a basic phrase book. **I do not recommend having a nanny or housekeeper in the home who speaks the child's native language as the child will bond to him or her first, and not to the patents.**

(8) Continually recreate as much as possible of the institutional environment for the first 3-4 months to gradually "detoxify" the child off the institutional mentality. This includes not only a gradual introduction to varying sights, sounds, colors and foods, but also to a new routine and new people. Think of it this way: rather than forcing the child to go "cold turkey," wean him or her slowly.

For example, in the institutional setting, children typically are very bored, isolated and withdrawn. The newly adoptive family may have a very difficult time continually providing boredom and isolation for the child, but this is what the child is used to and needs. Do not enroll the child in all types of activities or take him or her on numerous outings. Gradually, this can be changed but not all within the first week.

When parents try to make the child go "cold turkey," it is likely the family is trying much harder than the child is. The older child will give the appearance that he or she actually likes the family who is providing new toys, television, videos and games, but , in reality, this is the start of the attachment-disorder cycle where children begin to use parents to get what they want.

Therefore, children's eating, sleeping, playing, studying, English lessons and behavioral modifications should be religiously and rigidly maintained. **There should be NO exceptions to this very important rule of consistency.** Change takes time and should be gradual. Families attempting to do too much too soon typically have failures in the long run.

(9) Another problem is that children from institutional settings want to come in and "take everything." Along these lines, do **not** initially take the child to department stores, shopping centers, grocery stores or, worst of all, amusement parks such as Disney World, where children can become completely disorganized and out of control. Again, the adoptive family may want to fix everything all at once and give a child all of these wonderful experiences about which the child could actually care less. A child place too early on in this situation will only want to break away and grab and touch everything (i.e. the start of indiscriminate attachment disorder). Along these lines, it is imperative that families do not overstimulate the child with such things as television, videos, Nintendo or multiple toys. What you do want to give your child are basic building blocks involving assembly and construction activities that strengthen fine and gross-motor coordination skills and sensory-perceptual abilities. Also, take your child to a playground or a shallow pool to get him or her moving around and exercising. Again, all activities are to be done under strict parental supervision.

(10) Regardless of the age of the child, the only television that should be watched are Walt Disney-type movies, as opposed to cartoons which can often aggressive tones. I recommend Disney videos because they combine humor and good language which the child can model. Television should be limited to no more than one hour a day, but only after the first month when the child has already experienced "adult" interactions. Parents watch television with the child—remember, **NO TIME ALONE**.

(11) Post-institutionalized children should stay at home, with a parent as opposed to another caretaker, such as a nanny or babysitter, for at least 3-4 months. During this time of complete "adults only" (which is outlined in the next chapter), children may have time outside at a basic playground to play solely with their parents or with one or two other children under <u>strict supervision</u>.

(12) If available, having the child socialize with a child from a similar institutional setting (provided the other child has just arrived to the United States and is also at the same level of adjustment and acculturation) can also be very helpful. This may make the child feel somewhat more at home since he or she will be able to relate to the other child in the native language. The Parent Network for the Post-Institutionalized Child and

Friends of Russia and Ukrainian Adoptees can help locate families in your area.

(13) It is also very important to have your child enrolled in a school program very soon after arrival, although parents should use their good judgement and not place a child who is severely socially delayed or out of control in school right away. Socialization and family adjustment always takes priority over education with the post-institutionalized child.

When placing your child in school, it is important to staff his or her special needs with school officials. This entails having the child take comprehensive specialized evaluations regarding his or her cognitive and emotional level. It is appropriate that the child begin school only a few hours at a time and then return home. It may also be necessary for a parent to be actively involved at the school to monitor social and behavioral adjustment.

It is very common for schools to only put the child in an "English as a second language program," which is not acceptable. This is only a portion of the needed educational care. The child may need to start off attending school two or three days a week. Often, the parent may want to attend school with the child to maintain attachment and help guide the child when he or she becomes over-stimulated or, in the worst situation, out of control.

Children seem to settle in very quickly with other children in a school setting. Having a child develop social-interactional skills is even more important than the child learning anything in the classroom setting. Therefore, it is not that vital for the child to be in a true academic program, but rather, the child needs to learn English and social skills, while also learning how to have fun with other children. School should be started very slowly and, over the course of the next three to four months, worked up to a five-day-per-week schedule. Detoxification from institutionalization takes priority over school.

(14) Food is a very important concept to discuss. Many children from institutionalized settings tend to be very defensive when it comes to various food groups. They are often rigid and inflexible in their eating and want only junk food and candy. It is certainly very important for the child to eat, but do not just let the child eat anything and everything he or she wants. Many children from institutionalized settings become fixated on American food: hamburgers, hot dogs, candies, sweets and soda. This is because they have never had this type of food and it becomes an obsession. Post-institutionalized children should eat at their own rate but have a controlled diet. The child may be sickly or have intestinal parasites which seriously interfere with the eating cycle.

Initially, parents should try to imitate and re-create the type of food which the child has eaten for the years in the institution, such as meals of just bread, cheese, basic meats, eggs, tea and cake. This will make the child feel at home. Over time, gradually introduce various food groups. The law of nature always prevails: a child will become hungry and eat. Do not let the child become in control of their food as this will result in a "power struggle."

(15) From the beginning, post-institutionalized children absolutely need to earn activities and privileges based on day-to-day routines. They should learn very early how to make their bed, clean up, sit down, pay attention, show good table manners, use the toilet appropriately and ask or signal when they want something instead of yelling and screaming. Parents need to remember not to quickly "give in" for the sake of avoiding a scene of screaming from the child. Firmness and discipline help the child feel safe and secure. Inconsistency and permissiveness cause the child to be needy and demanding.

Parents must give up their need to give love and indulge the child as this only contributes to more problems in the long run. Remember, your child did not have maid service in the institution, so why begin that now?

(16) Families need to have training in "holding time" for safety and security, bonding and reattachment therapy, in addition to cognitive and behavioral training. (Please see the following chapter for a complete overview.)

(17) Families need to consistently rehearse and practice with the child facial expressions, eye contact, tone and pitch of their voice, body language, and self-control. Maintaining boundaries and a family hierarchy is essential. These kids need to know who is in charge and running the family as, in the institution, no one or everyone was in charge.

(18) Absolutely NO indiscriminate friendliness allowed. The child should not be allowed to touch, grab, push, shove, cling or make contract with anyone except under strict parental supervision. Indiscriminate friendliness can become a very large problem because children may use their seductive appeal and clinging behavior as a way of manipulating others into giving in to their requests before they put forth adequate diligence and effort. Furthermore, indiscriminate friendliness can create definite risks for these are the children who become targets for sexual predators.

The best parent is one who can remain somewhat detached, aloof, objective and extremely business-like during the initial adjustment with the newly-adopted child. This requires a tremendous amount of self-control on the part of the parents as, again, everyone wants to "love the child" and hope that this alone will make everything better. Parents must keep their space and distance from the child and vice-versa. The child under 2 years old needs the parents' closeness; the post-institutionalized child over 3 will use closeness (hugging/ kissing/touching) as a primary vehicle of communication as opposed to actions, behaviors, words and genuineness.

I know this all sounds impossible and cruel. Peggy and Bill found it very difficult to begin the program. "I don't want to be this type of mother," Peggy would say. But they kept with it and today, are grateful they did.

(19) We must assume the older post-institutionalized child will be developmentally-delayed in either (or both) cognitive and social-emotional areas. Therefore, the child may require immediate and intensive strategies. Children who show developmental delays, especially in their native language, will most likely be delayed in their English language transition and acculturation.

These special needs children will benefit by cognitive (or brain) rehabilitation strategies during their "detoxification from institutionalization." This approach will help to appropriately stimulate their brains "sensory register" in a way to teach more appropriate logic, reasoning and ability to follow a plan of action (See Chapter 6-Adjunctive Treatments). Proper adjustment takes proper thinking!

(20) Following a multi-discipline evaluation or your newly adopted child (which should be completed immediately after arrival), families should secure solid professional assessment regarding bonding and attachment issues. It will help parents greatly if they have an initial understanding of their new child's ability (or capacity) to comprehend and manage emotions. It is certainly taken into account the "adjustment factor", but families should assess "bonding potential" continually. Comprehensive evaluations by specialists should be done at 6 month intervals—up to 3 years, to be certain "residual" issues have disappeared.

For example, a child who displays intellectual/cognitive or speech delays will have a much slower development of solid emotional attachments than the child having a "strong brain." Parents should be prepared to offer the cognitively challenged child more of a brain and behavior retraining approach as a first step in creating family bonding on an emotional level. For the child having strong brain capacities, traditional bonding and attachment approaches can be utilized and "processed" by the child over time (not over night). Remember, all children develop and learn the fine art of emotion at different rates—it is our job to find the best avenue of teaching these skills. A strong brain will ultimately yield better results both at home and in subsequent school years.

Summary

To appreciate the full dimensions of an institutionalized orphan's medical, cognitive, and emotional difficulties, we need to understand the road traveled by such a child and what has happened along the path of decline.

Imagine how this child came into being. Imagine the child in the mother's womb, assaulted by malnutrition, environmental poisons, nicotine, alcohol and perhaps life threatening medical conditions. Imagine the child born into a totally impoverished family, without enough food, shelter, clothing, or medical care. Imagine that child abandoned, without the love and affection of a mother and father. Imagine the child placed in a stark and sterile hospital, with little human contact or stimulating activity, often kept tied to the crib. Obviously, such neglect can lead to psychological problems, but health problems are also a serious threat. As with any baby or young child left unattended for too long, neglected orphans tend to chew or eat anything in sight, some of which may be contaminated by neurotoxins that can cause brain damage.

After you have brought the child home, the concept of recreating the institutional setting and gradually detoxifying off of the institution is the most recommended treatment program. Implementing all of the other assessment and treatment strategies outlined in other aspects of this book are also very critical. Consistency and a willingness to make a complete commitment towards the best interest of the child, as opposed to the immediate needs of the parents, will promote long-term change and stability in the post institutionalized child.

Chapter 5
Family Intervention

For the family having a difficult child, starting a new and creative treatment may seem daunting or may arouse fear of yet another failure. By now, you have already engaged in a thorough assessment phase and you finally understand the true depth of your child's cognitive and emotional difficulties; and therein lies the hope of better recovery from the appearance of "hopeless" problems.

What I am proposing next, and what I facilitate in my practice to thousands of families, is an aggressive family intervention called "Adults Only." This program, which will require a parental commitment of at *least* three months, and perhaps as much as six months, of very intensive, often round-the-clock, consistent supervision of the difficult child. The program should be undertaken after efforts to correct the child's problems through discipline, discussion and talk, or professional counseling have failed. In addition, the parents should first consult with a professional therapist skilled in many of this program's techniques. As we discussed before, find professionals who will agree to try new, innovative and aggressive treatment, as opposed to more "traditional" approaches. You will want to be sure the therapist has training and experience working with the very difficult child, such as one who has done work in a psychiatric institution or in a juvenile home or who has a reputation for taking on very challenging and difficult cases.

The program consists of the three levels of treatment which are briefly described below. More in-depth information will follow.

LEVEL ONE:

Adults Only Holding Environment. Adults Only is actually based on a very simple concept: children are with at least one parent at all times so that the child is continually trained and educated about new and more appropriate behaviors. This may sound quite difficult, and I am not going to try and tell you that it will be anywhere near easy. In fact, many parents often need to illicit the help of relatives or close friends throughout this treatment program.

On Adults Only, the child must stay within three feet of a parent at all times and will be under complete supervision 24 hours a day, 7 days a week, for a minimum of four to eight weeks. If you are shaking your head in disbelief right about now, do not worry, that reaction is normal. When I first proposed the idea to Chris' parents, Anne and Richard, they were about ready to get up and walk right out of my office. But, six months later, although exhausted, they owed everything to this intensive program for they had their son back.

Why such severe guidelines? Because in Adults Only, parents must take complete control of an out-of-control child's life by putting a new "government" in place to rehabilitate the child. Often, this also requires therapeutic holds. There are Sequence One and Sequence Two holds which may seem scary and even barbaric at first, but which will, by the end, turn into welcome close time and interaction between you and your child.

LEVEL TWO:

Early Family Reintegration. Your child must remain within your sight, but can earn limited time away from you. Also, the child is given specific assignments and chores that must be completed. Limited participation in family activities is permitted. You will still be actively supervising your child's activities at all times except for when he or she is "assigned" to other family members or responsible adults. The concept of "EARNING EVERYTHING" is introduced.

LEVEL THREE:

Increasing Self-Control. Your child moves from being told everything to exercising more self-control based on rewards and privileges. The terms of acceptable and unacceptable behavior and the consequences for the latter (being returned to Level One or Level Two) are set forth in a "family contract" and are rigidly enforced.

It is probably very clear by now that nothing about working your child through this program will be easy. I can tell you, however, this program works and has been used successfully with all types of children, both at home and in institutional settings. All three of the children and their families whom we have followed so far have achieved amazing success through these methods. Not only that, but the thousands of children I have seen in my office have also been helped, and the majority of them emerge from the program new children.

This program will involve plenty of patience and discipline on the part of both the parents and the child. Sticking to the exact program is the key. I can almost guarantee you that it will get frustrating, so much so that quitting may seem an attractive option. I cannot caution you enough against giving up—DON'T. Even though, at points, you may want to stop or take time off, it is crucial to stick it out and complete each of the three steps back to back, in their entirety. This is the only way long-lasting results will be achieved. Just remember, This program *is* difficult, but workable. It *will* produce positive change if you are persistent, energetic and creative.

A Pep Talk: These pep talks are designed to give you inspiration throughout. Please re-read them whenever you feel like giving up.

Remember Angela? The 13-year-old who had been raised by a drug-addict mother and who had been shuffled from foster home to foster home, destroying each relationship by her uncontrollable screaming, misbehaving and later, by her sexual acting-out. Well, she completed the program while living at a residential girls' home. She now is excelling at high school and is actually leading a group therapy for disturbed adolescents.

Level One: The "Adults Only Holding Environment"

The starting point in this treatment program for the difficult child, the Adults Only phase, means the child is with you at all times. It requires your total commitment as well as total commitment from immediate family members (and, possibly, extended family). It is the means by which you prepare your child to re-learn and reintegrate back into a family system and society.

In Level One, you keep your child under total and complete supervision. Whenever your child exhibits out-of-control behavior, you will be called upon to exercise safe physical restraint until he or she calms down. This restraint is called **Sequence One Holding**. In the meantime, you will also need to engage in physical closeness with your child. This involves joint activities, role playing, affectionate contact, and learning to interpret and correct your child's emotional and thinking patterns. During Level One your child is:

(1) "Linked" to the parents. It is extremely important that you keep your child within three feet or less of you at all times.

(2) Keep home from school, if necessary. It is not far-fetched to consider pulling the child out of school temporarily to work through this program. The worse the child, the more likely it is that he or she will need to remain home from school in order to get the full effect of the treatment and in order to intensively work this new program. If the child acts out at school or is a chronic under-achiever, it is a sign that you might want to consider keeping him or her at home. I know it is a big decision, but a big problem will not be solved unless there is total commitment. It does not pay to do only half of the treatment. You must assess how bad the situation is and go accordingly. Often, this means temporarily taking the child out of school. School assignments can be sent home so that you can work with your child in a one-on-one setting. In some cases, it may be necessary to inform the school that, because of your child's emotional difficulties, only "home-bound instruction" is possible at this time. In that instance, parents will need to work with the school on developing proper curriculum for the child. If the child does remain in school, however, parents should inform the authorities that the child is undergoing a creative and unconventional treatment program. It is vital that school authorities know since many difficult children will attempt to "split" the authority at home and at school. They may, for instance, say, "It's so horrible at home" in order to gain sympathy and privileges from their teachers. Parents need to enlist the help of the child's teachers and guidance counselors and ask them to provide a degree of extra supervision at school. You do not want your child to be allowed to engage in the same

bad behavior at school that you are trying to break at home. Suggestions to pose to the teacher might include: moving thc child close to the teacher and away from any other children who might be negative influences or distractions, and asking for additional supervision of the child during recess and lunch. You NEED school support.

(3) Involved with the parents only. This is extremely important. In other words, your child is not allowed to have any type of extraneous distractions such as television, radio, video games or time with other friends or siblings. A difficult child prefers to be involved with inanimate objects or other distractions as opposed to the primary authority figure. You must break the child of this pattern.

You may feel that this degree of control is too drastic. The purposc, however, is to create a safe and consistent "holding environment" for your child. Your objective is to completely contain your child's unruly behavior. Then within this highly structured environment, you will re-educate your child in moral values, standards, positive and responsible behaviors and appropriate communication patterns. You will be training your child in various modes of thinking, reasoning, behavior, conduct and manners. Think of it this way: what sense does it make to send your child out into the world when his or her "home base" of family is not stable? It is the parents job to re-teach the child appropriate behaviors. Teaching does not mean long, drawn out lectures or repeated instructions. Remember, we are getting right down to the heart of the problem. Think of how far your past "lectures" have gotten you?

I like to compare it to boot camp. When soldiers in training enlist, they must first go through the treacherous journey of boot camp. In this situation they are deprived of life as they know it and are under constant supervision. And for what reason? So that they can basically be re-trained and so that they can build a bond with those around them. Suddenly, it is only the bare minimum that becomes important: food, shelter, sleep. Luxuries no longer matter. They learn a sense of honor and respect and they learn how to follow rules. This is what you want to accomplish with your child. You want to once again gain control over your child. You want them to develop a sense of what is important and that they must work for what they want. Non-negotiable rules and limits.

Chris' parents, after months of convincing, decided to alternate taking time off work so they could be with Chris around the clock. Finally, they had come to realize that their family needed to take priority over their careers. Interestingly, when they made that commitment, something else surfaced: their marriage had also been having long-term problems and that led them to even further engage in work. In addition to the program for Chris, they also began marriage counseling.

The Level One program should be catered to the age of your child. Children under the age of two require total parental involvement in the way of teaching speech and language, walking and exploring the world. Therefore, this type of family intervention program is not geared to the infant or young toddler, but more toward the child who is moving towards the preschool years and above. Parents should be able to effectively deal with a child under the age of two or three by providing constant supervision, protection, training and appropriate role modeling. The following sections outline the Level One program per age group:

Two to six years old: Adults Only must be maintained for a minimum of 4-to-8 weeks. There needs to be a lot of room for flexibility for the younger child, such as time left open in case Adults Only needs to be continued beyond the two-week mark. Also, the child will often require constant parental intervention and holding time, since children of this age tend to be extremely active, easily distracted and prone to prolonged temper tantrums. Children in this age group will also need a tremendous amount of direct physical and emotional contact. Parents absolutely need to maintain the child at arms length (in actual distance) and engage in frequent behavioral rehearsal and role playing (more on that later). This close time you spend with your child will certainly increase bonding and attachment and will allow you to serve as a consistent "role model" and ultimate educator. STOP the long lectures and academic debates. Instead, get concrete, specific and consistent. Teach and rehearse new behaviors with the toddler-aged child. Do this 5, 10, or 20 times per day until it works. This is behavioral rehearsal and "shaping or conditioning" appropriate behaviors at its best. Again, absolutely NO DAYCARE or other caretakers. Is is your job!

Parents also need to provide consistent rewards such as stars, stickers, tokens or another type of "tangible positive reinforcement" for any pro-social or appropriate behaviors. Selected foods and treats work wonders as reinforcers. You may be surprised how rapidly the younger child will begin to give up anger, rage and defensiveness, and strive to please and imitate you. Remember, <u>any</u> behavior that looks good should get immediately positively reinforced. Be generous and consistent with rewards and discipline.

Seven to eleven years old: The same principles as above apply to the child in this age bracket; however, parents may also be able to engage in more dialogue and discussion with the child. Hopefully, the child will be able to follow directions and be able to better understand the concepts of work, behavioral rehearsal and holding time. Children in this age bracket must learn to think, interact and respond to spoken language. Children in this age bracket are <u>excellent</u> candidates for the three tiered program which follows. Children ages 7-11 are at a rapid stage of learning as they never seem to "miss a detail" in their life. Just remember how persistent they are when they want something. This is a great stage to give them what they need, not what they want.

Twelve to seventeen years old: This is likely the most difficult age to work with as it requires a tremendous amount of close physical proximity and a great deal of conversation between parent and child. Here, there still needs to be behavioral rehearsal (practicing appropriate behavior and communication patterns) but also, include written assignments. It also needs to be anticipated that the older child/teenager may be very resistant and hostile. Therefore, it is extremely important for parents to be consistent and to expect that Adults Only may be at least three weeks long, if not significantly longer. Both parents will usually be required at all times to deal with a child in this age bracket as they can be highly resistant in their moods and behaviors.

During Level One, a child of almost any age will *often* become very angry and out of control when their activities are very drastically restricted. Children with significant emotional difficulties, particularly those with bonding and attachment deficits, become easily bored and frustrated with relationships. They will, therefore, try to sabotage the close emotional contact you are trying to encourage on Level One. During these episodes, the parents need to carry out a holding sequence which involves short periods of physical restraint and attachment therapy through physical closeness. Parents are often tempted to quickly give up, saying, "It's not helping, it's worse!" This is normal. Keep going. It always gets worse before it gets better.

As can be seen, Level One will be a very difficult initial stage of treatment for you, other family members and the child. Both you and your child will easily become frustrated and bored and "make excuses" for bad behavior or allow exceptions to the rules. While this stage of treatment is extremely demanding and taxing, the alternative is failure to bring about fundamental change. If you allow this to happen, the child deemed helpless and hopeless will make you and your family feel helpless and hopeless.

This is why, if you are to pave the way for fundamental change, you must be absolutely firm in curbing the child from acting out emotional rage. This requires practicing physical restraint and physical closeness, and teaching verbal expression of anger. I recommend beginning the program with a family contract that outlines exactly what is expected of the child and the consequences he or she will face if rules are broken. This contract keeps both parents and children on track, structured *and* committed to the program.

Family Contract for Level One

RULES

(1) You must remain within 3 feet of a parent at all times.
(2) You will have no contact with anyone besides your parents.
(3) Your parents decide what you are required to do each day.
(4) There will be no television, radio or any other distractions.
(5) Level One will last for at least 4-6 weeks before you have the opportunity to go to Level Two.
(6) For each day you do not follow by the rules, another day will be added onto Level One.

Sibling Roles During Adults Only

As a general rule, siblings should not be involved during Adults Only. You will achieve the greatest results if the child interacts with the parents only. Siblings may be involved if there are family activities that occur during Adults Only time, but they need to be asked to limit the time they spend playing with or conversing with the out-of-control child. Under no circumstances during Adults Only should a sibling be allowed to spend time with the child without adult supervision. For Peggy and Bill this was most difficult as they had another son, Brian, who was four years older than Sergei. Brian often felt left out and ignored throughout the entire treatment program but relatives and family friends took extra pains to provide much attention to Brian and to take him on many outings. Peggy and Bill also made sure to explain everything to Brian and to consistently praise him for his patience. Provide siblings increased reinforcements when providing positive role models and cooperating fully. Always put the tougher sibling in charge: good reverse psychology. A perceived sense of power will empower them to take charge as opposed to taking charge by being disruptive to the family plan.

Many families have found it useful (but not fair) to put all their children on a family program. While a newly adopted child may need a more intensive program, all children need work on one behavior or another. By involving all children, parents can work on the entire family restructuring. Your other children will say "that's not fair". Life is not fair, do move on.

Bedtime

Although the child needs to be with a parent at all times during Adults Only, there are exceptions when the child goes to sleep. If a child is able to maintain some responsibility regarding a normal sleeping cycle, he or she can sleep alone, in his or her own bedroom. If , however, the child is unable to follow a sleeping routine and tends to stay up all night or gets up at odd hours which disrupt the family, a parent will literally need to "camp out" with the child by sleeping in the child's room throughout Adults Only. It is important that a child feel bonded, attached and nurtured during the time that he or she is falling asleep; therefore, it is not absurd to ask that a parent sleep in the child's room. Bedtime can be one of the times that produces the highest amount of anxiety in children. This anxiety often turns into acting-out behavior. For children who have emotional and behavioral difficulties, falling asleep can produce high stress since it is the time to "relax," and often, these children are just too wound-up to do so. Subsequently, the child becomes agitated and may turn disruptive. In clarifying what sleeping together means, it is the same room, but not in the same bed. Sharing a bedroom with a child is a temporary intervention which may jumpstart the rest of the treatment program as this may be the beginning of a close and trusting relationships which provides "hands on" safety and security.

It is also important for parents to remove any type of stimulation from the child's room for the duration of Adults Only. This includes books, television, games and toys. Strip things to the bone and start over with the child. Emphasize that "nothing in the world is free" and that everything must be earned. When the child gets into bed at night, he or she can be allowed to listen to soothing music or books on tape which may help induce relaxation.

Management of Aggressive and Assaultive Behaviors

It is almost inevitable that very difficult children will resort to highly aggressive behaviors such as kicking, spitting, biting, shoving and throwing objects when they do not get their way. These behaviors are both grossly inappropriate and very dangerous as even the youngest child can hurt an adult. Many parents that I have worked with have allowed their child to strike them or injure them in some way stating, "What else was I to do-hit the child back?"

It is extremely important to emphasize that absolutely no one should be hurt—parent or child. The more aggressive and violent the child tends to act, the more probability exists that this type of child definitely requires a degree of medication to help manage impulses and moods which may be beyond the child's conscious control. It is sometimes very helpful that conservative medications be implemented as it is of paramount importance that the child have enough reality perceptions and self-control to at least make it through the program (see medication issues in Chapter 6).

Still, Sequence One holds must be used for every incident of aggression. Remember, the disturbed child's goal is to sabotage the treatment plan any way possible. Being totally belligerent and assaultive is one way children get the parents to give up as they may literally try to "beat the parent into submission."

To Spank or Not to Spank: That is the Question

Many people may be thinking at this point that it would be just as easy to spank or whip the child into submission as opposed to using a therapeutic Level One or Level Two hold. Additionally, many of us from the "old traditional school of thought" may be thinking that it is just as easy to spank and/or beat it into the child's psychology to comply with parental directives and to not act out. Recent studies have supported that there is no long-term damage to a child whose parents occasionally use spanking as a form of discipline.

There is a time and a place for spanking but never should objects such as belts, spoons or paddles be used; also, never should a child be spanked to the degree that marks, bruises, welts, cuts or bleeding occurs. The use of corporal punishment can be a tool, but should be reserved for "crisis intervention purposes." For example, a very firm swat (or two) on the rear with the parent's hand can often disrupt reckless behaviors such as running around aimlessly, trashing the house, running across the street or blatant verbal abuse. Corporal punishment of this nature is best reserved for children under the age of ten years old as beyond that age bracket their rear-ends are much harder than your hand. This is an important consideration as many parents may feel they must just strike the child with even greater force to make a point. This is when accidents and injuries occur and Child Protective Services becomes involved with your family.

Sequence One: Therapeutic Holding for Safety and Security

Much has been written about "holding therapy," and many forms are controversial and ones that I do **NOT** advocate. The ones I do not utilize involve taking a calm or detached child and holding them to the point the child becomes enraged and out of control. Many therapists continue to exert more physical holding during these evoked rages and have even gone as far as to roll a child in a sheet or blanket in an effort to contain them. There have been cases reported of bizarre holding-rebirthing techniques which require ample restraint in an effort to push the child through a makeshift birth canal to "re-enter" their family a "bonded" member. Even more concerning, are reported cases of therapists and parents attempting to recreate a scenario of the child's prior physical, sexual, or emotional abuse, by putting the child in a closet or isolated room to induce the feelings of trauma they may have experienced. I believe these techniques are more likely to re-traumatize a child, particularly a child with developmental disabilities, such as autism, retardation, or major mental illness. There is certainly a need for holding a child, but I believe strongly that holds should only be for safety and security, as opposed to evoking rage or reliving past traumas. Holds should only be performed as part of an overall treatment program, following very thorough assessment of a child's psychological and cognitive profile.

The type of holding therapy I advocate involves a two-fold approach: Sequence One Holds are designed solely for safety and security and should be instituted when a child is actively out of control or unmanageable. Sequence Two Holds are a gentle form of reconnection and re-integration from parent to child.

As I have noted earlier, children with attachment and bonding disorders likely will be very superficial (they can be charming in relationships when they want something, whereas any attempt at a deep relationship often results in conflict, tension and turmoil. On Level One, these issues will rapidly surface. In all likelihood, the child will make continual attempts to sabotage and negate the relationship. This is the hallmark of both attachment and behaviorally-disordered children. Therefore, in addition to being kept under total supervision and in close proximity to the parents, the child may require physical restraint or a Sequence One Hold during uncontrollable episodes.

To carry out an appropriate holding sequence often requires two adults who have been trained in the proper technique. This is a MUST. If it appears that the child is becoming verbally and physically out of control during the Level One stage of treatment, you must immediately initiate a holding sequence *without* nagging, discussing, or debating it with your child. As soon as you announce that a holding time is mandatory, a child will often say "I'm sorry, I won't be bad again" or attempt to run away. To back down and allow the child another chance or to abbreviate the hold sets a precedent for continuing manipulation by your child to avoid a hold. Parents must move towards inappropriate behaviors, not run away from the behaviors.

You should complete a therapeutic holding time in a physically firm, but gentle, manner without aggression on the part of the parent. The hold should last for a period of time that equals the child maintaining a totally calm position plus five minutes to make certain the child has relinquished control ("Calm plus Five"). Parents may need to practice with the child prior to an actual hold so that the child understands what will be occurring. In addition, you will become familiar with the amount of pressure and weight that can be safely applied. You should consult a qualified therapist concerning the proper methods. Check whether the therapist has experience in a state hospital with severely disturbed children, since holding is a common practice in institutionalized settings. (Therapeutic holds are also often used in children's psychiatric hospitals, residential programs or any treatment program emphasizing attachment therapy.)

The procedure for the therapeutic hold is as follows (see diagram):

(1) Each parent should position him or herself on opposite sides of the child (regardless of the child's age). If necessary, three adults may be needed (especially for the older child).

(2) The child is told that a hold is to begin. Say something like: "It is now time for a hold based on your defiance and uncontrollable behavior. Mom and Dad are going to put a hand on your shoulder and one on your wrist. We then expect you to get down on your knees. Then we will gently help you down to the ground where we will hold you until you are calm and get yourself under control. We will help you do this."

(3) More often than not, the child will resist. At this point, one parent firmly reaches out, and, using one hand, applies gentle but firm pressure on the shoulder in a small "pinch" manner (remember Mr. Spock's famous Vulcan shoulder grip from Star Trek? Think of this.). With the other hand, the parent pulls down one of the child's arms by the wrist toward the ground until it is straight down. The other parent then places one hand at the shoulder/base of the child's neck, then pulls the other arm until it is straight down.

(4) Next, you instruct the child to go to his or her knees and ultimately lie face down on the floor with arms at his or her sides and legs stretched outward.

(5) During the hold, the child should be consistently told: "This is a hold, and you must be Calm Plus Five Minutes before we let you up and talk with

SEQUENCE ONE HOLDING TECHNIQUE

you." There should be no other talking with the child as this is the time for the child to calm down and become more rational and for the parents to be in complete control and help the child regain composure.

(6) If the child is still resisting, one parent should lift up the child's legs while the other parent gently guides the child down to the ground, face first. If a pillow, jacket, or towel is available, place it under the child's face because it is very important for the child to lie face down during the therapeutic hold to prevent spitting, biting or direct eye contact. It is often overwhelming and guilt-inducing for the parents when direct eye contact occurs with the child. In order to avoid the tendency to abandon the holding time technique, make sure the child is lying face down.

(7) While one of you jockeys your weight over the child's buttocks and lower legs (thus straddling the child), the other parent lies across the child's upper torso and pins the child's arms down by the sides of the body to avoid arm flailing. Parents must learn to trust their instincts and not apply harsh pressure or heavy weight. While straddling, do not sit on the child's back or chest, as this may injure the ribs. Injuries are NOT the goal of holding time. This is meant as restraint and control, not abuse or punishment. During the time the child is physically being held, parents should not engage in dialogue or discussion. You should, however, repeatedly tell the child that it is all right to express any and all feelings during this time. Your statements should be short and concise, and you should gradually remove pressure and body weight. It is to be hoped that, as the child calms down, he or she will be very insecure, crying, and in need of emotional support and nurturing. Keeping a child in a more infantile state after a hold will serve as a starting point for moving toward appropriate attachment to the parent. Many children who act out have often missed the stage of immaturity in which they are completely deferential to the parents.

(8) The hold should be gradually removed after the Calm Plus Five interval. It should not be completely removed, however, until the child has made a firm commitment to being calm, cooperative, and nonaggressive. At the first renewal of struggle or aggression, the holding time should be immediately reinstated. Begin again the 8 steps.

SEQUENCE ONE HOLDING TECHNIQUE

If possible, tape record or videotape your child through the difficult episodes. Viewing the tape step-by-step during later role playing is extremely helpful and serves as a powerful intervention (see Role Playing and Behavior Rehearsal). It may be very difficult to actually tape or video a child during the episodes as this may make the child only more enraged, but parents are encouraged to work together as a team. One parent deals with the child while the other parent tapes or films.

You may stop at this point and think: "This approach is way too aggressive." Also, you may remember being advised by a therapist to try to "talk your child down" from aggressive behavior. You cannot always avoid the use of force, however. Unfortunately, force is often the only thing that works with the difficult child. That is why you must persist. Remember, attachment-disordered children will do everything they can to "push others away." That is what is denied to the child in a holding environment: the child cannot push anyone away because the child literally cannot move. This hold, although it seems extreme, allows the child to act out rage and emotional confusion while at the same time, recreating a strong physical bond and safety net between the child and the parents. Children need external controls when they are internally out of control.

Sergei often took two or three people to restrain him. At first, I trained Peggy and Bill in my office how to do the holds. They seemed confident there, but when they were on their own they were terrified. Often, Peggy would revert to tears. She said she had to force herself to not think about the actual moment while she was initiating the hold, but to think instead of a time, a year from then, when they could all be a happy family. This was the only way she was able to do the holds in the beginning. Eventually, it became much easier.

For Chris and his family, the hold was the most foreign thing they had ever done. It made Richard and Anne realize how little they had touched their own son throughout his life. Chris was also twelve at the point I began seeing him. So his age, coupled by the lack of affection the family had, made holds all the more awkward and difficult. Just being in the same room with each other was difficult, let alone touching! Anne and Richard frequently wanted to give up and go back to the medication as Chris "drugged" was more calm and complacent. After many hours of convincing the parents, they finally realized the DRUGS WOULD NEVER SOLVE the problems; they would only MASK them. We needed to finally solve the problems. Anne and Richard then set up a system where they would alternate who was strong and dominant and who was more patient and tolerant. In other words, neither one would ever be the "bad guy" all of the time.

Some children can require holding for a quite a long period of time, up to 30 minutes or even an hour, until they reach calm plus five. There is no way of telling how long you might have to hold your child since each child is different. The longer the holding time, the more the child clearly needs bonding and attachment therapy of this nature. Parents who are reluctant to use the hold should look at the experience this way: If a child truly did not like the holding time, then why would he or she prolong the period? Remember, contact is contact and the difficult child who is internally out of control desperately needs external and parental controls. In order to succeed with this program, you must succeed with these holding techniques.

Sequence Two Hold: "Holding on for Your Lives, Love and Attachment"

This next hold forces the child to completely and totally accept and experience bonding and attachment within the family system. This is essential since we already know that children who are out-of-control tend to push others away via their disruptive behaviors. They therefore have very little need or appreciation for emotional contact aside from using people to gain their way. The child who has been emotionally traumatized and damaged is afraid that any attempt at intimacy or emotional closeness will only lead to rejection or abandonment.

Unlike the Sequence One hold, this hold emphasizes physical touch, nurturing and sensory-integrative techniques. Although this hold may feel good to the parents, many difficult children will still fight this type of holding until they realize it can actually be a refreshing time together for the entire family.

Close physical contact is the key. For a Sequence Two hold, parents and the child should engage in very close physical proximity on the couch or floor, with the child sitting in a parent's lap. Older children should also be in very close proximity of parents or between both. There should be complete closeness; no distance, no detachment from primary caretakers. During this phase, two purposes are served: (1) the day is reviewed for both problems and improvements and (2) the child is taught to become accustomed to pleasurable sensory contact though brushing or stroking of the hair, upper torso, and back and neck muscles (which are typically stiff and rigid under anxiety). In addition, you give the child practice in methods to hug, hold hands and maintain eye contact. Communicate directly with an entire range of emotions. No blaming, nagging. Totally empathic listening: you listen first, then I will listen. Listen for meaning and depth. Be direct. Combine physical closeness with emotional closeness.

The most critical elements in a Sequence Two hold can be summarized by the **"Four C's":Contact, Cooperation, Connection and Communication**. Children who lack the Four C's will require the most amount of Sequence Two holds because their preference is to remain detached, and they need to rehearse, repair and reconnect with their parents.

Sequence Two holding should be done a minimum of 6 times per day during Level One for at least 5 to 15 minutes per session. At least one, if not both parents' complete support and cooperation are necessary in order to assure that the required Sequence Two holdings are completed. Involve the whole family if possible. This may take the form of a game or be done during cooking or cleaning, so long as the child is practicing being physically close.

Even the older child or teenager needs physical closeness and positive holds.

As children grow, they take on more challenges and stressors which require more guidance, structure and support. Parents need to use themselves and family relationships as the key sources of support and nurturing—not outsiders. The older child may be too big for a lap, but find a way for physical contact. Any way works. It is very important to remember that difficult teenagers tend to act like difficult 6 year olds. They resist people telling them what to do as they always have "all the answers." I find it very important to never debate or negate what a teenager says. During the physical closeness time in Sequence Two holding, parents need to be all ears and learn to accept (and tolerate) statements, ideas and at times rather unusual logic as opposed to being critical or telling the teenager they are wrong. Who really wants to be told they are wrong when they have their own creative idea?

Linking Sequence One and Sequence Two Holds: Reintegration

You have now completed both a **Sequence One Hold** for the period of Calm Plus Five. In this next step, you must immediately move toward a **Sequence Two Hold**, which focuses on talking with the child about what has happened that necessitated physical restraint. Remember, this is the first time you are talking with the child since you avoided all dialogue during the hold and are now making it absolutely clear to the child that you, the parent, are in control and the child must learn to calm down and give up aggressive verbal and/or physical behaviors. During the Sequence Two Hold period, your child (as well as you, the parents) will typically be exhausted. This is precisely the time to allow your child to talk about his or her feelings and for you to explain what is required to avoid further holding. Before beginning, parents should become extremely affectionate and nurturing, regardless of what the child did or said to make the hold necessary. You should encourage a two-way flow of information. The precise content depends on the situation, but in general you want to obtain information about the child's feelings and wants. In turn, your child needs to learn from you what makes holds necessary as well as what behavior will prevent them.

Getting information from the child. The vital pieces of information you want to get from your child are:

(1) His or her feelings about losing control and being held down. Ask your child directly: "Do you feel angry at us? Sad? Frustrated?" Try to get any verbal expression: positive or negative as long as there are no aggressive behaviors.

(2) What you can do to make the child's life better. Very often, children end up in a hold because they want something before they earn it and have thrown a tantrum in the hope of getting it. This is the time to explain the roles of parent and child and the expected requirements within the home.

(3) If the child cannot or will not verbalize feelings, he or she still needs to sit close to parents during this mandatory "processing period." Sitting

quietly can still be a very powerful form of communication. Remember, "silence is golden."

Giving information to your child. Stress that the family will continue to work through problems in the same manner. No excuses. No exceptions. No giving up. The child must work towards things before getting them and that you, the parents, are in charge. It is very important at Level One not to lecture the child. If the need arises to lecture, you should keep it as brief as possible because difficult children tend to "shut down." It is important to make sure your statements are short and concise, and that the child is allowed to respond. These are typical messages you want to get across:

(1) Discussion time is a step up from holding time, but you will begin another hold the minute the child becomes aggressive, defiant or out of control again. Explain there will be no exceptions: unmanageable behavior will be immediately dealt with for the protection of the child and the family.

(2) Getting behavior under control comes first. Explain that the reason is to ensure the safety and security of the family and to establish a closer relationship with each other without the child becoming aggressive or out of control.

(3) Certain things need to be done to avoid another hold. For example, you may say something like: "When you are becoming angry or disruptive, we need to develop a way to take a break, talk about the situation first, or find another way to deal with your anger and frustration when we tell you, "No."

(4) Disruptive behavior will not be tolerated. You can say, for instance: "We will simply not allow you to continue this type of behavior no matter what you say or how many times you act up."

Statements like these give your child the clear and consistent message that while you are interested in helping your child with problems, any that any reoccurrence of unmanageable behaviors will not be tolerated. The child should understand that, no matter what, you will enforce the family rules, guidelines and methods of discipline by immediate holds.

What began happening in Chris' family is that on one level, the holds felt very good to Chris. The attention and the closeness were what Chris had been craving all his life. The holds and Adults Only in general, opened the door for the family to spend long-needed time together. They made a point of using the time wisely, cutting down on mindless activities such as TV or computer games, and instead doing things around the house together (usually chores that the hired help would have done). Chris <u>needed</u> the external controls. The family needed safety.

It seemed that, although frustrating and tiresome, the entire family was getting much out of the program. Surprisingly, one of the most difficult things was explaining the strategy to others who had been involved in their high-society life. People began to whisper it seemed as if Anne and Richard were keeping a huge "family secret." This is where the simultaneous marital counseling really helped. Anne and Richard learned to focus on their own personal issues, something they had never really done before, and to stop worrying about social status. It was really tough, but worth it in the long run.

Keeping the Child Busy

Since in the Adults Only program the child must be with a parent at all times, there will be many instances where the child simply has nothing to do. This time should be filled with tasks or just being still with you and role playing. You do not have to entertain the child. Keeping busy is your definition. There is always something the child and you can do—routine work, chores, or just sitting together. Children on Level One that have been very difficult and defiant need to have extensive time learning how to share personal space with their parents without being demanding or always wanting something. The psychological message of "I will keep you busy" on Adults Only is far more ominous than the actual description or implementation of tasks for the child. Keep the child guessing. You owe no explanations. It is most corrective--yet most difficult--for the child to spend one-on-one time with a parent because the child learns firsthand through role-modeling and rehearsal of appropriate behaviors. At the start of the Adults-Only program, don't be surprised if your child requests any other form of discipline; being sent to their room or restricted is much easier than spending their entire time engaged with the parent.

Tasks and Activities: "The Luxury of Hard Labor". Parents should assign the child hourly, daily, and weekly activities. These may involve doing tasks or any type of work activity required in the home with you or other family members; doing homework or writing about experiences and feelings in the home or just learning how to be an active participant in family relationships. Doing household tasks such as cleaning up, cooking dinner, going to the store or helping out with siblings activities are excellent ways to provide bonding time. The child may feel that the restriction of desired activities is a punishment, but he or she will soon realize that the parents are providing undivided attention through mutual activities. Remember, the more time spent together most always yields positive results in the long run by increasing bonding, attachment and mutual cooperation. A difficult child needs to re-learn the concept of hard work, commitment and task completion.

However, it is not uncommon for a child to totally refuse to do the assigned tasks. If this happens, you must be persistent, firm and demand that the child remain within arms distance at all times, whether or not he or she joins you in the activity. It does not really matter if the child does or does not do the task. What is most important is that the child realizes that there is no "escape" from being actively involved in family activities. It is very important for parents to not engage in "physically forcing" the child to do the activity, but continually being firm that the parent-child closeness will remain throughout the designated period.

Role Playing and Behavioral Rehearsal. One of the luxuries of Level One is that you have the child with you 100 percent of the time. While this may seem overwhelming, the time together provides an excellent opportunity to retrain and recondition your child's negative behaviors, thought and reasoning patterns. Additionally, this is a very important phase in which you work through issues of bonding and attachment, since the child literally has nowhere else to go.

During this time when your child is completely bonded to you, you can accomplish a lot in changing thinking patterns via role playing or "acting out" emotions, or communicating about problems your child may have with any person. Furthermore, it gives your child the chance to "practice" ways of communicating, asking, maintaining eye contact or discussing feelings directly. You should do this regularly on Level One whenever there is time. Force yourself to practice with your child even when he or she is being "good." Record any and all behaviors, reactions and successes/failures on a chart, video, audiotape, photos, journal, etc. These "visual cues" will be used to train and rehearse until the child gets it right. Record and document <u>all</u> family members this way--remember, it is a "team effort".

During role playing and behavioral-rehearsal phases, parents should continually shift roles, often letting the child play the parent. You will need to become highly involved, aggressive and attentive to detail. You should imitate or exaggerate the child's out-of-control behavior and literally "assume the child's role." This gives your child the opportunity to see how he or she actually appears (via your direct imitation). In addition, the child learns what it feels like being the parent. This is particularly important for the child who has never really spent time listening to the parent. Difficult children often have lost perspective, and have very little appreciation, empathy or sensitivity for the feelings of others. Rather, they have spent most of their time demanding attention and immediate gratification.

While it is impossible to prescribe the exact procedure and content for role playing, some common features and techniques follow. Before beginning, give your child specific instructions as to what you will do and what you expect. Then, try to say the following:

(1) "I want to show you how you look and sound when you are angry and defiant."

(2) "I want you to look at yourself to observe your own behavior, the way your body moves when you are angry or frustrated."

(3) "I want you to listen carefully to how you talk to us, your teachers or anyone else in authority."

(4) "I want you to look in the mirror and see how your face looks right now when you are angry."

(5) "We want you to play a game with us and practice different ways of talking and behaving so you will not make the same mistake again."

(6) "I want to help you practice how to talk not just with people in authority, but also with your friends so that you will get along better with them."

(7) "I want you to pretend to be a mom or a dad, and I will pretend to be your child. You try telling me how to do things and answer me when I talk back to you, disrespect you, or don't do what you ask me."

(8) "I want you to practice using the right words, phrases, answers and comments. Here is your "word list" for the day or week. Here is what you may or may not say. Practice speaking this way with this tone, etc."

(9) "We are going to use these feeling charts and games to help you better identify which feelings you understand and can imitate in future family and social situations."

(10) "Before we go anywhere or do anything in public, we are going to practice and rehearse what you can and cannot do, and what the consequences are if you violate our practice sessions."

Make sure the child is sitting down face to face with you when you are communicating. Work on one topic at a time. For example, if your child has a problem in listening, demonstrate how the child "presents" in terms of facial expression, body language, verbal statements and gestures. Doing this over again gives your child a measure of how he or she looks and interacts.

Show how it has been for you as a parent to deal with such intense, uncontrollable behaviors. Do not just talk about it—act out the feelings and emotions. Have the child play back the parents' feelings over and over again. The idea is to "imitate" the parents body *language* and *expressions*, even if the child does not yet fully understand what the movements convey. Repeat words and phrases used, inflection, tone and pitch. Show how to speak correctly. Be animated, interactive and entertaining. Interact with and captivate your child's attention.

Now is the time to play back the actual video or audio tapes of your child's out-of-control behaviors. During the playback, you should go over the episodes slowly, step-by-step, providing critiques in a positive and constructive manner. Do not be surprised if your child, after seeing or hearing him or herself, completely denies being the child in the video or on the tape. This is extremely common among difficult children. (For example, a young boy was videotaped stealing money out of a bank machine. In the juvenile court proceeding, he completely denied the evidence from the video even though it was staring him in the face.) This shows how the unattached and difficult child often lives in his or her own sense of reality (or fantasy). That is why the child needs to be repeatedly shown the actual chain of events in his or her out-of-control episodes.

Involve various family members or even the entire family unit in role playing and behavior rehearsal. Remember "practice makes perfect." The "practice effect" is still one of the best ways of learning, even if the initial understanding is not there. At least your child can be taught to go through the motions, with the hope that later the emotions will actually make sense. Initially, all this is "behavioral conditioning". Eventually, we will get to cognitive and emotional reconstruction.

Parents may quickly tire of post-hold discussion, role playing, and shared activity; however, it is important to remember that these all contribute to rehearsing, reframing ideas and continually reinforcing the child. Be patient! It took years for your child to learn to be out of control. Give the needed months and interventions a chance. We keep telling you this is **hard work!**

Chris' family role-played out how they would liked to have treated each other had they had the opportunity to re-do life together. Anne and Richard both wished they had given more nurturing and attention to themselves and to each other, as well as to Chris. They all wished they could have had stronger family ties in which family came first rather than work or social events. It also became apparent that Anne and Richard were raising Chris in the manner they themselves had both been raised. They did not realize they could break the "family cycle" and teach Chris that family, people and relationships come before desires, material possessions or others' opinions.

For Sergei, the struggle was different. Sequence One was not about unlocking and rediscovering feelings and family. It was about bare-bones shaping up. To begin with, Sergei was placed on the proper antidepressant medication. Right away, this showed promise. It stabilized his moods and emotions and helped reduce his rigid, inflexible thinking patterns. Next, his room was stripped of toys, comics and games. Then he was isolated from everyone but Peggy and Bill. Sergei reacted with rage and both parents had to consistently hold him for the first three weeks before he finally realized his parents were in control. Over the course of those few weeks, Peggy and Bill's marriage strained. Bill felt they were being too hard on Sergei. Peggy, who was the one who had quit her job to care for Sergei, wanted to continue with the aggressive plan. Difficult children take their toll on the family.

Mutual Story Telling. Out-of-control children typically have lost perspective about themselves and how to function in their environment. This is why mutual story telling and therapeutic games are extremely important. The healing power of story telling is easy to recognize. Difficult children find it very helpful to share the struggles of growing up as well as the ways they have solved problems (or made terrible mistakes). They can benefit from fictional or real life stories. Look for stories in books or journals, magazine articles or even old home movies that will teach a child that everyone makes mistakes. It is extremely important for parents to share their own strengths, weaknesses and history of "mistakes" which they made as a child and how their parents helped them through the difficulties. Children need to realize that everyone has struggled at some point in their life and they should be no different. Remember, the goal is to "brainstorm" and work towards creative solutions to problems based on past experiences which are typically "trial-and-error."

Many excellent therapeutic books are available for use with children of all ages. Any type of story with a moral ending is useful. Please see the appendix for a list of recommended books. You may be completely surprised to find that out-of-control children love to have stories read to them, especially at bed time. Even many adolescents completely regress and allow parents to sit on their bed and read books to them at night following a terrible day. You should also be sure to take turns with your child in reading to each other. In addition to storytelling, therapeutic games can be very helpful. A multitude of therapeutic games are available which focus on constructive ways of dealing with anger, frustration, aggression, social skills, families, impulse control and conflict resolution. Please See Psychotherapeutic Games in the Appendix. These are great bonding experiences for the entire family.

In summary, proper therapeutic holds and Adults Only serve a much better purpose than the sole use of corporal punishment for behavior control. For those still desiring to use corporal punishment, which is part of their family's upbringing and philosophy, please use extreme caution, good judgement and self-control. Do not use corporal punishment when you, as a parent, are out of control.

Level One Summary: Moving to Level Two

Level One can teach a child to "think" about his or her emotions. This will only work if parents are diligent, consistent, and unrelenting. Remember, the goal is to change the child's deviant behavioral and emotional patterns. The more you tell or show your child what good behavior, mannerisms, and reasoning are, the more pressuring the child will feel to change. Eventually, the child will agree to parental and family demands in the hope of "fitting in" rather than remaining ostracized from everyone. Keep remembering the old adage "short-term loss for long-term gain."

The child must have been on Level One for a minimum of four to six weeks (depending on the child's age) and symptoms and problems need to have been absent for at least two weeks. Ultimately, you must use your judgment about when your child is ready to move to Level Two. Before Sergei could move up, he had to answer questions in his journal. He sometimes wrote out his answers and read to his parents whereas other times he role played out his responses by dramatic expression. His parents would ask why trust is important; what it means to care for somebody; how do you treat someone you love; and how do you treat someone you dislike. He also was required to write about his life in the institution. This was very difficult for him and he would often throw or stomp on the notebook. But eventually, it felt good to get it all down on paper and to share it with his parents.

Before moving your child to Level Two, however, the child must understand that certain violations will mean immediate return to Level One and start over.

They are:

(1) Violent and aggressive behaviors (striking self or others; destructiveness)
(2) Blatant and guilt-free disregard for rules and regulations
(3) Gross lying, manipulation and distortion of the truth
(4) Stealing or taking ANYTHING without permission
(5) Running away from home
(6) Disruptive behavior in school, resulting in the parent being called in
(7) Alcohol or substance abuse
(8) Sexually inappropriate behaviors
(9) Inappropriate screaming or yelling
(10) Verbal abuse to any family member

Level Two: Early Family Reintegration

With the difficult child, Level Two requires at least four to six weeks, unless your child regresses and returns to out-of-control behaviors; then, he or she must be placed back in Level One and start the program over from the beginning. Keep in mind that an overall treatment program takes a minimum of three to six months of very intensive and consistent work before results can be seen. Keep remembering that you must never, ever, give up.

To review, on Level One your child has had a "crash course" in relearning values, moral standards and positive behaviors through direct communication with you or through the experience of physical holding time. If you have not observed "breakthroughs" in which your child seems to be "picking up" parental behaviors, additional time in Level One is required. Remember, it is better to start over on Level One than to give a false "promotion" to Level Two.

Again, there may be times during Level Two when you must return the child to restart Level One. In the case of serious infractions and violations, such as inappropriate language, leaving messes, poor hygiene, and aggressive body language, Level One should be resumed for a minimum of two weeks, but up to four weeks if needed. Parents must use their discretion, but error on the side of requiring a longer "review period" on Level One. Many difficult children often need to return to Level One in order to recondition themselves back into reality. Many children actually like the "safety" and "undivided attention" available on Level One. Life is simplified which is the *key* to success. Level One is safe for the child—that is why they may "ask for it" by regressing in behaviors.

During Level Two, the child:

(1) Needs daily and weekly goals and objectives charted, graphed and contracted.

(2) Is gradually introduced to incentive systems.

(3) Gains some freedom and privileges. Anything and everything, however, must be earned. Setting up a system where tokens are rewarded for good

behavior and accomplishing assigned tasks is a good idea.

(4) Visualizes his or her progress or remaining areas of difficulty via charts, graphs, or any other type of "road map to success."

(5) Receives homework assignments to help solidify new behavior and thinking. This involves keeping a journal of feelings, making drawings of emotions or problems, making tapes about feeling angry, or just practicing new behaviors. Parents continue to record all responses in the same manner as on Level One.

(6) Gradually moves away from the parents for one or two hours daily but must still remain in sight of the parents at all times.

(7) Is assigned to other family members or responsible adults who will still consistently tell the child what to do and will not let the child pick and choose his or her own schedule and activities. Caution is maintained in the use of childcare or in-home nannies or au-pairs.

(8) Sleeps alone, unless situations arise (such as nightmares or night terrors, aggressive outbursts, running away, or other destructive actions) that require an adult to be in the room.

(9) Continue the role-playing games and behavioral rehearsal of Level One. This is vital as the difficult child will quickly lose these skills. What must be understood is that all of the "skills" acquired on Level One set the foundation for likely success overall.

If Level Two still seems too restrictive, remember that rebuilding childhood development and proper social and family behavioral patterns takes time and practice. Your child is gradually moving away from you in Level Two (towards slightly greater independence), but should not become detached too quickly. Although the child gradually earns time alone, he or she must remain attached to the family, and all activities are maintained within the parent/family rules, guidelines and moral standards and values. Overall, you must still keep your child very close and continue constant monitoring and grading their performance on all aspects of Level Two tasks. Because incentives and rewards are the major new element in Level Two, these require special attention at this stage.

Again, you may want to start with regular family meetings and the creation of a "Family Contract" which clearly and consistently lists out all of the goals and objectives on both sides (parent and child). Remember, the basic rules discussed on previous pages regarding a child immediately returning to Level One. To once again **reiterate** the infractions which place a child immediately on Level One are:

1. No physical violence such as hitting, kicking, biting or destructive behaviors

2. No running away
3. Blatant disrespect and defiance/verbal abuse
4. No lying
5. No stealing

A special note to parents must be made at this point. Once again, it is imperative that parents allow no exceptions to the rules or second chances. Remember, people may be tired of the program by now and have a normal temptation to "give a break." If you give the infamous "break" at this point or at any point in this program, it will come back to haunt you later. Hang in there and be consistent, firm, and non-negotiating. Level Two does not mean more breaks or freedom for the child and family. Level Two means that the child is now to take on more responsibilities and parental expectations. Everyone must grow up and progress forward and take on new challenges.

Incentive Systems (See Appendix for Examples)

Charts and Tokens. During Level Two, incentive systems are gradually introduced. All requirements and behavioral expectations should be listed or posted in the form of a chart or graph. These visual aids should be placed in various locations in the household. If a child is very young and not able to read, you can draw pictures outlining the behavioral and emotional requirement.

A token or point system can use various objects, such as poker chips, pennies or stickers. Many children can handle a simple "point on the board", but a tangible token representing a point is always better. They are used to reinforce daily and weekly goals and objectives. Tokens are awarded only for performance of a task or for conforming to behavior that meets your specifications. If the requirement is to make the bed, the child must do it properly. If the bed is not made properly, no token will be awarded, however, the child must still re-do the task until it is done correctly. Tokens should be put in some type of box available in a central location. You should explain when you introduce the system what rewards can be earned and that these rewards are still subject to your control. The token system gradually teaches the child the concept of earning privileges, freedoms, or favorite activities or treats through effort and diligence.

You may initially object to the token system, saying "bribes do not work." Bribery has nothing to do with this system. Many families tend to buckle under the pressure and allow a child to have a treat, watch a little television, read a comic book, or stay up late. These types of "violations" only serve to confuse the child and give him or her the message that the parents are basically giving in as opposed to sticking to a non-negotiable program. Your child must understand that limits and guidelines are in effect at all times and that every privilege must be earned. Your responsibility is to be very consistent and emphasize what your child's responsibilities are.

Keeping control over the child while giving him or her some freedom creates what may seem to be conflicting goals, but what is actually happening is that the child will develop a sense of independence and autonomy by earning privileges, while at the same time, will learn that they must check in even closer with you in order to earn tokens. At the end of the week, when the child's overall level of performance is graded, he or she may be able to cash in some of the tokens for basic privileges.

On Level Two, your child maintains an illusion of freedom and privileges that are available to them. What they often forget is that everything is still ultimately decided upon by the parents, including whether the child must return to a previous level or advance to a new one. It is the parents who set the terms for what behavior earns tokens, and when and for what the tokens can be used. Families are in charge. It is always a good psychological "trick" to give a difficult child the illusion of being in control and that they have choices when the ultimate choices are actually those of the parents. This is how a family structure needs to be maintained.

It may be difficult for the young child to understand the concept of "earning"; however, parents should continually emphasize the importance of tokens and the practice of completing tasks to earn them. Parents must use a great deal of "memory drills" for the young and sometimes older child so they will commit every aspect of their earning program to memory. Children have great memories for what they want; we are just expanding their memory for what they need to do. You may want to supply the younger child with a list of easy requirements that need to be repetitively practiced in order to earn tokens. Over time, gradually increase the responsibilities, adding more work, chores and new attitudes and behaviors to practice.

The older child certainly has the ability to work toward specific goals and objectives and should complete a good deal of work and chores, as well as writing assignments, such as journal entries. It is important for children to begin using language and the written word as vehicles of appropriate communication. The "new language" is the family's language. Rehearse, Reprogram, Rehearse, Reinforce. Basic training and persistence will prevail.

During this level, the child may become frustrated and say, "I have earned all these tokens and what do I get?" The answer is simple: All basic freedoms and liberties are now earned privileges. You can say: "Now that you have earned your tokens, you can have your bedtime fifteen minutes later, or you may have dessert, or play alone or with a sibling." Rewards such as toys, television time or going outside, however, must be reserved for Level Three.

Difficult children will resort to negotiation and manipulations, including ploys such as becoming overly nice and cooperative. This usually lasts for a short period of time and its only purpose is to gain privileges and freedoms and then immediately go back to old patterns and behavior. All children try to get what they want, but difficult children will manipulate even harder and will superficially comply to parents requests. These superficial behaviors usually last for only a short period of time as the main purpose is for the child to gain the privileges and freedoms they desire immediately and then, after getting what they want, going right back to their old patterns of behaviors. Parents need to be very firm and on their guard to not overly negotiate, or better still, do not negotiate at all. Also, parents must never think that things can get better without long-term change. It is still very important to be strictly "contract oriented" and to abide by goals and objectives and to NOT give in. NEVER negotiate, only reinforce or consequence. Children need "black-and-white approaches." The more one talks at the wrong time, the more room the child is given to talk back. Remember, we are done with that previous pattern of interaction which got us into trouble in the first place!

Review, Repeat, Practice

You may be feeling completely overwhelmed and frustrated at this point in "accepting" Level Two as an improvement. However, you must not give up. Long-term repetition is the key and even if everything seems to be going fine, your child will resort to the old out-of-control behavior if the program is stopped prematurely. Remember, you should be practicing what I call the **"Four R's": Rehearsal, Re-enactment, Repair and Reintegration**. The appropriate amount of Sequence One and Sequence Two holds must continue; however, Sequence Two holds should be increasingly positive for both the parent and child.

For Angela, the program was taking place in a therapeutic girls' home. She engaged in art therapy and heavy role playing where she would pretend to confront her biological mother (whom she rarely saw at that point). As the therapy continued, Angela became increasingly depressed and overwhelmed. It had truly been easier for her to push away the feelings of rejection and abandonment and replace them with acting-out behavior. This, however, to me, was a definite sign the therapy was working. She was required to look at her life and describe, year by year, what had happened. This helped Angela to put a life of sexual abuse and extreme neglect into some sort of format that made as much sense as it was ever going to make. Eventually, anti-depressants were prescribed as Angela began to have trouble sleeping. Again, a sign that the therapy was working. Angela was finally beginning to develop a genuine conscience, sensitivity and empathy towards others as opposed to thinking only about her own traumas and angers. She was learning to trust again.

Addition of Penalties and Demerits:Give Something Instead of Taking Away

If you have been working diligently on your level program but are encountering a very stubborn and resistant child, it is still very important to stick with the entire "earning concept" without exceptions. But you may want to incorporate penalties and demerits which serve as an additional reinforcer and discipline technique. I prefer "adding" consequences as opposed to "take away" points or other privileges. I also like to use thc word "adding hard labor" as this has a very strong connotation to the difficult child and will certainly gain his or her attention. Remember, children will attempt to sabotage the treatment program in any way they can as getting better requires motivation and effort which the difficult and unmanageable child refuses to produce.

Examples of hard labor and penalties are as follows:

1. 30 or 60 minutes of repetitive, boring, hard work activities such as scrubbing, cleaning, writing assignments, standing alone or anything that the parents deem fit. Families often become very creative and make the child work extremely hard in an activity or chore which they absolutely hate. This is an example of the best type of penalty.

2. Forget the idea of taking things away as a punishment at this point. Tough children have tough attitudes and get used to losing everything as they only torture with their anger and resentment. This is why it is very important to place in the program a long list of potential hard labor penalties which the parent or child can pick when the time is right and an additional "reminder" regarding the fact that inappropriate behavior will not be tolerated at any time throughout the program.

3. It is important to keep the concept of "double jeopardy" alive. This means that the program will require the child to continually earn levels, lose levels, earn privileges slowly and by hard work in addition to enforcing immediate and, hopefully emotionally painful hard labor penalties which will captivate their attention immediately. It is also very important to advise the child that penalty points will continue to "stack up". For example, doubling and tripling penalties for the same type of inappropriate behaviors until these behaviors become extinct is a recommendation.

4. Many people may ask "What if the child refuses to do the hard labor?". This makes no difference if the child refuses or not. Stay out of the power struggle about who will do what. Even if the child refuses, make it very clear that their penalties-hard labor time will then be converted to even more intensive adults only time. The child will love you even more when they realize they cannot get rid of you and that you are relentless in your pursuit for compliance and attachment. Actually, periodic addition of hard labor not only gives the child something to think about immediately, but it may also give the parents the needed extra time with the child during a critical "melt down". You must prove you are stronger, persistent and definitely in charge.

As cruel as it sounds, Peggy and Bill had Sergei scrub the bathroom floor when he seriously misbehaved. For repeat offenses, he had to scrub with a toothbrush. Angela spent ample time in doing repetitive writing drills, house work and chores, in addition to journal entries which involved writing out better solutions to her problems. Chris required a tremendous amount of hard labor activities outside of the home as he was often very belligerent if kept inside. He often refused to engage in the repetitive hard work penalties which he clearly deserved, but he still "did his time for the crime." Both Sergei and Chris learned very quickly that it was by far easier to behave and comply with parental expectations and terms of the contract than to spend the afternoon on hands and knees scrubbing or engaged in equally boring and repetitive tasks separate from the rest of the family. It certainly was a "contest of wills," but parents prevailed with the children realizing there was literally no way out.

Level Two Summary: Moving to Level Three

Level Two focuses on re-education and re-training, as well as a gradual separation of child and parent—but only after the child has shown appropriate social and moral behaviors and can be left unattended for short periods of time. Level Two must be consistently maintained for at least four weeks and may last as long as six months. The average stay is often around four months.

Under Level Two, the token system has been implemented to provide specific, tangible reinforcers and to teach the child the concept of "earning" everything, since, in the real world, nothing is free. As parents, can you think of what is free in your adult lives? I cannot.

Parents must clearly list all requirements of the child, such as basic work, chores, routines, homework, respect and responsibility. Also, time management and punctuality should be consistently graded.

Your child is ready to move to Level Three only after he or she has mastered Level Two activities and requirements for a minimum of one month (however, in most cases this time-frame will be much longer). If you feel you child is still "shaky," keep them at Level Two for a period of two or even three months. Keep them safe and successful and gradually push to the next level.

It is very important for parents to be formal in "grading" the child's Level Two activities. Parents sometimes make the mistake of quickly giving up and of prematurely trusting the child's good behavior. While the child has had some time to be on his or her own during Level Two, a continual emphasis must still be placed on adult supervision and frequent times where the child "checks in" with the parents regarding progress and performance.

Pep Talk

Repeat over and over whenever you feel like giving up: Short-term loss for long-term gain. Remember, more times than not, this program has proven to work on even the most hopeless children. Something is bound to "break through to your child," it may just take a while—longer than you would like. Patience and persistence are needed virtues.

If you find yourself at the point of exhaustion, keep reading, keep trying, and keep up your optimism. Your child will not improve if you are not committed to this program and committed and attached to your child. Besides, what are your other options? Allow the child to totally destroy your family? Take a step back.

Maintain a more objective, business-like approach. Lean on other family members for a while. Remember, the loss and hardship now will only continue for another several months—certainly nothing compared to a lifetime of problems if you give up.

Also remember that this is not the time to use logic, reasoning or fantasies on how the child might possibly get better "on his or her own." It is the family that makes the child better. Lastly, improvement does not mean "perfection." Improvement may actually mean manageability, tolerance, mutual respect and admiration.

Level Three: Increasing Self-Control

There are ten critical areas of inappropriate behavior and thinking that difficult children must continually work on during Level Three in order to prevent relapses and to foster healthy, stable and secure growth. They are:

(1) **Power Thrust**. Resisting authority, refusing and arguing, physically and verbally abusing others, intimidating, threatening and attacking others, feeling that he or she must always win, sulking and cursing.

(2) **False Pride**. Having an inflated self-image, feeling superior, fearing put downs, holding unrealistic expectations, mistaking views about success and failure, acting stubborn, and refusing to admit wrongdoing.

(3) **Irresponsible Decision Making**. Failing to plan ahead; acting first, thinking later; displaying inability to delay gratification; acting impatient or hyperactive; and being hooked on criminal and delinquent excitement.

(4) **Failure to Accept Obligation**. Being withdrawn, silent, or isolated; lacking effort or energy; possessing an "I can't" attitude; procrastinating or saying "I forgot"; doing a poor-quality job; refusing to honor commitments; blaming others for lack of trust; and making excuses for negative behaviors.

(5) **Inability to Empathize**. Displaying no concept of injury to others, setting people up against each other; hearing only what he or she wants to hear; being inconsiderate; using poor manners; negatively influencing others; and aggravating, bugging, insulting, and teasing.

(6) **Victim Stance**. Blaming others for own behaviors, feeling sorry for self or playing "poor me," and seeking rescue and help from others to avoid consequences of bad behavior.

(7) **Being Dishonest**. Attempting to confuse, lie or minimize wrongdoings; feeding others what they want to hear; displaying total or partial inattention; and saying "yes" but not meaning it.

(8) **Impulsivity**. Attempting to obtain what they want without waiting. Being impatient and demanding immediate gratification.

(9) **Negative Thoughts**. Constantly complaining, whining, or stating how terrible everyone is or how horrible life has become since parents have taken charge.

(10) **Passive-Aggressive Behaviors**. Being avoidant of openly expressing frustrations, anger and depressive feelings. Acting out these behaviors by being coercive or by trying to manipulate and find a short cut.

It is very important that you do not move your child to Level Three too soon as he or she may become quickly bored and begin to manipulate you by behaving well for a week, then causing problems that require going back to either Level One or Level Two. If you are not sure whether your child should be moved to Level Three, it would be wise to keep him or her in Level Two.

In Level Three, the child will:

(1) Spend brief times being independent and away from family members and primary caretakers.

(2) Choose for him or herself activities and/or the times to do them. This is a big change from Level Two where everything was dictated by the family.

(3) Have more numerous and complex goals and objectives in order to earn tokens.

(4) Have written or verbal homework assignments that are longer and more detailed. The assignments should involve more oral presentations of feelings and problems.

(5) Have daily and weekly exercises, such as writing exercises, where your child can actually show what has been learned by putting it down on paper. This can reinforce the concepts of morality, caring and sensitivity, family systems, relationships, love and affection and honesty.

(6) Have outside social activities. The difficult child will prefer to be alone and self-absorbed so parents need to insist on a minimum of two outside social activities, such as sports, religious groups, clubs, scouts or volunteer work. Such "social therapies" are essential to the rehabilitation program at this level and should be part of the token reward system.

Your child may become frustrated on this level because he or she knows there has already been improvement and complains, "Why do I have to work harder?" Emphasize to the child that there needs to be a continual increase in behavior requirements, work and chores, conduct and attitude, and academic performance. You can get this principle across by calling a family meeting and saying: "Our family's goal is to all work hard so that we can move to higher levels. Life will always be filled with more work and chores, and you will always need to learn to be more helpful and cooperative in order to be successful. That is why we are assigning you more work, in order to prepare you for life."

Often, what may be required is that the child be returned to Level Two in order to be closer to the parents and to have requirements and standards which are more manageable. You may find that you are placing the child back on Level Two quite frequently—this is normal and often required. Remember, too, that Level One regression is also always an option if the child becomes out-of-control or violates any of the "cardinal rules" which have been previously set forth.

What I would like to stress it that the difficult child needs to be taught to "think differently." The child's irrational beliefs, false perceptions and distorted thinking patterns need to be challenged and corrected. The child then needs to "practice" thinking and verbalizing correctly. Remember, you as parents must become "reality" for the child.

Difficult children often become defiant and refuse to cooperate during this stage. Initially, you may choose to help your child get started by organizing a journal or notebook for home assignments. Having regular family support meetings and reinforcement sessions every night can also be helpful. There may be times when a child needs one parent more than another for help on certain tasks, such as homework. This should be anticipated and not to be taken personally by either parent. Just be cautious with your child trying to play one parent against another. Remain a "united front".

It is very common for child to try to manipulate the parents or demand that he or she be given a break and not be forced to return to an earlier level. Additionally, children with emotional difficulties are very well-versed in manipulating to get out of requirements. Parents need to remain firm in their stance that each level must be completed "by the book" in order to be successful. There is no room for flexibility or negotiation on any of the levels in this program.

Verbal communication is extremely important in Level Three. Difficult children often have significant trouble communicating emotions. Their principle responses are coldness and indifference or anger and negativism. To overcome these unproductive emotions, parents should use trial-and-error techniques which allow the child to continually practice new, appropriate emotions. The goal is to make the child feel more comfortable with emotional expression via words as opposed to using physical actions and inappropriate behavior. They must also learn to work for everything. Nothing is free in the world, is there?

Also, the token or point system should be in full effect. Tokens can be defined as anything "tangible" that can keep track of a child's performance on any given day and will accumulate to determine what they have "earned" for the following week and level-grading system. It is a "week-by-week process". Younger children often prefer tangible tokens such as stars, stickers, pennies, marbles or poker chips (what I use in my family), whereas the older child's tokens are more in the category of a regular "tally" of actual points accumulated on a chart or board. On Level Three, tokens or points can increase to 20 per day, 5 days per week. This makes it very simple as 20 points per day times 5 days per week equals a nice even number of 100 possible tokens or points a week. An even number of points calculated at the end of the week (tally time is typically done Fridays around the dinner hour) makes it much easier for both children and parents to count up and assess the appropriate level earned. Any and all privileges, freedoms and activities should be solely based on the actual amount of tokens earned. Parents should not succumb to the child's statements "I came close." Close only counts in horseshoes. We must go by the book because if we allow for a "break" in the contract without the child actually earning everything as prescribed, it is just a matter of time until the child is back in control of the parents by gradually wearing them down via manipulations and coercive techniques.

The following table outlines how levels are determined (see examples in Appendix):

90-100 tokens or points allows the child to "pick" a family activity, or a specific privilege or freedom. Extra game and recreational time, television or other visual entertainment can also be earned, although television and Nintendo activities should be kept to a minimum as they often become self-reinforcing and preoccupying. If a child chooses specific television shows, video or electronic games, you should closely limit the duration to 15-30 minutes each. Time outside the home is certainly earned, but shorter in duration. Initially, only one or two hours at most should be granted. Gradually, the time can increase. Earned tokens buy what the child thinks is free within the family: privileges, freedom, socializing, independence, activities. Children must learn that nothing is free in the world.

80-89 tokens or points allows the child approximately two-thirds of the privileges, freedoms or activities. This means that the child has two-thirds of desired free time; two-thirds of desired privileges; and two-thirds of desired options for rewards and overall activities.

Below 80 tokens or points - Level One all the way. This is a full week of the "good old days" of just Mom and Dad; closeness without distractions and "hard labor" to pay for a rough week. This is a lesson in life and reality--no work, no pay!

If one looks at this grading criteria, 90-100 is typically an "A," 80-90 is a "B," and below 80 is a low-average/below average score. School, home and life in general are all judged and graded based on our performance. Giving children an actual "score" regarding their performance provides an immediate acknowledgment of how they are doing and also prepares them for the inevitable aspects of life when all of our attitudes, behaviors and "outputs" are, indeed, assessed continually.

How long are the privileges gained from tokens to last? For the child four to six years old, tokens can be calculated daily for a level the next day. For children seven years and above, levels are earned (or *not* earned) a week at a time. Levels earned are calculated Friday evenings after points or tokens are accumulated and tallied by the parents, and last until the next Friday. You have the option of making a level go from Friday evening through Sunday evening and then starting fresh Monday morning. I recommend you do this "earned weekend level" for the child six to ten years old, until he or she fully understands the program. Once they understand (which usually occurs in a short period of time), move to the week-by-week earned level system (Friday evening through the next Friday evening which finalizes the next grading period). Remember, earning and maintaining a level should be an effort and struggle. If it becomes too easy, increase the demands. Work is good! Hard work is even better!

Throughout the program, there were many times when Sergei had to be brought back to total Adults-Only. In fact, at one point on Level Three, the pattern of bouncing back and forth from Level One lasted for three weeks. Finally, Sergei decided that he was willing to work hard. He knew what he had to do. He had a chart were the levels were clearly listed. He knew if he earned 20 points a day, 5 days a week, (which totaled 100 points) he could move to Level Three. If he only earned 90 he only received Level Two privileges and if he earned below 80 points he immediately went back to Level One, no privileges, no freedom. Eventually Peggy and Bill stiffened the requirements and even added demerits, whereby Sergei would be docked another point for every point he lost to bad behavior. This double jeopardy finally got the message across to Sergei that consequences would increase if he did not push forward and maintain appropriate behaviors. Likewise, they instituted bonus points for proper behavior which Sergei tried very hard to earn. Peggy and Bill referred to it as the "carrot in front of the horse technique."

Throughout this all, Sergei was also being tutored by his parents in speech and problem solving, areas that he was deficient in and that needed to be gone over and over. I trained both Peggy and Bill to use only highly specific, concrete and focused sentences and orders with Sergei, rather than drawn-out explanations and discussions.

Level Three Summary

Level Three strongly emphasizes dealing with negative and deviant behaviors and increasing decision making and responsibility through specific homework and role rehearsals. There may be frequent times when a child is required to return to Level Two for a "refresher course" since Level Three is very demanding and requires a tremendous amount of effort on the child's part.

Graduation at last!

Almost six months passed and Sergei began to earn success. By no means was the program complete or the problems solved, but Sergei was able to maintain significant amounts of time on Level Three. Peggy and Bill threw a graduation party which made Sergei feel very positive and gave him an additional flavor of how it is to achieve. Peggy and Bill continually emphasized that Sergei had choices and that it was their obligation to be very strict with him so that he would make the right choices. The contract system was reinforced on a daily basis. And every week, they would review where Sergei had started out and where he was at now. They continued family therapy with me and we focused on being consistent and maintaining open, honest communication. Sergei was prescribed long-term conservative medication for mood swings and irritability and was closely followed by his attending physician. Sergei was also placed back in school and his teachers followed a "contract" that was coordinated with the one at home. The school was very supportive and maintained the proper level of strictness. There were, however, still times when Sergei acted out and was pulled from school to work at home for a couple weeks under stricter supervision. Sergei also received a lot of tutoring, when in and out of school, since his cognitive weaknesses often contributed to his behavior problems. Sergei was encouraged to socialize with others and was enrolled in soccer and swimming. After a year, the family was exhausted, but life was beginning to settle into a state of normalcy. Finally they had their family back in a more functional capacity while accepting that improvement had been approximately "80%" leaving a remaining "20%" of expected problems to work on throughout Sergei's development.

Angela's graduation was truly remarkable. She was able to realize that all her acting out behaviors were just representations of how bad she felt about her life and that she had never viewed people as more than objects. Her insight and strength prompted her to actually become one of the leaders at the group home where she held a group therapy lesson for disturbed adolescents. But the best gift of all was that Angela was eventually adopted by a wonderful family. Angela let go of her hold on the past and embraced the present. She said that if it was not for the treatment program she would have killed herself and that some of her reckless behavior was also geared toward the hope that someone would just kill her. Angela also acknowledged that her treatment needed to continue, probably for the rest of her life. She found herself bonding to people who were most aggressive and directive in dealing with her during difficult times. Because of this, she kept in touch with me. Occasionally, during her teenage years, there were gradual "slips." When these occurred she would call and tell me she needed a "tune-up."

The most remarkable thing was that Angela made a full commitment to herself to live completely opposite how she was raised. She is now excelling at school and looks forward to going to college.

Chris was started in public school and slowly, but surely, learned that from now on, everything had to be earned; no longer was anything just going to be handed to him. Everything was on a strict schedule and was considered a "reward." For six months Chris had ups and downs. He often tested the limits but finally realized he had been acting out for attention and that he was no longer going to be able to do what he wanted, when he wanted. Chris continued frequent therapy for three years. Adolescence had its share of bad times for Chris, but there were good times as well. The entire family began doing volunteer work together. They became active in their church and worked on expressing feelings to each other, no matter how much it hurt. Then, as a family, they mourned for their loss of the early years of what should have been family closeness. This was critical for it helped them to realize they still had may good years ahead. Anne and Richard maintained a reduced work load and were committed to working on their marriage as well. Chris did vacillate between happiness that things were going well now, and intense anger at his parents for his past. Never, though, did it get to the point where Chris required medication. Over time, things evened out. There were a few crisis calls, but they were few and far between compared to the letters I received from them saying, "Thank you for helping us create a real family."

Parents can be more persistent than an unmanageable child.

Summary

Working with difficult children is tremendous effort for any family or professional. Demanding treatment programs, such as this one, often come under criticism as being too hard, too dispassionate or just too much for parents to handle. The key to success with the most difficult and, at times, the most hopeless child is commitment and dedication (as well as sacrifice) from parents, other family members, and support systems. Anything and everything must be tried to assist the child. If the family is hopeless, the child remains hopeless.

Yes, aggressive treatment and commitment is both painful and long-term, but so are the ramifications of giving up. This approach may not be the "quick fix" of medication, the "new fad" or the traditional therapy, but it will offer hope, guidance, structure and, above all, an aggressive and highly focused way to repair old problems. Even if the child improves 50, 60 or even 80 percent (success!!), we accomplished a great deal. Just keep thinking how far you have come. If you have any doubts, just compare the number of infractions now and at the start of the program. And think of how much more "in control" you feel. We wants the parents stress level lower than your child, and, your child doing the hard work and moving forward day by day to a more rational, compliant and "bonded" member of the family.

Chapter 6
Adjunctive Treatments

Families with difficult children often feel alone and afraid which contributes to their wanting to give up and abandon any and all hope that the situation will improve. It is extremely important to involve adjunctive services and individuals who can provide professional guidance, support and practical treatment.

Adjunctive services basically mean anyone and everyone who can be of assistance to the family and, primarily, the child. Not everyone who can provide help and support needs to be a formal "expert" in a medical or psychological specialty, although the more experts involved, the better. We hope that experts are truly "experts" in the understanding of the unique child and family structure as opposed to an "academic expert" who has "heard about these situations" but has not actually treated a child or family. Along these lines, the standard psychiatrist or psychologist who only worked with a few children here and there cannot be really called an expert for the family. Children's issues need to be handled by experts in *children*. The general therapist often does not have enough practical experience in understanding all the intricacies and nuances of children, let alone the difficult child or the child from a post-institutionalized setting who has experienced catastrophic circumstances and losses. (Please refer back to previous sections of this book which have outlined specialists and qualifications.)

Many families have exhausted all financial and insurance benefits, and are often left to their own devices to seek help. Because of financial burn-out many families resort to complete reliance on state-run or city-based counseling programs. While there may be good people working in these programs, the majority are not licensed or sub-specialized which may be non-productive for the child and family.

However, it is important to keep in mind that any treatment is better than no treatment at all. If families are just not able to afford any services, it is very important for them to check with their local community mental health center or community-based counseling programs to find help. At the very least, families should maintain family and/or individual counseling for support and structure.

Another option for families on a limited budget is to seek out a University Medical Clinic or teaching facility in which there is a "sliding scale." While the treatment team may be composed of students-in-training, they are under very strict supervision from professors and experts. These treatment programs are often staffed by very aggressive and diligent students who want to help and learn their profession. Always "interview" perspective therapists for qualifications and experience.

Within every community are state-run social services and child protective service agencies that provide help and interventions for families in distress. It is also possible that families can request county or state assistance. Many agencies have "referral lists" of experts which they utilize. Sometimes, families need to sign a "temporary entrustment" in which they are entrusting a portion of their child's care to a county agency. Many families may feel that they do not want to have anyone tell them what to do or what decisions to make for their child but, when desperate, the county agencies are often trained and staffed to deal with children who are out of control. It is a lot better for county agents to work on "prevention and treatment" as opposed to having families fall apart and put the difficult child in foster care or up for adoption; or, in the worst scenario, for the families to lose patience and control and abuse and neglect the child.

Additionally, children and adolescent therapeutic homes are often available, but application needs to be through the social service agencies or court service unit. The county can often help guide families to state-run intensive psychiatric or treatment programs or residential care programs. Funding is often arranged through a combination of county and state sources. Also school systems allocate special funding for residential placements, but this can be a long and arduous process to convince them of the need.

County-run agencies often have "in-home" supportive family services which can allocate one or two staff members to work in the home many hours per week with the family (I have seen therapists spend 15-20 hours per week doing excellent "in home" therapy). This is a very good option for the family who feels totally overwhelmed and needs tremendous professional support. Again, county funding is often utilized; ask around your local school district or department of social services for agencies which provide this service.

Social Security disability may also be a possibility for the family with limited funds in great need of services. The criteria to qualify for Social Security disability is quite strict based on the parents income, but it is certainly something to consider for families having a child who has a great deal of educational and emotional difficulties to where additional financial support is required.

Cognitive Rehabilitation Techniques for the Child with Brain Dysfunction.

Learning disability services are certainly very important for the child with brain dysfunction, but it is also very important to consider even more intensive cognitive rehabilitation to improve the child's deficits in logic, reasoning, auditory and visual information processing, and overall problem-solving skills. Remember, if a child's brain is damaged or dysfunctional at any level, these deficits often result in improper "input and output" of human emotions. We know very well that neurocognitive deficits produce impulsivity, mood agitation, irritability and periodic rage which can be destructive to interpersonal relationships. Language deficits make it very difficult to adequately express emotions. Processing and memory deficits make it very difficult for children to fully understand instructions and directions and to benefit from past experiences (i.e. they make the same mistakes repetitively at home, school, and in relationships).

The following list of cognitive rehabilitation strategies are recommended for the child with both learning deficits and, primarily, neuropsychologically-based attachment disorders:

Cognitive and educational skills assessment. Specific testing of a child's intellectual strengths and/or limitations is necessary in order to design an accurate treatment program. For example, if a child is a slow learner, parents will need to scale down the level of assignments, requirements and the mode of discussing and rehearsing thinking strategies and behaviors. If a child is extremely bright and has excellent educational abilities, however, you must leave no room for negotiation or manipulation; otherwise, the child will clearly use these intellectual abilities to gain his or her way. Try to obtain evaluations through the school district or try to find a specialist in neuropsychology to evaluate cognitive and educational problems. Please review Chapter 2 of this book which outline specialists in neuropsychology, educational, and speech and language assessment. Obtaining an educational advocate is often quite helpful for parents needing to arrange the proper special education curriculum for the child.

Language therapies to improve receptive and expressive language abilities, with an extra emphasis in addressing auditory-processing disorders and semantic-pragmatic language usage. Language evaluations and therapy should be in the child's native language and English. There has been a great deal of emphasis on English as a Second Language remediation as being the main treatment for older internationally-adopted children who have language delays. Many schools adopt the "wait for language transition and acculturation" before giving therapy. Language therapies for the internationally adopted child should begin immediately upon arrival for an child who is delayed in their native language.

Children who have struggled with attachment and behavioral difficulties often have undiagnosed language processing or expressive deficits. These disabilities significantly limit appropriate interactional skills and produce a tremendous amount of frustration in the child as they are unable to follow verbal instructions and directions or communicate emotional needs. Language interventions which emphasize both the mechanics of language and "emotional language" (love, hate, frustration, sadness, sensitivity, caring, etc.) are critical if a child is to learn better ways to interact and attach.

Auditory Processing therapy aims to improve five critical areas of language: 1) auditory awareness and recognition of sound; 2) auditory decoding and phonemic awareness/sound discrimination; 3) auditory attention; 4) auditory sequential memory and learning; 5) auditory integration and organization of abstract verbal concepts and reasoning skills. Remember, a critical part of emotional language is to be aware of tones, pitch, intonation, inflections and nuances in the speech patterns from primary caretakers. Auditory processing therapy should also be aimed at increasing or decreasing sound sensitivity and working towards captivating a child's attention for better listening skills. (See additional detailed description on subsequent pages.)

Traditional learning disability interventions will provide remedial work in all standard academic areas such as reading, reading comprehension, spelling, written language organization and mathematics reasoning/numerical operations. Additionally, children with neuropsychologically-based learning disabilities require intensive remediation and retraining in the areas of concept-formation, the development of higher-level logic and reasoning, sequential thought, categorization abilities, and organizational skills.

Visual-Perceptual training is a relatively new concept and recommended for children with learning and attentional disorders. Visual-perceptual training often involves computer-assisted programs that help strengthen visual discrimination, visual-spatial relationships, visual figure-ground, and visual memory/visual sequential memory. Many children who have significant learning disabilities, particularly developmental dyslexia and attentional disorders, have a great deal of difficulty in visual scanning, tracking, sequencing, and memorization.

Materials available through Learning Fundamentals provide intensive remediation in all academic subject areas (see Appendix), especially in the areas of visual and auditory attention, informational processing, linguistics and problem solving.

Children who have neuropsychological and behavioral problems need a tremendous amount of work in increasing their visual awareness of environmental and interpersonal stimuli. For example, increasing facial recognition; becoming aware of body language; and becoming aware of interpersonal space and boundaries can increase a child's social skills and appropriate behaviors.

Basic assembly tasks such as assembly of block designs, puzzles, models and Legos which require the child to follow a visual-plan of action are very good ways to strengthen, focus and organize work habits. Board games can also be very helpful in teaching a neuropsychologically-impaired child how to pay attention and follow a plan of action which has a start and finish.

Training to improve copying and writing tasks (both with paper-and-pencil and with the use of a computer) strengthen fine-motor coordination along with visual-perceptual analysis and organization. There are many children who have significant weaknesses in fine-motor coordination involving paper and pencil output and will not learn to write in any legible manner. Keyboarding techniques are highly recommended for the child who has developed basic language skills. For those children unable to write, dictation devices are a viable option. For children with limited speech and language skills, using the "Picture Exchange Program" (PEC's), or even sign language are additional options.

Increasing memory and retention skills is a critical rehabilitation technique for difficult children. Remember, children who act out seem to continually "forget the rules." Whether or not a child has a brain dysfunction, it is extremely helpful for families to strengthen a child's auditory and visual memory by various techniques, such as having them memorize words, phrases, sentences, goals and objectives (specifically the ones set forth in their contracts, rules and regulations). Memory games can be created by the use of flash cards, repetitive writing and reading drills and the making of cassette tapes which can be played over and over to enhance retention by providing auditory redundancy. Children need to list out and post all of their day-to-day activities. Keeping daily and weekly planners, journals, charts and graphs also strengthen memory skills.

There are many excellent board games (available at educational learning centers) which teach a child new ways to memorize via mnemonic strategies. Basically, mnemonic strategies are "tricks" which help increase memory for new material by relying heavily on visual imagery and visual "cues" in order to create a mental picture of new information. Since it is very important for children to learn by having both auditory and visual cues presented at the same time, mnemonic strategies are extremely valuable as children often prefer drawing pictures or using fantasy images as a way of learning new material as opposed to just the traditional way of "studying the facts." For example, certain auditory cues (words or short phrases) can trigger a memory just like a small visual cue (picture) can trigger the recollection of a concept, idea or task.

Improving Critical Thinking and Problem Solving helps build on logical, rational and organized thought patterns necessary for organized problem solving. Many children with learning disabilities and emotional problems tend to be very concrete and primitive, seeing the world in a black-and-white manner. Improving abstractive logic, organized thinking and creativity will enhance academic and emotional success. The material available through "www.criticalthinking.com" is excellent in developing higher-level thinking skills.

Learning-Disability and Attention-Deficit Intervention at Home. Working with a child having learning and attentional difficulties requires a great deal of patience in addition to structural and strategic modifications both at home and in school. These special students learn in a very special way and require a wide variety of "accommodations" and "modifications" for both child and parent. The following may be beneficial and can be included in your child's "Individualized Educational Program" or Special Education Curriculum:

FAMILY AND SCHOOL ACCOMMODATIONS FOR CHILDREN WITH ATTENTION AND PROCESSING DISORDERS

1. Classroom placement is very important. Child should be seated centrally in the class and away from as many distractions as possible such as windows, doorways, other noisy students, heating or air conditioning, pencil sharpeners or any other type of distraction.

2. It is very important for parents and teachers to gain the child's undivided attention before giving any type of instructions or directions. Speaking slowly and clearly without over-exaggerating speech will be helpful in addition to giving directions in a logical and time-ordered sequence with words which make the

sequence clear such as "first", "next" and "finally".

3. Gaining undivided attention can also be obtained by calling the child's name or a gentle touch/nonverbal reinforcer which will serve to alert the child and to focus attention upon the classroom activity.

4. It is also very important to continually check comprehension by asking the child for a brief summary after key ideas have been presented in order to make certain he/she understands. Paraphrasing instructions and information in shorter and simpler sentences rather than only by repeating will be helpful.

5. The child should be encouraged to ask questions for additional clarification.

6. It is also very important to emphasize key words when speaking or writing, especially when presenting new information. Brief instructions with emphasis on the main idea being presented may also be effective.

7. Use gestures that will help clarify information in addition to varying the loudness of the voice to increase attention may also be beneficial.

8. It will also be very helpful for the child with an attentional disorder to sit next to a student who has very good attention and focus.

9. It is very important to shorten assignments or work periods to coincide with span of attention. Using a timer which can break down tasks into small and manageable sections with specific time limits, such as 15 minutes, will also be very beneficial.

10. It is important to give assignments one at a time to avoid work overload and also reduce the general amount of in-class and at-home material or break it down into very small segments in order to prevent the child from feeling overloaded.

11. It is very important for children with attentional problems to be on a daily and weekly set of goals and objectives which clearly list out and/or post all of their requirements. For example, a daily and weekly "planner" and a notebook which can be coordinated between parents and teachers is recommended. This way, the child will be able to review specific requirements, goals and objectives.

12. It is also very important to provide consistent and concrete examples and specific steps in order to accomplish each task. It is also very important to make certain that parents and teachers give one direction at a time and prioritize assignments and activities.

13. It is important to continually address messiness and organizational skills. In addition to a daily, weekly and monthly assignment sheet, parents and teachers should list out all materials needed daily in a consistent format in which homework needs to be turned in. Frequent checks and reward points for homework and appropriate behaviors should be done throughout the day at regular intervals

(approximately 15-30 minutes).

14. It is very important to provide auditory and visual cues at all times as children with attentional problems have difficulties with visual attention. Therefore, it is very important to carefully explain in a concrete and direct manner all of the goals and objectives in addition to providing additional visual handouts which can summarize classroom activities and requirements.

15. It is very important to continually teach the child with an attentional disorder "there is a place for everything and everything belongs in its place". Frequent checks/rechecks on a daily and weekly basis need to be done in addition to continual positive reinforcement for organizational skills, adherence to time constraints and appropriate task completion.

16. It is very important for parents and teachers to practice with an attentional-disordered child to continually "look at me while I talk and watch my eyes while I speak".

17. It is very important for children with attentional disorders to sit in close proximity to teachers and parents when completing tasks so visual and physical and monitoring of behaviors can be done. Also, consistently state in a calm and rational manner the behaviors that need to be completed.

18. It may also be very helpful to have a small note-card with specific goals and objectives taped to the child's desk such as eyes forward, sitting down, pay attention, and, complete task on time. This may be one way for the teacher to nonverbally redirect the child by pointing to the note-card when the child with an attentional problem appears to be off task.

19. A contract or "level system" which can be implemented at home will be very beneficial. While it is certainly acknowledged that children with attentional problems have difficulties with consistency and self-control, they need to learn to be taught to strive for betterment/improvement and keep track of daily and weekly academic behavior, home behavior, task completion, attention and concentration, self-control, motivation and general attitude. It should be emphasized that there is most always a correlation (connection) between a child anxiety, motivation and general emotional development and the amount of attentional and concentrational difficulties that are presented.

20. Organizational rules need to be emphasized as part of the family contract.

21. It is also very important for parents and teachers to have regular desk checks and checks for notebook neatness with training and redirection if problems surface.

22. It may also be very important to allow additional time to complete timed in-class examinations or standardized tests as this will give a better measure of abilities. Additionally, a proctor can also be helpful in addition to allowing the child with an attentional disorder to complete their in a quiet setting.

23. Children with attentional disorders need a great deal of visual aides and cues which can be posted around the home and in their room. This will keep them on-task and continually remind them of daily and weekly goals and objectives. It is very important for parents to write out instructions and requirements.

24. It is also very important for parents and teachers to recognize times that a child with an attentional problem can become fatigues and frustrated and require time for alternate movements such as stretching or standing in the back of the class.

25. It is very important for continual praise and reinforcement for self-control, positive attention and motivation. It is also very important to ignore minor inappropriate behaviors or disruptions, and to use appropriate discipline, time outs or positive reprimands as opposed to lectures or criticism. It is extremely important to continually attend to any type of positive behaviors in order to shape appropriate responses.

Learning-Disability and Attention-Deficit Interventions at School.

Throughout my treatment program for treating the challenging child, families must be aware of and sensitive to any learning disabilities or attention-deficit disorders, and must seek special education interventions from the school or other community and private resources. Aside from learning disability interventions, many schools provide group counseling to help children adjust with learning disabilities, ADHD, children who have chronic academic underachievement, depression or other emotional problems sometimes related to family difficulties such as divorce or children who just lack social skills and need training in this area. Both at school and at home, make sure the child is rewarded for any and all positive effort and motivation and not just the grades they produce. Utilize school personnel to create the appropriate special education curriculum. If needed, families should seek out an "educational advocate" who is typically a professional who has worked in the school system and can assist the family in negotiating with school officials to arrange the most appropriate school-based special education and psychological supports.

Many school programs are utilizing innovative methods for rehabilitating learning disabilities. For children having significant dyslexia (struggles in reading, writing and math), the Wilson Reading Methods or the Lindamood-Bell Programs are outstanding and work extensively in phonics and visual-perceptual skill remediation.

Additionally, schools have the ability to make accommodations in a child's workload. Untimed examinations for the child with significant attentional and processing difficulties can be very beneficial. Using computer assisted programs with a "spell check component" may make it much easier for the child who just cannot organize written language. When parents and school officials get together to arrange a special education curriculum, it is very important for the families to fully understand all of the school's psychoeducational evaluations and arrange the most intensive learning disability remediation program for the child with highly specific goals and directives that can be "tracked" on a weekly basis.

The following are recommendations for teachers to utilize with children having attentional and learning disorders:

PLAN FOR TEACHING SPECIAL NEEDS CHILDREN

Interventions for improving attention

- Seat student in a quiet area
- Seat student near a good role model
- Seat student near a "study buddy"
- Increase distance between desks
- Seat student away from distracting stimuli (for example, air conditioner, high traffic areas, etc.)
- Allow extra time to complete assigned work
- Shorten assignments or work periods to coincide with span of child's attention (a timer may be used)
- Break long assignments into smaller parts so that the student can see an end to work
- Give assignments one at a time to avoid work overload
- Develop a checklist of important steps to help the student self-monitor their progress and provide cues when a step has been missed
- Pair written instructions with oral instructions
- Provide peer assistance in note taking
- Give clear, concise instructions
- Increase saliency of lesson to student
- Look at student when talking
- Seek to involve student in lesson presentation
- Provide written outline of lesson

- Pair students to check work
- Cue student to stay on task, e.g., private signal

Interventions to reduce impulsivity

- Ignore minor, inappropriate behavior
- Increase immediacy of rewards and consequences
- Use time-out procedure for misbehavior
- Supervise closely during transition times
- Use "prudent" reprimands for misbehavior (i.e., avoid lecturing or criticism)
- Attend to positive behavior with complements, etc.
- Acknowledge positive behavior of nearby student
- Seat student near good role model or near teacher
- Set up behavior contracts
- Instruct student in self-monitoring of behavior, (i.e., hand raising, calling out)
- Call on only when hand is raised in appropriate manner
- Ignore student who calls out without raising hand
- Praise student when hand raised to answer question
- Implement classroom behavior management system
- Implement home-school token economy

Interventions for decreasing excessive motor activity

- When appropriate, allow student to stand wile working
- Provide opportunity for breaks that get the child out of their seat, (i.e., run errands, etc.)
- Provide short break between assignments
- Supervise closely during transition times
- Remind student to check over work product if performance is rushed

Interventions for improving written work

- If written language is weak accept non-written forms for reports (i.e., displays, oral, projects), accept use of typewriter, word processor, tape recorder, do not assign large quantities of written work; test with multiple choice or fill-in questions; instruction in "brain storming" to generate ideas

Interventions for increasing organization and planning

- Allow student to tape record assignment or homework
- Write main points on board in lesson presentation
- Use visual aids in lesson presentation
- Ask for parental help in encouraging organization, (i.e., routines for homework, check if student has needed work each morning, help organize materials)
- Provide rules for getting organized
- Encourage students to have notebook with dividers and folders for work
- Provide student with homework assignment book
- Supervise writing down of homework assignments
- Check homework daily
- Send daily/weekly progress reports home
- Regularly check desk and notebook for neatness, encourage neatness rather than penalize sloppiness
- Allow student to have extra set of books at home
- Provide peer assistance with organization skills
- Give assignments one at a time to avoid confusion
- Assist student in setting short-term goals in completing assignments
- Do not penalize for poor handwriting if visual-motor deficits or organizational deficits are present

Interventions for improving mood

- Provide reassurance and encouragement
- Frequently compliment positive behavior and work product
- Speak softly and in a non-threatening manner if student shows nervousness
- Review instructions when giving new assignments to make sure the student comprehends the directions
- Look for opportunities for the student to display leadership roles within the class
- Focus on student's talents and accomplishments
- Conference frequently with parents to learn about student's interests and achievements outside of school
- Send positive notes home
- Assign student to be a peer teacher in an area where he or she excels
- Make time to talk alone with the student
- Encourage social interactions with classmates if student is withdrawn or excessively shy
- Reinforce student frequently when signs of frustration are noticed
- Look for signs of stress build up and provide encouragement or reduce work load to alleviate pressure and avoid temper outbursts
- Spend more time talking to students who seem pent-up or display anger easily
- Provide brief training in anger control; encourage student to walk away; use calming strategies (deep breaths); tell a nearby adult when feeling angry

Occupational and Sensory Integration therapy. This form of occupational therapy has become extremely popular and effective with post-institutionalized children. It strongly emphasizes increasing a child's sensory awareness of environmental and interpersonal stimuli such as human contact, touch, holding, balance, coordination with space and eating. Brushing, stroking and movement activities are very important in sensory integration, as well as gradually teaching the child to lower hyper-sensitivity and defensiveness to hot and cold, various food and liquid groups, clothing, and hygiene activities. In addition, thc child will gradually learn that human bonding and attachment on a physical level should be a pleasurable experience as opposed to anxiety provoking. The child learns to allow others into his or her personal space. Children from institutional settings are typically deprived of sensory stimuli, making this form of adjunctive treatment an integral part of the overall recovery program.

Neurolinguistic programming (commonly known as NLP) is a very creative concept in cognitive rehabilitation which is founded on several basic tenants involving thinking and reasoning. The NLP therapist can assist the child and family by teaching them that all behaviors stem from true neurological processes (the "N" or Neurological mode of NLP) of seeing, hearing, smelling, tasting and feeling. Language is used to direct all of the person's thoughts and behaviors so that they learn to communicate more clearly and effectively with others. By increasing this ability to establish and maintain rapport with anyone very quickly and easily will deepen emotional bonding and attachment (the "L" or Language mode of NLP). The messages that we give ourselves as the result of the interaction between the way we use our mind and the way we use our language helps develop ways to facilitate changes in one's own behavior, thinking and belief systems in addition to resolving internal conflicts and achieve a deeper sense of self and self-respect. This leads to personal evolution in identity (the "P" or Programming mode in NLP).

Neurolinguistic programming can often involve use of clinical hypnosis or deep muscle or body relaxation techniques to place an individual in the most optimal mode of "absorbing" new thoughts, ideas and suggestions (otherwise known as post-hypnotic suggestions). NLP therapists aim at identifying the perceptual and cognitive patterns which underlie all forms of human communication and interaction (particularly bonding and attachment) and hope to provide ways to "undo" illogical and irrational perceptions and belief systems. In NLP, it is extremely important to "replace" old patterns of thinking with new, creative and optimistic insights and ideas. This is an excellent form of therapy which must be done by a qualified therapist trained by the Neuro-Linguistic Programming Institute based in New York and Washington, D.C. (see Appendix under Professional Organizations).

Private tutors. Families must often seek out the assistance of private tutors who have experience with various learning disabilities, ranging from language disorders, visual perceptual deficits, dyslexia or multiply-handicapped conditions. There are many private tutors who specialize in children with multiple handicaps. Nowadays, there are private therapists available to help within the home as well as to provide families with in-home training for attachment therapy. Consult your local schools department of special education for a list of teachers/tutors who offer private learning disability and tutorial services. Also, local universities having a Graduate Program in Special Education often allow students to work with children as part of their training requirements. These graduate students typically provide excellent and inexpensive services as they are closely supervised by university professors.

Navigating the special education maze. Families often have to deal with school officials regarding the child's academic, learning and behavioral problems. It is extremely important to request a full "child study" to assist in arranging the most suitable educational program for a child's specific condition. This is a multi-discipline evaluation to assess psychological, educational, physical and sensory-perceptual abilities.

Under public law, children who display any type of learning disability in which there is a "severe discrepancy between achievement and intellectual abilities" or an emotional disorder which "impacts a child's educational functioning" should be able to qualify for supportive services. Parents need to be persistent and informed as a child with a learning problem is entitled to special education services. Go to all meetings and do not take "no" for an answer.

If the school turns down a child for special education interventions, parents have the right to appeal and seek out a "second opinion" to help mediate the process. The second opinions are often the financial responsibility of the school system if parents are unable to pay This second opinion is important because often schools will erroneously claim that the child is either not showing problems, that the child should first be on medication for things such as attention deficit disorder, or that the child's disability is not severe enough to warrant action.

Children with atypical or borderline learning disability patterns, or children who have ADHD typically can qualify for a 504 Accommodation Plan, or categorization as "Other Health Impairment" as ADHD is termed a "medical condition". Under this program, the school officials have an obligation to help provide any and all practical accommodations, such as preferential seating, smaller classroom size where the child can be afforded a better teacher-student ratio, behavioral modification programs or school-based counseling. For example, children with attentional and learning problems, particularly in spelling and writing, often need extra time in order to complete assignments. Children with severe learning disabilities or severe ADHD may require training in study skills, in addition to supportive counseling services. It is recommended that families write up their "wish list" and then work on a joint contract with school officials.

Many children who have severely disruptive ADHD or serious emotional problems also have coexisting learning disabilities and often wind up in placements for the emotionally disturbed. This should not be quickly ruled out since these small, self-contained classes can often provide intensive structure and guidance for the out-of-control child while, at the same time, allow for additional help with academics. There are many children who truly have serious emotional problems which interfere with their overall ability to function in an academic environment. A formal psychiatric and/or psychological syndrome must be present in addition to an emotional disability that clearly affects the child's performance in school before categorization as "Seriously Emotional Disturbed" can be utilized. It is also very important to simultaneously treat any and all learning and cognitive disorders. Therefore, some children may need categorization as "Multiply Handicapped" as more than two areas of disability may be present.

School systems also have the provisions to continually "review" a child's individualized educational program and upgrade treatment if warranted. If a child is severely impaired and non-functioning both at home and in school, the school and parents can work together to try to arrange a self-contained special education program or, in the most extreme cases, a residential program.

Many families have been told by school officials that these provisions do not exist. But under public law, families with seriously disabled and disturbed children still have the right to the most suitable educational program and curriculum. Parents must be advocates for their special-needs child.

If the school says that the only option is residential treatment (which is typically warranted only if a child is non-functional and out-of-control at school), then families have the right to appeal all the way to the superintendent. Usually school systems have a special committee that reviews residential placement applications. Many families may request residential care programs as a last resort.

Many families seek out an educational advocate or legal counsel to help support them through the special education process, and in working collaboratively with school officials when arranging a comprehensive and long-term educational treatment program. This type of negotiation is often required as difficult children with both learning and emotional problems may not always respond to traditional in-classroom supportive services. These special children typically require a more aggressive special-educational curriculum.

A national support and information center named "The Parent Educational Advocacy Training Center" or PEATC for short, provides an excellent newsletter on all of the laws and national policies pertaining to special education. For those interested in joining, they can write to: PEATC at 10340 Democracy Lane, Suite 206, Fairfax, Virginia, 22030; Phone: 703-691-7826.

Role models and Trainers. Utilize coaches, responsible adults at church or synagogue, neighbors or anyone who is a positive factor in the child's life. Anyone strong, consistent and supportive to the family can be a helpful role model. Honor students at local high schools or colleges are often very strong influences for difficult children, particularly the gifted underachiever. Children who are struggling both academically and behaviorally often respond much better to strong peers either their age or slightly older. This is particularly important for the only child who may desperately desire an older sibling figure to look up to and model. Single parents should seek out individuals willing to mentor your child and support the family treatment program.

ADDITIONAL PSYCHOLOGICAL INTERVENTIONS:

Reality therapy. The principle framework for the child is to adhere to and function "within reality." Working on improving reality is a lifelong goal, especially with difficult children. In the Level Three program, the written and verbal homework assignments are part of reality therapy. Many parents report constant fights over homework. This is absolutely unnecessary. Homework struggles often lead to family conflict. It is much more important to have positive family relationships and cooperation as opposed to lamenting when the child fails to complete homework. Education is certainly important, but "emotional education" must take priority at this point. The goal is to establish a working relationship with your child. Over the course of time, this will translate into completing homework or doing other tasks which are required.

As part of reality therapy, the following three reality principles need to be continually emphasized to the child :

(1) Understanding the difference between right and wrong.
(2) Taking responsibility for all actions with no blaming or avoidance.
(3) Respecting yourself and others at all times.

Parents and professionals alike will find the basic principals of reality therapy to be extremely straight forward and common sense oriented. Michael Glaser's book "Reality Therapy" in addition to "Using Reality Therapy" written by Robert Wubbolding (see Reading List) provide excellent guidelines and a "flow chart" for reality therapy principals which need to be incorporated into a child's home and therapy treatment plan.

In condensing reality therapy into the most basic and helpful forms, responsible adults need to train the child to function in reality at all times; be responsible at all times; and always know the difference of right versus wrong. Henceforth, the three major "R's". Also, children need to be taught the most important basic needs that all of us living in reality need to master:

1. To learn to give love and accept love.
2. To feel worthwhile to ourselves and others.
3. To maintain a positive standard of behavior at all time without excuses.

Parents and therapists need to tap in to a child's (and family's) basic human needs. Reality therapy focuses heavily on principals of simple responsibility and active participation with others. The following are basic principles (per Wubbolding's "Using Reality Therapy, 1988) that should be an integral part of my three tiered level system, particularly when a child reaches levels Two and Three:

1. Human beings are motivated to fulfill their needs and wants. Human needs are common to all people. Wants are unique to each individual.

2. The difference (frustration) between what human beings want and what they perceive they are getting from their environment produces specific

behaviors which can be both positive but often negative as they perceive they are being "shorted" from their basic needs.

3. Human behavior is composed of doing, thinking, feeling and physiologic behavior. Human behavior is purposeful and is designed to close the gap between what someone wants and what they perceive they are getting. Therefore, behaviors come from inside and are based solely on the choices we make.

4. Doing, thinking and feeling are inseparable aspects of behavior and ones we generate from within ourselves. These are all choices we make freely. No one influences us as we make our own decisions.

5. Human beings see the world through perceptions. Some of our perceptions are accurate and some are distorted reality. All people must learn to perceive reality the way it is. Remember, reality is right in front of us and we must respond with respect, responsibility and knowing the right thing to do when dealing with a frustrating situation.

Throughout the use of reality therapy principals, an individual is continually confronted and asked "what are you doing NOW?" It is the therapist's and family's responsibility to suspend judgement and criticism The focus needs to be on a continual redirection to follow all principals of reality, responsibility and doing the right thing. It is very important for the individual to focus on how they will get what they want and need by strictly following the "three R's" of reality therapy. In reality therapy there is no room for excuses, blaming others, or making partial promises such as "I'll try" or "I'll think about it." Reality therapy requires an absolute commitment and continual practice via homework assignments and supervision in addition to continually staying in the "here and now" which, again is the reality we all live in.

Cognitive therapy. This is a specialized type of reality and individual therapy which focuses very heavily on teaching the difficult child different ways to think, reason, problem solve and apply logic instead of acting out. Within cognitive therapy, the child is often given a great deal of written homework assignments which list out goals and objectives and require brainstorming in order to create a larger repertoire of solutions to common problems. In addition, these assignments teach the child and family to "attack" irrational and illogical thought patterns and beliefs. It is a very focused and directive form of therapy which puts pressure on the child to replace negative and pessimistic thought patterns with more optimistic and affirmative statements, leading to more productive behaviors.

Contracts are a critical part of this therapy as children, families and therapists work very closely together to make certain that a new set of words, phrases and overall thought patterns become part of day-to-day interactions and replace the previous non-productive attitudes and communications. Part of the contract requires that all family members keep close track and "score" each individual's performance, successes and failures. Cognitive therapy promotes the creation of healthy competition between family members by motivating with positive thought patterns and leadership.

A famous Greek philosopher in the first century made a profound statement:"Man is disturbed not by things, but rather by the views he takes of them." Parents and therapists alike need to understand that negative feelings and destructive patterns of behaviors are founded in how individuals view themselves, others, and their world. Becoming familiar with the most common cognitive errors and logical fallacies will help to control negative emotions and change destructive patterns of behaviors by taking a more realistic and less disturbing "view of the world."

The following are a few examples of cognitive errors that are countered by thoughts that are less distorted and more realistic:

1.	Catastrophizing	"It would be terrible not to get this job."
	Realistic Thought	"I would be disappointed, but I will find another job."
2.	Perfectionism	"I must always do things perfectly."
	Practical Thinking	"I know it is not possible to do everything perfectly, but I will do the best I can."
3.	Overgeneralization	"I am a total failure at everything—everyone is better than I am."
	Realistic Thought	"I may not be the best, but I am trying as hard as I can."
4.	Personalizing	"Everybody is out to get me—everyone is against me."
	Practical Thinking	"It is just not possible that everyone in the world is out to get me. I am sure I am having trouble with certain people."
5.	Fault-Finding	"It is my parents fault that they don't understand me."
	Practical Thinking	"I have a relationship with my parents that needs to improve in terms of communication. We may both be responsible (not at fault) for the problems."
6.	Pathologizing	"My child (or my parents) are crazy—they must have a serious psychiatric problem which is making them act up."
	Practical Thinking	"There might be an emotional problem involved, but we everyone in this family is responsible to help resolve this problem since there are treat-

ments for psychiatric difficulties."

7. Overpowering — "You will do whatever I tell you all the time or else. You will obey my orders."

   Realistic Thought — "I am the parent and am in charge. This is a family that will work together."

8. Entitlement — "They are children and they are going to make a lot of mistakes, and they will grow out of their problems. They were deprived and need a lot of now."

   Realistic Thought — "There may have been problems with our child's early years, but they must learn to work through their difficulties and not feel entitled to get what they want when they want."

Classical and Operant conditioning. Classical conditioning has been around for many years and can be taught by a skilled behavioral therapist. Think of Pavlov who was able to condition an animal to perform a new response by continually emphasizing a positive reinforcement attached to a "cue." Well, when trying to teach a child a new behavior it is very important to "condition" the child with a specific cue, such as a hand or facial gesture which indicates that a behavior must be performed immediately. This takes a great deal of practice, training, and positive reinforcement.

In operant conditioning, the goal is to continually reinforce any and all pro-social behavior. This desired behavior must be continually coaxed until it becomes an automatic response for the child. A gradual reduction of reinforcements should take place over time; for example, giving reinforcements at intervals, such as at the end of the day or week. After achieving a regular pattern of desired behavior, it becomes very important to maintain reinforcements at varying intervals, while also alternating the type of reinforcers to prevent the child from becoming bored. For example, children get tired of just getting to watch television or just receiving outside privileges or, even allowances. Parents may wish to be creative and use various other reinforces, such as extra-special activities with the family, rewards (within reason) that the child may request, extra activities with peers, special foods, or other reasonably priced items which can be distributed daily or weekly, based on practicality.

Applied Behavioral Analysis (ABA). These techniques, pioneered by Dr. O. Ivar Lovaas, have often been reserved for the treatment of autism but are extremely beneficial concepts for any family with a developmentally disabled, mentally retarded, brain damaged, autistic, or even a severally behaviorally and psychiatrically disturbed child.

ABA therapy is not harmful when delivered properly and consistently, as the emphasis is on systematically introducing small, measurable units of pro-social behavior. Every skill is broken down into small and manageable steps with appropriate responses that are followed by either intense reinforcers or immediate consequences. These lessons are repeated multiple times throughout the day. Rewards are used until the child is able to respond spontaneously and consistently. Consequences also fade out, but are reinstituted if there are any signs of regression or noncompliance. It is extremely important for parents and ABA trainers to record and evaluate the child's hour-to-hour and day-to-day progress in order to keep up with the timing and pacing of "teaching sessions" that are determined individually for each child. Under the ABA model of rehabilitation, a child can be said to have mastered a skill when he or she provides the appropriate response at least 80 percent of the time over a two-day period with at least two different teachers or trainers (parents included).

Individual and Family Therapy. It is highly recommended that the difficult child be involved in adjunctive psychological care with a trained and competent child and adolescent psychologist and/or psychiatrist who has direct and extensive experience in dealing with behavior-management programs. The traditional therapist who seeks to use only "talk therapy" or very passive interventions will only set the family up for another failure and frustration.

Family support groups. It is very important for families who have difficult children to rely on each other for support and exchange of ideas. Multi-family support groups on the Internet are very helpful as families having children with similar problems often link into various chat rooms and exchange ideas, research, names of professionals who have helped and lists of reading materials and national conferences.

Play therapy. In a counseling setting, the difficult child can often benefit by working with a play therapist to address problems of aggression, defiance, social skill deficits and bonding-attachment disorders. A qualified play therapist will often utilize special toys, dolls, puppets, various therapeutic games, drawing/art therapy and role playing. This is a very useful intervention and can be performed in the therapist's office, or with the therapist's instruction, at home. Difficult children often "open up" and talk more freely if play therapy is introduced and the quality of the play interpreted for the parents to better understand the child's emotional struggles.

A therapist should regularly review with you the child's conflicts, strengths, and weaknesses, and also provide families with homework assignments which are a continuation of therapy to be worked on with the child in the comfort of their own home. Make sure you talk with the therapist after every session so that you are closely monitoring progress and problems. Some children and therapists get very caught up in the play interaction and leave out parents. Therefore, play therapy requires the parents active involvement at periodic intervals as opposed to just having the child attend therapy on their own for onc hour a week.

Art Therapy. A very integral part of play therapy is art therapy. Most all children love to draw which is a way of expressing themselves. Art therapy needs to be structured by providing the child both free drawing time and specific assignments such as drawing various family members, scenes and situations from their lives, or any type of problem which has occurred. For example, many children who are depressed and angry will draw very revealing pictures. The child who has been abused and neglected or deprived as the result of living in an institutional setting will draw incredibly painful pictures. Art therapy can also emphasize the drawing of "comic strips" which list out sequences of events and problems in the child's life and another set of pictures which may outline possible solutions. The use of colors which the child selects can also help understand their emotions. In general, art therapy is a great way to interact with difficult children, particularly children who are emotionally "shut down" or the child who has prominent language delays which make it difficult to express themselves verbally.

Therapeutic games. While children are working their way through the program, therapeutic games can provide a way of reaching them. Games such as the "The Talking, Feeling and Doing Game" created by Dr. Richard Gardner, a child psychiatrist, are excellent for family use. (See Appendix for companies making therapeutic games). Children actually enjoy therapeutic games. They provide an outlet for anger and frustration as well as an alternate way of interacting with family members. Positive completion of therapeutic games should be regarded as another goal and objective for the child and should be rewarded with tokens.

Animal Therapy. The single most important thing about pets is that the majority give unconditional love and affection which everyone needs, particularly difficult children. While many troubled children can be cruel to animals, arranging for the child to take charge of the animals care and training may make the difficult child feel empowered at some level. Also, even the most difficult child needs someone to talk to, and it is amazing in watching a belligerent and unmanageable child speak kindly to an animal and treat it with great affection. Big dogs seem to work the best as they are not fragile, but any animal may do. Try to find an animal which is relatively low maintenance as the difficult child is already high maintenance and parents most likely do not need additional work.

Social-interactional therapies. It is very important for difficult children to become involved in a wide variety of social therapies such as sports recreation, or music and dance. These difficult children need a great deal of work in learning to follow directions in a group setting while also learning to appropriately interact with peers. Small group activities are usually the best, such as marshal arts, gymnastics, swimming and non-aggressive competitive sports like soccer or baseball.

PsychoDrama. Children who are just learning to deal with their emotions often do very well in theatrical activities. Getting these children involved in musicals, dance, or plays where they can act out roles and social themes can often be very helpful in building self-confidence and assertiveness. PsychoDrama is a great form of family therapy (and entertainment) which can be done at home. This is a great way for family members to interact and work out emotional conflicts via fantasy exchanges as opposed to directly confronting each other in an accusatory or provocative manner.

Sports and Recreation. Martial arts, gymnastics, swimming, soccer or any vigorous activity helps a child focus while building self control. Being a "star" is not mandatory, only healthy efforts and cooperation with the team.

Medication, Medication, Medication. Before undertaking any type of medication, families should go back and reread the section on Comprehensive Assessment since it is important to really know the problem before treating it. It is imperative a family should start with a comprehensive multi-discipline evaluation by all the recommended specialists **before** medication begins. Specifically, in order to properly diagnosis the difficult child, we must initiate comprehensive medical, pediatric-neurological, neuropsychological and psycho-educational evaluations. Medication is only one part of a treatment program—it is not the solution. **All medications must be carefully monitored by the child's physician on a monthly basis**.

Medications can be extremely helpful if handled properly. For example, ADHD children often develop coexisting problems such as depression and mood disorders. It is often better to treat the larger problem— the emotional difficulties. Or, I recommend treating the problem that causes the most distress for the child and family. With these factors in mind, the more difficult child may better respond to treatment for depression and unstable moods. Medications for ADHD such as Ritalin, Dexedrine, Cylert, Concerta, Strattera, Metadate and Adderal are frequently used and can be very effective if we know exactly that the child has only ADHD. Stimulant medications for ADHD certainly target attention problems and hyperactivity, but can have a great deal of side-effects such as appetite suppression, sleep cycle disturbance, irritability, depression, restlessness, crying spells and a general "rebound or sling-shot effect" when the medication wears off (usually anywhere from 3-to-6 hours later). Rebound effects are often described as a resurgence of hyperactivity and impulsivity and a child who appears even more out of control than when they took the medication. This is why ADHD and ADHD medications need to be very carefully assessed and monitored for both effectiveness and appropriateness.

The newer antidepressants which are termed Selective Serotonin ReuptakeInhibitors (SSRI's) are Prozac, Zoloft and Paxil. These are very good medications, especially Zoloft based on its action with dopamine (reduces agitation) which can target children who have a high level of irritability, mood agitation, negative thought patterns and behaviors, in addition to obsessive and compulsive traits. Caution needs to be maintained in giving SSRI's to children. While the drug certainly helps moods and emotions, it can often cause an "activating effect," making the child hyperactive and restless. These medications can be used in low doses and then gradually increased until the child responds. They should be given at the lowest possible dose that produces a response. This category of antidepressants has been extensively studied and found to be very safe for use with children. The myth that these medications cause suicidal behaviors is just a myth, although this category of medication should not be given for individuals who clearly have manic depressive illness or a psychotic disorder.

There is a new category of antidepressants known as "atypical antidepressants" which have been going through extensive research and study for the treatment of difficult or "atypical" cases. Many very depressed and agitated children who have coexisting attentional and conduct problems have been found to do very well on Wellbutrin and sometimes Effexor as long as they have been cleared by their attending physician for seizure disorders or any type of neurological problem. These medicines are very unique in that they "target" specific brain receptors that rapidly reduce mood agitation, aggressive outbursts and, to a degree, improve distorted thinking due to clinical depression. There are a multitude of new antidepressant medications such as Cylexa and Remeron which target different brain neurotransmitters with the ultimate goal of finding the correct "match" so that a child's grossly inappropriate behaviors and volatility can be reduced to a manageable level so that traditional behavioral and psychological interventions will be more effective. It is a good idea to steer clear of the majority of the older tricyclic antidepressant medications such as Imipramine, Desipramine or Elavil as these medications have a lot of side effects which make children feel physically ill. Also, This category of tricyclic antidepressants requires a lot more medical management in terms of blood tests and heart monitoring. Remember, children hate medication in general and they hate blood tests. Keep antidepressant medication focused and simple, and know what you are medicating.

Children who have been diagnosed as having a volatile mood disorder which may be in the category of Bipolar illness (manic-depressive disorder) can benefit from trials of Lithium, Tegretol, Depakote, Trileptal or a combination of mood stabilizers with other classes of medications. Children with Bipolar mood disorders often do well on mood stabilizers combined with psychostimulant medication if there is coexisting ADHD. It is very important to remember, however, that the more medication produces more side effects. With this factor in mind, families with a possible Bipolar child need to be very conservative with medication and very aggressive in the management to avoid side effects.

Nowadays, physicians often prescribe medications which have been used for blood pressure such as Clonidine (Catepress) or Tenex. These are very good and safe medications to use in the early stages of assessment and treatment since they rapidly produce a state of calmness and decrease volatile moods, agitation and aggressive outbursts. Also, This category of medication greatly helps agitated children sleep better. Anti-hypertensives such as Clonidine and Tenex are also used when there is a question of ADHD, particularly with extreme hyperactivity and impulsivity which has not responded well to the stimulants. Clonidine or Tenex are often used to augment stimulant use due to their calming effect and assistance during the rebound stage and can be used on an "as needed basis".

Children who have neurodevelopmental syndromes, such as autism or multiple and severe learning disabilities, Tourette's or tic disorders, or even the post-institutionalized child who is over-stimulated will do very well on Clonidine or Tenex. Again, this category of medication is very conservative and a recommended starting point although major pharmacological research has been done on using broad spectrum psychotropics to target the difficult behaviors of autistic spectrum disorders..

In the case of the volatile and aggressive child, possibly with a diagnosis of Bipolar illness, Schizophrenia or even brain damage may respond to low-dose anti-psychotic medications. The older/more traditional anti-psychotics such as Haldol, Thorazine, Stelazine, Mellaril are not used as frequently due to side effects. There has been tremendous research in the areas of Neuropharmacology to develop a new category of anti-psychotics termed "atypical anti-psychotics." Risperdal (Risperidone) and Zyprexa (Olanzapine) are two of the newest anti-psychotic medications which have been found to be very helpful with out-of-control children. These medications target several brain neuroreceptors and seem to "clean up" negative, depressive and aggressive thinking and behaviors while also providing an appropriate amount of mild sedation needed for rest and sleep. Three new medications, Seroquel, Abilify and Geodon are showing promise for chronic and medication resistant children with major psychiatric and behavioral disorders. All of these atypical anti-psychotics are sometimes used at a conservative level for the treatment of very severe ADHD children who have not responded to other medications.

Again, it is very important to realize that children often hate medication and the side effects. Many medications do have side effects requiring close monitoring by a child psychiatrist or pharmacologist. It is extremely important to stress that medications are helpful, but children should not be treated like drug depositories and given a medication for every symptom that emerges. If this occurs, one is only asking for trouble in terms of medication compliance and potential medical risks.

Sometimes the treatment is worse than the illness when it comes to medication.

Medications Helpful for the Treatment of Chronic Enuresis (bedwetting) and Encopresis (soiling behaviors/problems with defecation)

After consulting with your primary physician and ruling out any type of medical problems, there are some medications which can be helpful for the treatment of chronic bedwetting or soiling behaviors. It should emphasized that these medications work in only a portion of the cases and need to be carefully monitored by the prescribing physician. Many times there is a medical or genetic component to a child's bedwetting behaviors with many physicians and professionals stating "they will grow out of the problem." This sometimes does not happen, and it the child is unable to leave the home in fear of having a "accident." When the child's self-esteem and social skills become compromised it is time to consider more of a medical intervention.

For example, enuresis or chronic wetting behaviors are sometimes treated with low-dose Imipramine (Tofranil) which is a tricyclic antidepressant that can sometimes have side-effects if the dose is too high. The exact action of this medication which is given right before bedtime is not completely understood, although its chemical action seems to target certain brain receptors and "timing mechanisms" which are irregular in the child who wets the bed. After just a few days of administration, many children report a cessation of the wetting behaviors although if the medicine is discontinued too quickly, the wetting reoccurs almost immediately. Should this medication be implemented, it should be utilized for at least 6 months.

Another medication often used is a nasal spray or pill named DDAVP. This medication involves a complicated exchange of neurochemical and hormonal activity in the brain chemistry, and is reported to help in at least 50% of the cases prescribed. Again, it is important to discuss this medication with your pediatrician or urologist.

Children who have chronic encopresis or soiling behaviors may have medical problems and require either aggressive or conservative treatment. Treatments can range from prescription medications to the simple use of mineral oil to ease the digestive and bowel movement process. Many children who are encopretic have emotional and behavioral problems ranging from anger, aggressiveness, rage, or highly immature and infantile behavioral patterns. Depression and mood disorders are frequently seen in children who have encopresis.

With these psychological factors in mind, many children can improve with medications that target mood agitation, irritability, anxiety or rage. SSRI medications such as Prozac, Zoloft and Paxil have been found to be helpful in many cases of encopresis. Conservative anti-anxiety medications such as Xanax, Serax, Buspar or Klonopin have also been found to be helpful. Hyperactive and impulsive children tend to have the highest degree of enuretic and encopretic behaviors so it is important to "target" their impulsivity in order for them to be in better self-control. Therefore, medications which can help the child calm down and relax may yield positive results.

Alternatives to Prescription Medication.

Nowadays, there has been mixed feelings about the use of prescription psychiatric medications. Many people are very interested in trying any and all type of medications, particularly Ritalin, whereas there is still a large group of parents totally afraid of trying any psychiatric medication for their child.

Alternatives to medication have gained great popularity. For example, the Feingold Diet Program is designed for Attention Deficit Hyperactivity Disordered children and children with mood and behavioral problems (Feingold Association in the United States, PO Box 6550, Alexandria, VA 22306, (703) 768-FAUS).

Food allergies have been widely studied but do not show a great correlation to childhood emotional and behavioral disorders, although there are certainly isolated cases. Many people spend thousands of dollars searching for a food allergy which is producing their child's difficulties, only to find out their children are tested as being allergic to everything. It is very important for families to consult a physician specializing in allergies in order to assess the need for further (and quite expensive) testing.

St. John's Wort, a natural herb and essential amino acid, has been used in other countries for hundreds of years as a natural treatment for depression and mood problems. St. John's Wort has gained tremendous popularity in the United States since being available as an over the counter, nonprescription medication. This natural herb, sometimes combined with Ginseng, has been found to be very effective in many children and adults who seem to have low grade depression, anxiety, restlessness or general nervous conditions. Adults typically take 3 pills per day with children of any age being able to tolerate anywhere from one-half to full adult strength without any incidences of side effects or drug interactions. St. John's Wort is safe and is now being studied on the national level and compared to prescription antidepressant medications.

Melatonin is also another natural amino acid which aides in improving the sleep cycle. Melatonin is sold over the counter in pill form having 1, 2 or 3 mg. The adult recommended dose is 3 mg one hour before bedtime, with children being able to tolerate either one-half the adult dose or even full strength if the child is older and has a significant sleep disorder (trouble falling asleep, staying asleep or waking up early). Melatonin appears to interact with serotonin centers in the brain which is an important neurochemical tied into both sleep and mood. Melatonin has been widely studied and found to be very safe without side effects, although there are skeptics regarding its use in children. Some feel children may be producing enough of their own natural Melatonin and that any addition places the child at risk for "serotonin syndrome" which can cause dizziness and mild confusion, and numbness and tingling in the extremities. While this mild side effect (which goes away immediately after stopping the Melatonin) may raise concerns, it has mostly shown up when someone is taking several other medications, particularly Prozac or other Selected Serotonin Reuptake Inhibitors.

It has been my experience that agitated, moody, depressed and irritable children do very well on St. John's Wort at the adult strength as a precursor or "stepping stone" to a more intensive prescription medication such as Prozac. It is certainly worth a try for those families wishing to be conservative with medications. Many homeopathic and naturapathic physicians are consulted and a host of other "natural substances" are often tried, all with varying success.

Summary

When handled properly, comprehensively and aggressively, medications can be extremely helpful for the difficult child as long as medication interventions are not the "starting point" or the only aspect of a child's treatment. All children on medication should be involved in the previously recommended therapies with close coordination between therapists and the medical doctor prescribing medication. It is also very important for families to find a medical doctor who will be open to other opinions, and who will be creative and aggressive, but who will not overmedicate the child or resort back to medications which have previously failed. The optimal treatment plan is for a "team" of experts (medical, psychological, educational, family therapy, and adjunctive personnel, such as physical therapists, occupational therapists, sensory-integrative therapists, etc.) to work together and consistently exchange information in order to update the child's progress and address problems before situations deteriorate and become out of control.

Chapter 7

Helping Hopeless Children: An Instructional Guide for Professionals

Professionals wishing to take on the challenge of a hopeless child <u>and</u> those who are willing to ascribe to principles set forth in this book (which are openly acknowledged as being aggressive, unconventional, and highly provocative and stimulating) need to be able to make a full commitment to engage in a treatment program that may fall out of the boundaries of their professional training and practical clinical experience.

The treatment professional willing to work with the most difficult children and families needs to have extensive experience in all areas of child, adolescent and family development and therapeutic principles. This treatment approach is <u>not</u> recommended for treatment professionals who: have only seen a few children; who do not have the educational background or willingness to research and seek out additional training in the areas of medical, psychological, psychiatric, and neuropsychological diagnoses; who are not willing to engage in very directive supervision from other highly qualified professionals who have been dealing with hopeless children for many years and understand the importance of an aggressive recovery program.

Additionally, This treatment program is <u>not</u> recommended for therapists who ascribe to older and more traditional approaches about treatment programs that focus solely on nurturing, communication building, and just using "time-out" techniques when a child is difficult. While many families do, indeed, benefit from traditional "family therapy," the child who qualifies for helpless and hopeless (per the terms and guidelines set forth in this book) clearly requires more aggressive interventions than have been traditionally taught in graduate-level treatment programs. Furthermore, with our understanding regarding the complexities of children who have come from very deprived and damaging environments, we have now come to realize that the only way a child will ever "recover" is to be challenged with very aggressive, somewhat provocative, and unorthodox treatment programs which may not be readily accepted.

Families seeking out innovative and aggressive therapists for their most difficult child must <u>absolutely</u> interview the therapist and go over professional background, training, amount of cases treated, in addition to personal and professional feelings regarding engaging in an unorthodox and aggressive treatment approach. This is a very important stage of treatment as many families with very difficult children have been in numerous treatment programs without positive results and do <u>not</u> need to go through the "failure cycle" once again as this only serves to make the parents feel helpless and hopeless themselves and not able to trust that anyone will be able to help them. This is a very sensitive matter as many therapists may feel somewhat insulted or even "put out" if they are interviewed as an appropriate treatment provider. One way to circumvent this uncomfortable experience is be very open and expressive and to ask what treatment programs the family has been through and what they really want to get out of this professional situation. Likely, the therapist will need to be creative and different from the approaches and will need to allow for a better (and more honest and direct) interchange between patient and family.

THE "IDEAL" TREATMENT PROVIDER

As stated in other sections of this book, the treatment provider most able to work with the most difficult child has to be an extremely direct and somewhat confrontational individual who is not afraid of anger, rage or uncontrollable behaviors. What I mean by this is that the treatment professional must have at lest some practical experience in seeing totally out-of-control children, or children who have failed in so many treatment programs that they truly meet the criteria for "helpless and hopeless."

Many treatment providers may state "I can try to help you," but unfortunately this is just not an adequate statement. The ideal mental health treatment provider must be highly skilled on several levels:

1. Extensive skills in working with the most disturbed child who is prone toward aggressive, violent, highly oppositional, and intensely manipulative behaviors. A treatment professional who is extremely kind, over sensitive, or even gullible is not likely to be successful.

2. The treatment professional must have extensive experience in highly structured, focused, and goal-directed therapy.

The therapist must be able to confront both child and family regarding any type of problems, improvements or regressions in treatment. Additionally, the therapist must be "action oriented" and provide constant homework assignments, reinforcements, review sessions, in addition to serving as a strong "guide." This is a very important consideration as many traditional therapists tend to be more laid back and "reflective." I tend to call a proper therapist-family relationship "the involvement" as this really signifies a form of attachment to each other in order to work towards both short and long-term goals. While there certainly needs to be a business component (i.e., schedules and financial arrangements), it is also very important for the therapist to be open and willing to discuss certain personal aspects with the family in order to "humanize" the therapeutic experience make the family feel more at home. This is a very important consideration given the fact that many families who have encountered therapists who have not been able to help them in the past, described them as "cold and detached," "disinterested," "uncertain," "not highly knowledgeable," "easily manipulated," or even "incompetent." Additionally, families have often described psychiatrists as only "pushing pills."

Along the lines with statement pertaining to psychiatry, it is very important for families having helpless and hopeless children to consider starting off with a formal therapeutic program and then moving back into a medication program. So many families try to look for rapid relief by medications which often serves to only "medicate the symptoms."

Proper treatment professionals must also be willing to seek out supervision from more experienced therapists. This may take the form of attending lectures, workshops, or contacting national experts for periodic phone consultation. There are excellent training programs available across the country which deal with very disturbed children. In particular, the Parent Network for Post-Institutionalized Child, and Friends of Russian and Ukrainian Adoptees run at least four or five intensive weekend training sessions a year for therapists and families who are dealing with adopted and/or post-institutionalized children. These workshops cover medical, neuropsychological, psychiatric, educational, speech and language, occupational and physical therapy, and new and aggressive psychotherapeutic interventions. There are many medical and psychological specialists across the country who specialize in "Adoption Medicine", meaning they are well trained in children coming from troubled backgrounds.

Male or Female? Preference is the Key

Many people ask about having a male or female therapist. This really does not matter as long as the therapist is qualified and meets the strict criteria for working with the most difficult cases. The only time it seems to be important is when there is a definite and documented need within the family structure. For example, in the case of a single mother who has a very difficult child, it would be very important to have a male therapist involved as the child may not have had the experience in their life to deal with a male figure, and this may be a very key factor in establishing and maintaining a strong therapeutic bond. The reciprocal may also apply to the single father who is raising a difficult child without a mother. A female therapist would be highly recommended in this situation.

There are also times in which co-therapists are recommended. For example, a family that is highly dysfunctional and has a large amount of children may often be an overwhelming task for a single therapist. Sometimes a male-female therapist team is an outstanding recommendation for the family that needs tremendous interventions. Along these lines, in-home therapy teams are sometimes assigned to families. There are many emerging "home-based" treatment programs that actually go to the family's home and work with the family on their own grounds as opposed to coming to a more sterile office situation. This is an excellent form of intervention for the more dysfunctional family.

It would be optimal if the treating therapist would devote the majority of his or her professional practice to working with the most dysfunctional children and families. This therapist would be very key in "linking" families together to provide group support and an open exchange of ideas. Along these lines, multi-family group therapy is a very good treatment option. Families would have to sign releases of information in order to disclose confidential material, but this can be an extremely helpful form of treatment for both family and therapist as much can be accomplished by utilizing the old term "strength in numbers."

Support for the Treatment Professional

There are certainly many treatment professionals who have excellent qualifications and years of experience. It should be emphasized in this section that no one (and I mean no one) is exempt from becoming burned out and overwhelmed.

Children in families who are extremely out of control demand tremendous attention and can often drain treatment professionals. It is very important for the treatment professional to continually analyze their own strengths, weaknesses, emotional and physical states.

Signs of professional burn-out are: fatigue, irritability, isolation, withdrawal, depression, and changes in their own family structure. The reason to discuss therapist "burn-out" is that it is very common to absorb a tremendous amount of emotions from disturbed children and families and it is difficult to get rid of these feelings after hours.

Therapists working with the most disturbed children need their own support and stress- reduction strategies. In addition to collaborating with other professionals to create a bit of a "group therapy approach," it is very important for therapists to take ample time off from and engage in a wide variety of recreational activities. Therapists sometimes need therapy of their own, and if that's the case, it is very important for to cut down the case load and refer out cases that may be overly demanding. Another way to assist the therapist who is going through stress is to provide co-therapists in the session under the auspices of providing even "stronger support" to the family.

It is never appropriate for the therapist to disclose to the family that they are overwhelmed and burned-out as the family will quickly lose faith and interest in pursuing yet another potential failure in treatment. While therapist-patient disclosure is important, there are some things that the therapist must work on their own and be able to be at a level of professionalism to know when it is time for them to quit and refer the family to another person, which is a sign of strength as opposed to weakness.

Hopefully, there will be a new subgroup of therapists who truly specialize in working with the helpless and hopeless child. Nowadays, there are so many different treatment options available, but families who have the most difficult child really need to find a treatment professional who has the title of "expert with the most difficult." Success in treatment is measured by the level and intensity of commitment between therapist and family, and willingness to try anything and everything that will help salvage the helpless and hopeless child. Anyone who believes that they can "fix the problem 100 percent" is really not able to fix the problem 10 percent. The therapist who ascribes to the "80 percent rule" seems to be the treatment professional of choice.

More specifically, if a difficult child can reach a level of appropriate and successful behavioral patterns 80 percent of the time that therapist has done an excellent job and truly meets the criteria for "expert" based on practicality and acceptance of a less-than-perfect situation and outcome. Sometimes families expect perfection, which is a totally unrealistic expectation. Hopefully, families and treatment professionals can both agree on the 80 percent rule and work collaboratively towards a mutually rewarding outcome. Therapists sometimes take the heat as they have the privilege (and difficulties) of providing to the family very direct and difficult material to digest. The therapist must not take the family's anger and rage personally or even the times that the therapist is blamed for the problems by "not helping fast enough." There is an excellent phrase that those of us who treat very disturbed children and families use regularly: "Please don't kill the messenger—we are just doing our job of delivering good or bad news." Experts have the professional and ethical obligation of delivering all types of information, whether it be good, bad, or painful.

Chapter 8

Where Do We Go From Here?

When Enough is Enough

Life sometimes distributes problems and challenges that require faith and stamina to overcome. There gets to be a time in the lives of every family with a difficult child where a break is necessary. Previous sections have talked about utilizing adjunctive services, including social service programs or respite care centers.

While the focus of this book is to encourage families to put forth 110 percent diligence, effort and faith in "starting over" to recondition their child, there are clearly times where everyone involved needs to take a break and gain a new perspective.

The difficult child takes a toll on marital relationships and the relationships of parents and other siblings. Signs of complete parental burn-out are: changes in the ability for a parent to function at work, symptoms of clinical depression, appetite and sleep disturbances, negative thought patterns and behaviors, and social withdrawal and isolation; these are all quite common in the burned-out parent. An increase in smoking or other types of reckless behaviors are also warning signs, as well as anger or rage directed toward the difficult child.

Often, parents need to work through their own attachment and re-attachment issues in separate therapy. Regardless of the problem or parental response, parents need to be supported and commended for any and all efforts, even if the efforts have thus far failed.

Parents also need to be encouraged to maintain a strong social support system. It is a good idea to try to find other families who have experienced or who are currently experiencing similar problems; it will make you feel much less alone.

Prevention and Changes for the Next Generation

I would like to conclude with some thoughts on future prevention and how it relates to the coming generation.

We now know that genetics have an effect on overall behavior and temperament, however, the focus needs to fall more on "nurture," rather than the "nature." Namely, an intensely bonded and dynamic family system needs to be created; one that is strong enough and in tact enough to whether any and all storms.

In reviewing the main principles of childhood development, the most important factor is the child's attachment to the parents. A child needs to be in close proximity, both physically and emotionally, to the parents. Problems set in when a child is abused, neglected, abandoned, or has not been allowed to form proper bonding and attachment. Therefore, the most important area of change and prevention for the next generation needs to be focused on building a strong and stable childhood development, with the core foundation rooted in deep physical and emotional attachment from the earliest point possible.

Each and every parent and caretaker has a huge obligation to commit to their child. Each parent must support the other consistently and completely, even when disagreements in child-rearing strategies surface. From the birth of the child, parents must make a conscious effort to strongly bond and attach to the child. They must build a sense of safety, security and stability within the family system. Therapeutic holding should be practiced throughout early childhood development so that the child experiences sensory integration and nurturing.

As the child reaches toddler stage and begins having temper tantrums, parents should practice Level One holds. Discussions and negotiations with children this young never work. Therefore, parents need to take a strong role in both the discipline of the child and the nurturing and emotional training of the child.

Throughout the child's life, frequent "tests" need to be performed. Children and families should undergo regular scrutiny and critical self-evaluation of their performance. The assessment of strengths, weaknesses, and failures can often yield a tremendous amount of understanding.

Never underestimate the power of the family. It is vital for proper development that the family in and of itself, remains as closely bonded and attached as possible. Separation and divorce has been shown to influence a child's acting-out behaviors. Families need to pay attention to spirituality, group cohesiveness, and community and recreational involvement. Also, families must stress the importance of morals, values, and standards. Teach the difference from right and wrong and the importance of taking responsibility for one's own actions. Teach self-respect and respect for others.

Children need supervision, support and education in a non-threatening and consistent manner. Children and parents both may feel that supervision and parental guidance is a cumbersome task, yet it is the fundamental principle in turning the child into an active member of the household; namely, children learn by example. Families need to be willing to put aside personal differences in order to maintain unity and to imprint upon the child that there is no problem which cannot be solved so long as the family works as a team with deep commitment to one another. There should be no room in the family system for avoidance, secrets or denial, and all problems should be "embraced" rather than ignored.

Early assessment is the key. Problems need to be checked the moment they arise. Prevention and change for the next generation need to be instilled in our children very early on. There is a need for early educational and psychological intervention programs that stress the importance of bonding and attachment and how to deal with early aberrant behavior.

It has been very common in our society to view children as completely "independent human beings" who should, in no way, be controlled. I don't subscribe to this philosophy. Children need both parents actively involved in their life to guides, educate, discipline, and at times, control. Especially children who become out of control, and who often need extreme measures to get back into control.

I want to end this book by paying my utmost respect to each and every family who has encountered difficulties, and also, to the numerous patients I have personally assessed and treated. You have provided me the most rich and stimulating educational experience of my professional career. Success is truly driven by experience and understanding.

Appendix

Suggested Readings

Neuropsychology and Learning Disabilities

Helping Children Overcome Learning Disabilities by Jerome Rosner, Walker and Co. (ISBN 0-8027-7396-6)

Unlocking the Mysteries of Sensory Dysfunction by Anderson and Emmons (ISBN 1-885477-25-5)

Reaching Out to Children With FAS/FAE by Diane Davis (ISBN 0-87628-8573)

So Your Child Has a Learning Problem: Now What? (ISBN 0-88422-015-X)

Complete Learning Disabilities Handbook by Joan Harwell (ISBN 0-87628-239-7)

The Hyperactive Child Book by Kennedy, by Terdal and Fusetti (ISBN 0-312-08815-9)

The Myth of the A.D.D. Child by Thomas Armstrong (ISBN 0-525-93841-9)

Helping the Hyperactive Child by John Taylor (ISBN 1-55958-013-5)

Medications for School Age Children by Ronald Brown and Michael Sawyer (ISBN 1-57230-316-6)

How to Reach and Teach ADD/ADHD Children, Sandra Rief (ISBN 0-87628-413-6)

Neuropsychology of Perinatal Complications by Jeffrey Gray and Raymond Dean (ISBN 0-8261-5890-0)

Screening Children for Brain Impairment by Michael Franzen and Richard Berg (ISBN 0-8261-6390-4)

Therapeutic Education for Children with Traumatic Brain Injury by McKerns and MotchkavitZ (ISBN 0-88450-591-X)

If Your Child is Hyperactive, Inattentive, Impulsive and Distractible by Garber, Garber and Spizman (ISBN 0-394-57205-X)

Natural Alternatives to Prozac by Michael Murray (ISBN 0-688-14684-8)

Late Talking Children by Thomas Sowell (ISBN 0-465-03834-4)

The Borderline Child by Kenneth Robson (ISBN 0-7657-009-5)

Childrens Psychological Testing: A Guide for Non-Psychologists by David Woodbrich (ISBN 1-55766-277-0)

Handbook of Clinical Psychopharmacology for Therapists by John Preston, John O'Neal and Mary Talaga (ISBN 1-879237-73-3)

Diagnostic and Statistical Manual of Mental Disorders: Fourth Edition (ISBN 0-89042-062-9)

Teaching Children with Autism: Strategies for Initiating Positive Interactions and Improving Learning Opportunities by Robert Koegel and Lynn Koegel (ISBN 1-55766-180-4)

How Can I Help My Child? Early Childhood Research Directory for Parents and Professionals by Irene Shere (ISBN 0-9658244-0-3)

Children with Disabilities by Mark Batshaw (ISBN 1-55766-293-2)

Maybe You Know My Kid: A Parents Guide to Identifying, Understanding and Helping Your Child with Attention Deficit Hyperactivity Disorder by Mary Cahil Fowler (ISBN 1-55972-022-0)

Children with Tourette's Syndrome: A Parents Guide by Jim Eisenreich (ISBN 0-933149-44-1)

Shelly, the Hyperactive Turtle by Deborah Moss (ISBN 0-933149-31-X)

Children with Mental Retardation by Romayne Smith (ISBN 0-933149-39-5)

The Special Needs Reading List by Wilma Sweeney (ISBN 0-933149-74-3)

LOCOTOUR Program: Attention and Memory Training. Learning Fundamentals 1130 Grove Street, San Luis Obispo, CA 93401, Phone Number 1-800-777-3166

Earobics Phone Number: (1-888-328-8199), Fax: (1-888-328-5881). www.cogcon.com

Autism

Children with Autism: A Parents Guide by Michael Powers (ISBN 0-933149-16-6)

The Out-of-Sync Child, by Carol Stock Kranowitz, (ISBN 0399523863)

Teaching Developmentally Disabled Children, The Me Book, by O. Ivar Lovaas (ISBN 9780936104782)

A Work in Progress, by Ron Leaf and John McEachin (ISBN 0966526600)

Behavioral Intervention for Young Children with Autism, by Maurice, Green & Luce (ISBN 0890796831)

How the Special Needs Brain Learns, by David Sousa (ISBN 0761978518)

Therapeutic Education for the Child with Traumatic Brain Injury, From Coma to Kindergarten, by Dorothy McKerns, Ph.D. and Leslie McKerns Motchkavitz, BA, BS, (ISBN 088450591X)

Teaching Individuals with Developmental Delays, Basic Intervention Techniques, by O. Ivar Lovaas (ISBN 0890798893)

Fetal Alcohol Syndrome

Bridging the Gap, Raising a Child with Nonverbal Learning Disorder, by Rondalyn Varney Whitney, (ISBN 0399527559)

Cognitive-Behavioral Therapy for Persons with Disabilities, by Cynthia L. Radnitz, (ISBN 076570238X)

The The Enduring Effects of Prenatal Alcohol Exposure on Child Development, by Streissguth, Bookstein, Sampson, Barr (ISBN 0472104551)

The Challenge of Fetal Alcohol Syndrome, Overcoming Secondary Disabilities, by Ann Streissguth and Jonathan Kanter (ISBN 0295976500)

Fetal Alcohol Syndrome, A Guide for Families and Communities, by Ann Streissguth (ISBN 1557662835)

The Best I Can Be, Living with Fetal Alchol Syndrome or Effects, by Liz Kulp (ISBN 096370723X)

Our FAScinating Journey, by Jodee Kulp (ISBN 0963707248)

Attachment

Facilitating Developmental Attachment by Daniel Hughes (ISBN 0-7657-0038)

Becoming Attached by Robert Karen (ISBN 0-446-51634-1)

Parenting the Hurt Child by Gregory Keck (ISBN 1576833143)

Handbook for Treatment of Attachment-Trauma Problems in Children by Beverly James (ISBN 0-02-916005-7)

Don't Touch My Heart: Healing the Pain of an Unattached Child by Linda Mansfield and Christopher Waldmann (Tapestry Books: 1-800-765-2367)

Adopting the Hurt Child by Gregory Keck and Regina Kupecky (ISBN 0-89109-907-7)

The Bipolar Child, by Demitri Papolos, MD and Janice Papolos (ISBN 07679-03161)

Bipolar Disorder, A Family-Focused Treatment Approach, by David J. Miklowitz and Michael J. Goldstein (ISBN 1572302836)

Childhood Development and Behavior

High Risk: Children Without A Conscience by Magid and McKelvey (ISBN 0-553-05290-X)

Treating Traumatized Children by Beverly James (ISBN 0-669-20994-5)

Cognitive-Behavioral Therapy for Impulsive Children by Phillip Kendall and Lauren Braswell (ISBN 0-89862-013-9)

Coping with Teenage Depression by Kathleen McCoy (ISBN 0-451-13663-2)

Play In Family Therapy by Eliana Gill (ISBN 0-89862-757-5)

The Emotional Problems of Normal Children by Stanley Turecki (ISBN 0-553-07496-2)

Post-Traumatic Stress Disorder by Raymond Flannery (ISBN 0-8245-1194-8)

The Role of the Father in Child Development by Michael Lamb (ISBN 0-471-11771-4)

Children with Conduct Disorders by Paulina Kernberg and Saraleah Chazan (ISBN 0-465-01055-5)

Play Therapy with Children in Crisis by Nancy Boyd Webb (ISBN 0-89862-760-5)

Conduct Disorders of Childhood by Richard Gardner (ISBN 933812-32-9)

Playing for Their Lives by Dorothy Singer (ISBN 0-02-928903-3)

Reality Therapy by Michael Glasser (ISBN 0-06-080348-7)

Using Reality Therapy by Robert Wubbolding (ISBN 0-06-055123-2)

Understanding Your Child's Temperament, William Carey (ISBN 0-02-861664-2)

Raising Your Spirited Child by Mary Sheedy Kurchinka (ISBN 0-06-092328-8)

The Oppositional Child by O. Randall Braman (ISBN 1-55864-017-7)

Winning Cooperation From Your Child, Kenneth Wenning (ISBN 1-56821-733-1)

Positive Discipline A-Z by Jane Nelsen, Lynn Lott and Stephen Glenn (ISBN 1-55958-312-6)

Winning Them Over: How to Negotiate Successfully with Your Kids by Bradley Bucher (ISBN 0-8129-1206-3)

The Magic of Encouragement: Nurturing Your Child's Self-Esteem by Stephanie Marston (ISBN 0-688-09467-8)

Loving Your Child Is Not Enough: Positive Discipline that Works by Nancy Samalin (ISBN 0-670-81362-1)

You Can Say NO to your Teenager by Shallov, Sollinger, Spotts, Steinbrecher and Thorpe (ISBN 0-201-60826-X)

Parent and Child: Getting Through to Each Other by Lawrence Kutner (ISBN 0-380-71368-3)

Play Therapy Interventions with Childrens Problems by Landreth, Homeyer, Glover and Sweeney (ISBN 1-56821-482-2)

I'm On Your Side: Resolving Conflict with your Teenage Son or Daughter by Jane Nelson and Lynn Lott (ISBN 1-55958-039-9)

Cartoon Magic: How to Help Children Discover Their Rainbows Within by Richard Crowley and Joyce Mills (ISBN 0-945354-07-X)

Growing Up Sad: Childhood Depression and Its Treatment by Leon Cytryn and Donald McKnew (ISBN 0-393-03827-0)

The Girls and Boys Book About Good and Bad Behavior by Richard Gardner (ISBN 0-933812-21-3)

Relation and Stress Reduction Workbook by Davis, Eshelman and McKay (ISBN 1-879237-83-0)

Anger Disorder by Howard Kassinove (ISBN 1-56032-353-1)

Acting Out by Lawrence Abt and Stuart Weissman (ISBN 1-56821-778-1)

My Name is Brian by Jean Betancourt (ISBN 0-590-44921)

Healing the Hurt Child by Denis Donovan and Deborah McIntyre (ISBN 0-393-70093-3)

Monsters Under the Bed and Other Childhood Fears by Stephen Garber, Marianne Garber and Robyn Freedman Spizman (ISBN 0-679-40858-4)

Dry All Night: The Picture Book Technique that Stops Bedwetting by Alison Mack (ISBN 0-316-54225-3)

Professional Organizations Offering General Information, Parent Support, Workshops, Specialty Books and Therapeutic Games

The Parent Network for the Post-Institutionalized Child (PNPIC)
Thais Tepper and Lois Hannon (Directors): e-mail: PNPIC@aol.com and www.PNPIC.org. PNPIC organizes intensive week-end workshops for parents of internationally and nationally adopted children. Books and training videos are also available. Referral base of international adoption medicine specialists.

Friends of Russian and Ukrainian Adoptions (FRUA), www. FRUA.org

Parent Educational Advocacy Training Center (PEATC), 10340 Democracy Lane, Suite 206, Fairfax, Virginia 22030, Phone Number: (703) 691-7826, e-mail: peatcinc@aol.com

Kids Rights 10100 Park Cedar Drive, Charlotte, NC 28210 1-800-892-KIDS, Fax Number (704) 541-0113

Adoption Tapestry Books: Adoption Book Catalog 1-800-765-2367

A.D.D. Warehouse 300 N.W. 70th Avenue, Suite 102, Plantation, FL 33317, Phone Number (305) 792-8944

Childs Work/Childs Play: A Catalog Addressing the Mental Health Needs of Children and Their Families Through Play Therapy, Phone Number 1-800-962-1141

The Center for Applied Psychology, Inc., PO Box 61586 King of Prussia, PA 19406 Phone Number 1-800-962-1141 (Excellent selection of therapeutic games, activities and parent training information for children of all ages)

Free Spirit Publishing: Self-Help for Kids, 400 First Avenue, North, Suite 616, Minneapolis, MN 55401-1724 Phone Number 1-800-735-7323 (Excellent selection of books, videos and therapeutic games for children experiencing emotional and behavioral difficulties)

Learn and Play, 45 Curiosity Lane, PO Box 1822, Peoria, IL 61656-1822
Phone Number 1-800-247-6106 (therapeutic and recreational games for children to use during play therapy)

Sherman Specialty Company, Inc., PO Box 401 Merrick, New York, NY 11566
Phone Number 1-800-645-6513 (inexpensive behavior management reinforcers)

Woodbine House Publishers, 6510 Bells Mill Road, Bethesda, MD 20817
Phone Number 1-800-843-7323 (books for special needs children)

LinguiSystems, www.linguisystems.com

Remedia Publications, 1-800-826-4740

Critical Thinking Books & Software, www.criticalthinking.com, 1-800-458-4849

Fiengold Diet Association of the United States, PO Box 6550, Alexandria, VA 22306 Phone Number: (703) 768-FAUS

The Neuro-Linguistic Programming Institute One Brittany Terrace, Rock Tavern, NY 12575-5105

Children of Intercountry Adoptions, in School, by Ruth Lyn Meese, (ISBN 0897898419)

The Complete IEP Guide, How to Advocate for Your Special Ed Child, by Siegel (ISBN -983386072)

Recommended Therapeutic Games

The following games available through Childs Work/Childs Play, which must be ordered through a professional:

The Talking, Feeling, Doing Game
The Conduct Management Game
The Anger Control Game
The Social Skill Game
Pictionary Junior
Look Before You Leap
In Control: A Book of Games To Teach Children Self-Control Skills
The Angry Monster Machine
You and Me: A Unique Game for Teaching Social Skills
The Good Behavior Game
All Feelings are Okay-It's What You Do With Them That Counts
The Angry Monster Workbook
Face Your Feelings
On Improving Self-Concept
You Decide: Right or Wrong
Alternatives to Anger and Aggression

Therapy Skill Builders, Assessment an dTherapy Resources for Occupational Therapists, Physical Therapists and Early Interventionists, from The Psychological Corporation, 1-800-872-1726, www.PsychCorp.com

RECOMMENDED PSYCHOLOGICAL AND NEUROPSYCHOLOGICAL TESTS FOR COMPREHENSIVE NEURODEVELOPMENTAL EVALUATIONS

Intellectual Testing

Wechsler Preschool and Primary Scale of Intelligence - Revised (WPPSI-R)
Wechsler Intelligence Scale for Children - Revised (WISC-R)
Wechsler Intelligence Scale for Children - Third Edition (WISC-III)
Wechsler Adult Intelligence Scale - 3rd Edition (WAIS-3)
Stanford-Binet Intelligence Scale: 4th Edition
Peabody Picture Vocabulary Test (PPVT)
Kaufman Brief Intelligence Test (KBIT)
Test of Nonverbal Intelligence - 2 (TONI-2)
Comprehensive Test of Nonverbal Intelligence (CTONI)
Leiter International Performance Scales
Universal Nonverbal Intelligence Test (UNIT)

Neurodevelopmental Testing for Infants and Toddlers

Vineland Adaptive Behavior Scale
Battelle Developmental Inventory
Bayley Infant Neurodevelopmental Screener
Child Neuropsychological History Form
Childhood Autism Rating Scale (CARS)
Gilliam Autism Rating Scales (GARS)
Autism Screening Instrument for Educational Planning-2 (ASIEP-2)
Developmental Tasks for Kindergarten Readiness
Screening Test for Educational Prerequisite Skills

Academic-Achievement Tests

Wide Range Achievement Test - III (WRAT-3)
Wechsler Individual Achievement Test (WIAT)
Woodcock Johnson Psycho-Educational Battery
Gray Oral Reading Test - III (GORT-3)
Test of Written Language - II (TOWL-2)
Norris Educational Achievement Test (NEAT)
Boder Test of Reading-Spelling Patterns
Test of Early Written Language (TEWL)
Test of Early Reading Ability-2 (TERA-2)
New Educational Aptitude Test (4 years old & up)

Speech and Language Tests

Preschool Language Scale-3 (PLS-3)
Test of Language Development-Primary
Test of Language Development-Intermediate
Test of Adolescent and Adult Language-3 (TOAL-3)
Comprehensive Evaluation of Language Functions (CELF)
Boston Naming Test
Decoding Skill Test

Neuropsychological Tests

Luria Nebraska Neuropsychological Test Battery for Children - Revised (Ages 7-11)
Luria Nebraska Neuropsychological Test Battery for Adults - Revised (Ages 12 & up)
Halstead-Reitan Neuropsychological Test Battery for Adults & Children (Ages 7 through Adult)
Adult and Children's Neuropsychological Questionnaire
Auditory Discrimination Test
Bender Gestalt Visual Motor Test
Beery Test of Visual-Motor Integration (VMI)
Booklet Category Test
Children's Category Test
Boston Naming Test
Memory Assessment Scale (MAS)
Test of Memory and Learning (TOMAS)
Boston Revision-Wechsler Memory Scale
Test of Prerequisite Skills (Kindergarten Readiness)
Childrens Auditory Verbal Learning Test (CAVLT)
California Verbal Learning Test (CVLT)
Childrens Memory Scale(CMS)
Graham-Kendall Memory for Designs Test
Hooper Visual Organization Test
Memory, Orientation and Amnesia Test (MOAT)
Neuropsychological Symptoms Checklist
Psychosocial Pain Inventory
Rey-Osterrieth Complex Memory Figure
Shipley Institute of Living Scale
Wechsler Memory Scale - Third Edition
Wisconsin Card Sorting Test

Yacorzynski-Northwestern Frontal Lobe Battery
Wide Range Assessment of Memory and Learning (WRAML)
Test of Visual-Perceptual Skills (Nonmotor)
Test of Memory and Learning (TOMAL)
Learning Efficiency Test (LET)
Test of Auditory-Perceptual Skills (TAPS)
GFU Auditory Memory Tests
Visual Search and Attention Test
Test of Auditory Reasoning and Processing Skills (TARPS)
Token Test for Children
Wide Range Assessment of Visual-Motor Abilities (WRAVMA)
Examining for Aphasia (EFA-3)
Neuropsychological Impairment Scale (NIS)

Motor Sills and Sensory-Perceptual Tests

Reitan-Indiana Aphasia Screening and Sensory-Perceptual Examination
Adult and Children's Finger Tapping Test
Grooved Pegboard Test
Purdue Pegboard Test

Computer Assessment for Attention Deficit Hyperactivity Disorders

Connors Continual Performance Test (CPT)
Test of Visual Attention (TOVA)

Psychological Tests

Beck Depression Inventory
Children's Depression Scale
House-Tree-Person Projective Drawings (HTP)
Kinetic Family Drawing (KFD)
Rorschach Psychodiagnostic Test
Thematic Apperception Test (TAT)
Children's Apperception Test (CAT)
Family Apperception Test
Roberts Apperception Test
Abuse/Neglect Apperception Test
Tell-Me-A-Story (TEMAS)
Piers-Harris Self-Concept Inventory
Minnesota Multiphasic Personality Inventory - II (MMPI-2)
Malingerers Personality Profile

Endler Multiaxial Anxiety Scale
Multiscore Depression Inventory (MDI)
Rotter Sentence Completion Test (Children, Adolescents & Adults)
Family Sentence Completion Series
Adolescent Sentence Completion Series
Personality Inventory for Children (PIC)
Personality Inventory for Youth (PIY)
Reynolds Childhood and Adolescent Depression Scales
Reynolds Childhood and Adolescent Suicide Scale

Rating Scales

Conners' Rating Scales for Attention Deficit Hyperactivity Disorders
ACTeRS Rating Scales for Attention Deficit Hyperactivity Disorders
Achenbach Child Behavior Checklist & Teacher Rating Scales
Differential Scales for Conduct and Emotional Problems
Childhood Autism Rating Scales
Attention Deficit Hyperactivity Disorder Tests (ADHDT)
Childhood and Adult Neuropsychological Questionnaire
Conners Adult ADHD History Form

IMMIGRANT VISAS ISSUED TO ORPHANS COMING TO THE U.S.

TOP COUNTRIES OF ORIGIN

	FY 2002	FY 2001
1	5,053........CHINA (mainland)	4,681........CHINA (mainland)
2	4,939........RUSSIA	4,279........RUSSIA
3	2,219........GUATEMALA	1,870........S. KOREA
4	1,779........S. KOREA	1,609........GUATEMALA
5	1,106........UKRAINE	1,246.......UKRAINE
6	819..........KAZAKHSTAN	782..........ROMANIA
7	766..........VIETNAM	737..........VIETNAM
8	466..........INDIA	672........ KAZAKHSTAN
9	334..........COLOMBIA	543..........INDIA
10	260...........BULGARIA	407...........COLOMBIA
11	254...........CAMBODIA	297...........BULGARIA
12	221...........PHILIPPINES	266...........CAMBODIA
13	187...........HAITI	219...........PHILIPPINES
14	169...........BELARUS	192...........HAITI
15	168...........ROMANIA	158...........ETHIOPIA
16	105...........ETHIOPIA	129...........BELARUS
17	101...........POLAND	86...........POLAND
18	67.............THAILAND	74.............THAILAND
19	65.............PERU	73.............MEXICO
20	61.............MEXICO	51.............JAMAICA and LIBERIA (both 51)

	FY 2000	FY 1999	FY 1998
1	5,053........CHINA	4,348.......RUSSIA	4,491......RUSSIA
2	4,269........RUSSIA	4,101.......CHINA	4,206......CHINA
3	1,794.......S. KOREA	2,008......S. KOREA	1,829.....S. KOREA
4	1,518.......GUATEMALA	1,002......GUATEMALA	911.......GUATEMALA
5	1,122.......ROMANIA	895.........ROMANIA	603........VIETNAM
6	724..........VIETNAM	709.........VIETNAM	478........INDIA
7	659..........UKRAINE	500.........INDIA	406........ROMANIA
8	503..........INDIA	323.........UKRAINE	351........COLOMBIA
9	402..........CAMBODIA	248.........CAMBODIA	249........CAMBODIA
10	399..........KAZAKHSTAN	231.........COLOMBIA	200.......PHILIPPINES
11	246..........COLOMBIA	221.........BULGARIA	180........UKRAINE
12	214..........BULGARIA	195........PHILIPPINES	168........MEXICO
13	173.........PHILIPPINES		151........BULGARIA
14	131..........HAITI		140.......DOMIN REP
15	106..........MEXICO		121........HAITI
16	95...........ETHIOPIA		103........BRAZIL
17	88...........THAILAND		96.........ETHIOPIA
18	83...........POLAND		84.........THAILAND
19	79...........MOLDOVA		77.........POLAND
20	60...........BOLIVIA		76.........LATVIA

	FY 1997	FY 1996	FY 1995
1	3,816......RUSSIA	3,333.......CHINA	2,130.......CHINA
2	3,597......CHINA	2,454.......RUSSIA	1,896.......RUSSIA
3	1,654.....S. KOREA	1,516.......KOREA	1,666.......KOREA
4	788.......GUATEMALA	427........GUATEMALA	449........GUATEMALA
5	621........ROMANIA	555.........ROMANIA	371.........INDIA
6	425........VIETNAM	380.........INDIA	351........PARAGUAY
7	352.........INDIA	354.........VIETNAM	350........COLOMBIA
8	233.......COLOMBIA	258........PARAGUAY	318.........VIETNAM
9	163.......PHILIPPINES	255........COLOMBIA	298........PHILIPPINES
10	152.........MEXICO	229........PHILIPPINES	275.........ROMANIA
11	148.......BULGARIA	163........BULGARIA	146.........BRAZIL
12	142........HAITI	103.........BRAZIL	110........BULGARIA
13	108........LATVIA	82..........LATVIA	98..........LITHUANIA
14	91.........BRAZIL	78..........LITHUANIA	90..........CHILE
15	82.........ETHIOPIA	77..........GEORGIA	83..........MEXICO
16	78.........LITHUANIA	76..........MEXICO	67..........ECUADOR
17	78.........POLAND	68...........HAITI	63..........ETHIOPIA
18	77.........BOLIVIA	64..........POLAND	63...........JAPAN
19	72.........HUNGARY	63...........CHILE	59..........LATVIA
20	66.........CAMBODIA	55..........THAILAND	53..........THAILAND
21		51.........ECUADOR,HUNGARY	51..........GEORGIA

	FY 1994	FY 1993	FY 1992
1	1,795......KOREA	1,775....KOREA	1,840....KOREA
2	1,530......RUSSIA	746.......RUSSIA	418......GUATEMALA
3	787........CHINA	512......GUATEMALA	404......COLOMBIA
4	483.......PARAGUAY	426......COLOMBIA	357......PHILIPPINES
5	436.......GUATEMALA	412......PARAGUAY	352.......INDIA
6	412........INDIA	360......PHILIPPINES	324.......RUSSIA
7	351.......COLOMBIA	331.......INDIA	309.......PERU
8	314.......PHILIPPINES	330.......CHINA	249......HONDURAS
9	220........VIETNAM	273......UKRAINE	212......PARAGUAY
10	199........ROMANIA	224.......PERU	206.......CHINA
11	164........UKRAINE	179......HONDURAS	179.......CHILE
12	149........BRAZIL	161.......BRAZIL	138.......BRAZIL
13	97.........BULGARIA	133......BULGARIA	121......ROMANIA
14	95.........LITHUANIA	124......BOLIVIA	117......EL SALVADOR
15	94.........POLAND	110......VIETNAM	109.......POLAND
16	85.........MEXICO	100......ELSALVADOR	91........BULGARIA
17	79..........CHILE	97........ROMANIA	91........MEXICO
18	77.........HONDURAS	91........MEXICO	86........THAILAND
19	61.........HAITI	70........POLAND	73........BOLIVIA
20	54.........ETHIOPIA	69........THAILAND	68.......JAPAN
21	49..........JAPAN	64.......JAPAN	64.......COSTA RICA

	FY 1991	FY 1990	FY 1989
1	2,594...ROMANIA	2,620....KOREA	3,544..KOREA
2	1,818...KOREA	631……COLOMBIA	736….COLOMBIA
3	705......PERU	440.......PERU	648….INDIA
4	521…..COLOMBIA	421……PHILIPPINES	465….PHILIPPINES
5	445…..INDIA	348.......INDIA	253.....CHILE
6	393…..PHILIPPINES	302.......CHILE	252.....PARAGUAY
7	329…..GUATEMALA	282……PARAGUAY	222….PERU
8	266......CHILE	257……GUATEMALA	202….GUATEMALA
9	234......HONDURAS	228.......BRAZIL	201.....CHINA
10	190…..PARAGUAY	197.......HONDURAS	131.....HONDURAS
11	175......BRAZIL	121.......ROMANIA	175.....BRAZIL
12	131…..THAILAND	112.......MEXICO	138.....ROMANIA
13	123…..El SALVADOR	105……COSTA RICA	109….THAILAND
14	97……MEXICO	103……EL SALVADOR	95..….CUBA
15	92……POLAND	100……THAILAND	94…...EL SALVADOR
16	87……JAPAN	66...…..POLAND	91..….MEXICO
17	61……CHINA	66...…..TAIWAN	80..….HAITI
18	60……CAMBODIA	64……..HAITI	78…...COSTA RICA
19	56……COSTA RICA	59...…..ECUADOR	75..….TAIWAN
20	54……TAIWAN	58…….DOMINICAN REP	74..….JAPAN
21	50…....DOMINICAN REP	57...…..JAPAN	74..….POLAND

World Total for Calendar Years

2002	20,099
2001	19,237
2000	17,718
1999	16,363
1998	15,774
1997	12,743
1996	10,641
1995	8,987
1994	8,333
1993	7,377
1992	6,472
1991	8,481
1990	7,093
1989	8,102

Examples of Level System

Children ages 4 through 6

Tokens earned	M	T	W	Th	Fr	S	Su
Get up on time (1)							
Clean up/be neat (1)							
No tantrums (1)							
Listen immediately (1)							
Proper answers to parents (1)							

Points are totaled daily to determine the level for the next day

LEVEL 3: All 5 points earned
LEVEL 2: 4 out of 5 points earned
LEVEL 1: 3 points or below

LEVEL 3: Extra snack, dessert, free play time, extra special time with parents
LEVEL 2: Routine day, only partial play time and extra time for activities
LEVEL 1: Early bedtime, no treats, no play time, no special time with parents

NOTE to Parents: Tokens earned can be tasks of your choosing or problem areas. Recommend use of tangible reinforcers such as stars, stickers, or anything directly posted on the chart that the child can see throughout the day. Also, parents can determine what are the most appropriate rewards for Level 3 and partial rewards on Level 2 in addition to the most suitable punishments for Level 1.

Examples of Level System

Children ages 7 through Teenager

	M	T	W	Th	Fr	S	Su
Tokens/Points earned							
Wake up on time-No second prompting (2)							
Clean up room and hygiene activities (1)							
Complete all required school work with appropriate conduct (4)							
Bring home and complete all assigned work and stay on weekly schedule (3)							
Listen to and follow all instructions the first time (2)							
Absolutely no excuses, backtalk or arguing (4)							
Home chores/clean up (2)							
Bedtime preparation/be organized for next day (2)							

There are 20 points to be earned per day, 5 days per week, which totals a maximum of 100. The level earned is determined following a tally of points Friday evening. The level earned begins Friday evening through the following Friday evening grading period (one entire week including Saturday and Sunday).

Remember, parents and children can decide on what are the most important areas to emphasize for point earning. For example, some families may wish to stress attitude, behavior, cooperation, peer relationships, cleanliness and hygiene, in-school and at home academics, communication patterns, tantrums, aggression and inappropriate behaviors, destructiveness, negative statements and behaviors, etc.

Level 3: 90-100 points
Level 2: 80-89 points
Level 1: Below 80 points

Level 3: Later bedtime, more freedom, privileges, time to play outside and inside, friends over to the house or possible sleep over, additional allowance or bonuses, earned video game time, special foods and family activities of their choosing, later curfews and generally less restrictive activities. For the older teenager, social and recreational activities are privileges to be earned. In general, Level 3 requires the most work and the most privileges consistent with pre-agreed upon rewards.

Level 2: Regular bedtime, regularly scheduled work and chores completed first before outside and inside recreational activities, one-half of the desired privileges, freedoms, movies or time with friends. Only friends over to house—no sleep overs or unsupervised activities. Partial allowance or bonuses. Only special food or activities available at parents level of interest, not child's.

Level 1: Total Adults Only. Isolation from any type of activity, friend or other sibling. Early bedtime, no talking to others, no television, play or any type of recreational activity. No hiding out in their room which is often preferred. Must stay in immediate sight and close proximity of parents or responsible adult at all times. Hard labor activities occupying any and all free time. Awakening early to begin work. Writing assignments or boring, repetitive tasks. Absolutely no stimulation. If parents must leave to go places, child must accompany them but not engage in any discussion or distraction. Again, Total Adults supervision, isolation and continual hard work is of paramount importance on Level One